From Sand to Circuits

AND OTHER INQUIRIES

From Sand to Circuits
AND OTHER INQUIRIES

Edited by
John J. Simon, Jr.

Harvard University
Office for Information Technology
Cambridge, Massachusetts

Harvard University Office for Information Technology
Cambridge, Massachusetts 02138

ISBN 0-674-32575-3

Designed by Eleanor Bradshaw
Composition and Presswork by the Harvard University
Office of the University Publisher

To
Nathan Oakes

CONTENTS

INTRODUCTION

Harvard University's relationship with technology, which harks back almost to the institution's founding in 1636, has had a persistently practical bent. Within a decade of becoming, the College put to work generating a meagre supplement to the modest income being derived from a corn crop and management of a ferry across the Charles River the by then two hundred year-old technology of Gutenberg embodied in a hand press with a small font of type.

Little more than a decade after Harvard assumed management of its small press, Zechariah Brigden (A.B. Harvard, 1657), using the College's first telescope, made observations published in the *New England Almanack for 1659* that took account of both the notion of the Earth as a planet and the semi-annual phenomenon of eclipse. Twenty-one years later, in his *Philosophiae Naturalis Principia Mathematica*, Issac Newton remarked that of the many observations made of the Great Comet those of "the observer in New England [Thomas Brattle using the same telescope], taking the position of the comet with reference to the fixed stars, are better." Thus, the "little college telescope, used by a careful and intelligent observer, contributed its mite to helping Newton test Kepler's three laws, to work out the law of gravitation, and to write his great work" (Morison 1936, 221).

Practicality is in evidence some two centuries later not only in a device, a then-uncommon steam heating system installed in Harvard's first library building, but also in the title held by its devisor, Daniel Treadwell, Rumford Professor of Applications of Science to the Useful Arts. Though lengthy by modern standards, Professor Treadwell's title conveys the essence of this modest volume's intent. The periodical from which this collection of articles is drawn professes its purpose to be "to inform its readers about information technology developments and services as they relate to Harvard University." Without forsaking this fundamental charge, the Harvard University *Information Technology Newsletter* mounted increasingly thorough and comprehensive inquiries into various technologies — taking account of their origins and relationships to the processes and institutions of learning, as well as of their natures — an expansion reflected in its transformation, in 1985, into the *Information Technology Quarterly*. The articles go about the task of providing intelligible introductions to various technologies with a conscious avoidance of the endemic plague of acronymism (except where it is simply unavoidable, as in the case of corporations or products that have no other name) and a gratuitous indulgence in illustration designed to enlighten rather than provide technical specifications.

Harvard's relationship with the subject matter is not everywhere explicitly stated; that was, and is, not the purpose of these articles. Rather, it is the objective of imparting to the broadest base of readers a general understanding of the forms and implications of contemporary information technologies that is maintained and generalized in this updated and revised selection.

If this book, which is consciously being published in the year of Harvard University's three hundred and fiftieth anniversary, continues in some small way a venerable institution's practical affair with a concurrently developing science and technology, it will have achieved the ends that its editor and contributors sought as they variously selected, critiqued, described, wrote, and sketched the material that comprises its contents.

ACKNOWLEDGEMENTS

An exhaustive enumeration of the many individuals at Harvard, at other universities and institutions, and in corporations and businesses large and small who made significant contributions to the compilation of the articles in this volume would be quite impractical. A more tractable task is that of identifying the individuals who conceived the home that these articles were originally written to occupy. The genesis of this book lies with the Harvard University *Information Technology Newsletter*, and the genesis of the *Newsletter* with Dr. Howard L. Resnikoff and Guy J. Ciannavei.

Collaborating and contributing authors are identified at the end. There, too, are credited the illustrators who consistently transformed the editor's stick-figure sketches into lucid illustrations, and the sources of the many other diagrams, drawings, and photographs that relieve the text.

The editor is also grateful to the Harvard and other libraries from which he obtained most of the many reference materials identified in the concluding, and only selected, bibliography.

To all who helped with this volume and find no acknowledgement in any of the foregoing, the editor says "thank you."

1

From Sand to Circuits: a Survey of the Origins of the Microprocessor

The sand on the beach in which you leave your footprints contains the very same materials from which microprocessor, and other, chips are made. Purified silicon, extracted from rocks and ordinary beach sand, is grown into cylindrical, single crystals. Sliced wafer-thin, and so selectively tainted with atoms of impurity that tens of thousands of discrete electronic elements are formed in an area only one quarter of an inch square, such crystals can yield thousands of identical integrated circuits, each one a complete microprocessor. Taking the discovery of the electron as a point of departure, the following article attempts to chart the course of events — scientific and industrial — that gave rise to the "computer-on-a-chip" and explain something of its nature and manufacture.

A typical contemporary microcomputer occupies only a corner of a conventional office desk. Yet it can outperform a room-full of electronic hardware of the sort that constituted its earliest predecessors. The agent responsible for this remarkable feat is the *chip*. Onto one of these slivers of silicon, roughly a quarter of an inch square, can be packed circuitry functionally equivalent to that which filled numerous large cabinets in early relay and vacuum tube computers. Under magnification, the surface of one of these chips presents a complex pattern of interconnecting pathways, resembling somewhat a city viewed from extremely high altitude. Scratching this surface (figuratively speaking) will uncover underlying strata of varying complexity. This chip *geology* is a consequence not of natural forces, but rather of a carefully conceived and executed manufacturing process carried out to exacting specifications in ultra-clean environments.

The chip is a child of solid state physics, a branch of a relatively young modern physics. The scientific inquiry that gave rise to modern physics occurred only around the turn of this century, whereas the parent science can be traced to the ancient Greeks, who put forth physical theories of the universe as early as 580 B.C.

A new physics

Modern physics rests on a way of looking at the universe formally referred to as *quantum theory*. The *classical* theories of physics, evolved over centuries of scientific observation and experimentation, had come to describe a universe that was extremely orderly. The past and future behaviour of particles and waves can be exactly calculated in classical physics if their motion at any one time is known.

A variety of experiments carried out during the latter part of the nineteenth and early part of the twentieth centuries yielded results that were discrepant with the predictions of classical theory. This dilemma precipitated the creation of a new theory. Developed over a span of a mere twenty-five years, the new theory of physics, in order to resolve the discrepancies alluded to above, is less presumptuous; the universe according to *quantum theory* is a place of fuzzy indeterminism.

Practical applications of electricity — in the telegraph, the electric generator, and the electric light — preceded Joseph J. Thomson's discovery, in the late 1890s, of the electron. Though he didn't call it that, the particle, at 1/1837th the mass of the hydrogen atom, effectively annulled the latter's distinction as the smallest building block in nature.

Discoveries relative to the nature of this new smallest-of-particles soon followed. Max Planck's discovery, in 1900, that small-scale energy changes are made in little jumps rather than continuous changes was extended to light by Albert Einstein, who, in 1905, suggested that light could be thought of as composed of small particles, each with a fixed, tiny amount (a quantum) of energy. Subsequently, Robert Millikan showed experimentally that the Thomson particle was accompanied by a basic unit of electric charge, thus establishing that electric charge exists in small, discrete quantities and was not, as had been thought previously, infinitely divisible.

A physical demonstration that electrical currents in metals are carried by electrons was provided by a "shocking" experiment carried out by Thomas A. Edison. Edison showed that one could obtain an electric shock by touching a metal plate inserted at the top of a light bulb above the filament. Conjecture supplied the electron as the "something" that had to be carrying the electric current through the vacuum from the filament to the plate.

Edison later discovered that when a positive potential was applied to the plate a greater number of electrons were attracted to it; that is, it drew a larger current. In 1906, Dr. Lee DeForrest extended Edison's discovery; by varying a small voltage applied to an intermediary grid he was able to produce proportional variations in a larger current passed from the filament to the plate. Initially, the three element vacuum tubes that emerged from his discovery, by virtue of their ability to amplify a weak current, or signal, found application first in radio and then in television. Later, recognition of the ability of such tubes to act as switches in an electronic circuit led to their extensive use in computers.

With increasing use, inherent limitations of the vacuum tube began to be in evidence. By comparison with contemporary solid state components, vacuum tubes consume a great deal of power, are relatively large and fragile, and are prone to fail fairly often. Of the eighteen thousand vacuum tubes employed in the mammoth Eniac computer of 1940s vintage, one could be expected to fail every seven and one-half minutes.

A substitute for the vacuum tube was to emerge as a result of the continuing study of the behaviour of electrons in solids.

The nature of metals

Most solids are crystalline, that is, their atoms are arranged in repeating, three-dimensional patterns called *lattices*. This orderly arrangement of atoms is in contrast to the completely random arrangement that is to be found in, for example, a dilute gas, and the state of modest disarray characteristic of atoms in liquids and amorphous solids. Identification of crystalline structure predates the discovery of the constituents of the atom — the nuclei and years, papers on crystallography having been published as early as the eighteenth century.

In 1913, Neils Bohr, by adding two conditions to a picture of the atom arrived at by Lord Rutherford in 1910 — of a small, positively charged nucleus surrounded by light, negatively charged electrons — was able to account for the stability of the atom, something that classical physics could not do. Whereas electrons, were they to follow unwaveringly the theories of classical physics, would rapidly radiate all of their energy as they circle around the nucleus and quickly become bound to it, Bohr postulated that only certain energy levels are allowed for atoms and that energy is given off only when an electron goes from one allowed energy level to another. Arguing for Bohr's stable atom is the extant universe; if matter, on the atomic and molecular scale, behaved according to classical theory the universe would have shrunk into darkness shortly after coming into existence.

Early attempts to explain the movement of electrons in metals were made by Paul Drude and Hendrik A. Lorentz. To Drude's picture of metal as an electrically neutral gas of positive and negative particles Lorentz added the assumptions that the mobile negative carriers were a single species of electron, the same in all metals, and that the positively charged particles remained fixed in the matter. In 1927, Felix Bloch put the electrons into the periodic lattice of a crystal, an idea he says was suggested to him by recollection of a demonstration in elementary physics in which many equal and equally coupled pendula were hanging at constant spacing from a rod and the motion of one of them was seen to "migrate" along the rod from pendulum to pendulum.

With Bloch's picture of the migration of electrons through a lattice and Bohr's concept of allowed energy levels, an elementary sketch can be made of the theory of electrons in metals. Most of the electrons in the lattice atoms stay close to their nuclei. However, a certain number tend to be found in the regions directly between two atoms. Together with the equivalent electrons from the neighboring atoms these form the *covalent bonds* that hold the crystal together and provide, from their number, the mobile charges that carry current. Each of these electrons has a certain total amount of energy.

Because of their wave-like nature, electrons can occupy only certain energy levels, or *bands*. Thus, there are bands that correspond to energy levels that electrons may possess (called *allowed bands*) and bands at energy levels that no electrons will have (called *forbidden bands*). The bands are interspersed, the magnitude of the forbidden bands that separate allowed bands constituting the *band gap*. Measured in electronvolts (eV), the band gap represents the amount of energy required to displace one of the outermost, or *valence*, electrons and effect its movement through the lattice. As can be seen in Figure 1, the band gap for metals is essentially zero; electrons can be displaced readily, hence conductivity is high. The greatest band gaps will be found in insulators (as much as 6-8 eV), with semiconductors having somewhat lesser band gaps (as low as 1-2 eV); because their electrons are much more firmly bound to their nuclei, their conductivities are very low, and low, respectively.

Semiconductors

The term *semiconductor* describes the electrical properties of a class of elements, also called semi-metals or metalloids, that occupy a diagonal slice through the periodic table between metals and non-metals. For reasons related earlier, semiconductors are neither good conductors, like

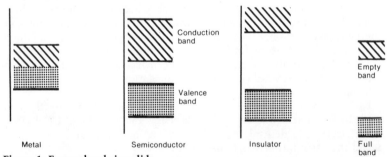

| Metal | Semiconductor | Insulator | |

Figure 1: Energy bands in solids

The regular arrangement of atoms in a crystal results in energy bands, allowed bands *being those which energies in the solid can have and* forbidden bands *being those which no electrons can have. In the illustration, the* conduction *and* valence bands *are allowed bands, separated, except in the case of metal, by forbidden bands. In order for electrons to move from the normally full valence band to the normally empty conduction band they must receive a "push" to get them across the forbidden band. The amount of push required, measured in electron volts, is determined by the extent of the band gap and reflects the nature of the substance, metals having essentially no band gap, semiconductors a modest band gap, and insulators a large band gap.*

the former, nor good insulators, like the latter. Their electrical properties lie between these extremes.

For a time it was believed that, in their pure state, semiconductors were really true metals. This idea was supported by work such as that of H. J. Seeman, who, in 1927, reported of his investigation of ten crystals of silicon that certain characteristics were on the same order as those of normal metals. Even after Johann Bernhard Gudden suggested, in 1930, that no pure substance is ever a semiconductor, and that the conductivity in such conductors is due to the presence of impurities, silicon continued, in many circles, to be regarded as a metal.

Gudden was correct, however, and in the 1930s researchers at the Bell Telephone Laboratories began to experiment with ways of directly altering the electrical properties of semiconductor material. Methods for growing pure single crystals artificially had begun to be worked out in 1925. Bell Labs' scientists discovered that by infusing controlled amounts of impurities into a pure crystal of semiconductor material a conductive path could be formed. Atoms of the impurity substance, heated to a gaseous state, would seep into the semiconductor material displacing some of the semiconductor atoms and modifying its pure crystal structure. This process is called *doping* the semiconductor, and the impurity atoms are called *dopant* atoms.

This research culminated, in 1948, in the creation of a complete transistor within a piece of semiconductor material by three Bell Labs scientists, Walter Brattain, Robert Bardeen, and William Shockley. Their transistor was the prototype for solid state electronic devices. By the mid-1950s, transistors were being produced for commercial use and, by 1954, when the U.S. Air Force was turning over the idea of synthesizing a complete circuit function out of a single piece of solid material, a scheme they called "molecular electronics," Texas Instruments announced the first commercial silicon transistor.

The integrated circuit

In 1952, Geoffrey W. A. Dummer, a British authority on radar, offered the following prediction at the annual electronic components symposium in Washington, D.C.:

> With the advent of the transistor and the work in semiconductors generally, it seems now possible to envisage electronic equipment in a solid block with no connecting wires. The block may consist of layers of insulating, conducting, rectifying and amplifying materials, the electrical functions being connected directly by cutting out areas of the various layers.

The theme of the symposium — which took place when the transistor was but three years old and the Korean War was at its height — was a need, felt particularly by the military, for greater reliability from existing electronic components. Although the Royal Radar Establishment (RRE) contracted in April 1957 with Plessey Company Research Labs to develop a "semiconductor integrated circuit," and Dummer, a few months later, exhibited at the RRE's International Components Symposium a metal model demonstrating how silicon crystals might be shaped to control properties in a transistor switch, the first functional integrated circuits were developed not in Great Britain but in the United States.

By the late 1950s, refinements in manufacturing processes had made it possible to put hundreds of transistors on a single slice of silicon. The significant strides made in component miniaturization seemed almost to cry out for a concomitant advance in circuit techniques. The printed circuit board — a flat, insulator surface laid with conductive strips connecting the mounted electronic components — was an improvement over wired circuits, but not on the order of improvement as semiconductor devices over vacuum tubes. Referring to the dense packing of transistors on silicon slices, one of the co-inventors of the integrated circuit, Robert Noyce, remarked in retrospect:

> People cut these beautifully arranged things into little pieces and . . . girls hunt for them with tweezers in order to put leads on and wire them all back together again; then we . . . sell them to our customers, who . . . plug all these separate packages into a printed circuit board.

Noyce, a physicist, was director of research and development at Fairchild Semiconductor Company in 1959 when he outlined a scheme for making multiple devices on a single piece of silicon. Just months before, Jack Kilby, an electronics engineer with Texas Instruments, had sketched out a similar scheme. By 1961, both firms were turning out production quantities of commercial integrated circuits.

The techniques needed for creating integrated circuits in silicon were the same techniques already employed by the semiconductor industry to manufacture transistors — diffusion, oxide masking, and photographic reproduction of fine geometric patterns. The "batch" process of manufacture — in which hundreds, and even thousands, of identical integrated circuits are produced on wafers of silicon only a few inches in diameter and then cut apart — lent tremendous economy to circuit production, and the tiny "chips" of silicon containing the individual integrated circuits which fell out of the process lent a generic name to the product.

Even more quickly than the semiconductor industry grew, and it grew quite rapidly, the size of the circuits being produced by it shrunk. Refinement of existing manufacturing techniques and development of new techniques yielded such tremendous increases in amount of circuitry per area of silicon that terminology to describe levels of integration was introduced. In terms of number of components per chip, or circuit, Small Scale Integration (SSI) encompasses those with up to 64, Medium Scale Integration (MSI) those up to 1,024. With Large Scale Integration (LSI) and Very Large Scale Integration (VLSI) the numbers are in the tens and hundreds of thousands.

An annual doubling of chip capacity has become an observed trend, yet the cost of a contemporary chip, after correcting for inflation, is the same as the cost of a 1959 chip, a decrease in cost per component by a factor of a million in twenty years.

A matter of 1s and 0s

Underlying the heady growth of the semiconductor industry is the remarkable simplicity of the digital circuit. Unlike an analog circuit, in which a proportional electrical signal represents another physical quantity (such as temperature, fluid level, or sound), a digital circuit operates on the basis of the presence or absence of an electrical voltage or current. To understand the distinction between analog and digital it is helpful to think in terms of continuous versus discrete. An analog signal is continuous and variable, and every value throughout the entire range of its variability is significant. A digital circuit generally has only two possible values, one resulting from the presence, the other from the absence, of a voltage or current. By way of analogy: music is analog, morse code, digital; a wailing siren is analog, a machine gun, digital.

Representing information in a digital circuit is accomplished with an extraordinarily elementary system called *binary logic.* As in morse code, in which everything is dots and dashes, in binary logic everything is pulses or absence of pulses, usually represented as 1s and 0s. Because the electronic components in a digital circuit are, by and large, all switches of one sort or another, one might also think in terms of on and off, up and down, etc. Internally, all of the information in a computer — from the stored instructions by which it carries out all the operations possible for it, through the data input to it via keyboard, disk, etc. — is represented in the voltage/no-voltage equivalent of binary logic.

For the military establishment that provided much of the impetus for its development the integrated circuit would have been worth any price. The reduced size and improved reliability and speed of a solid circuit with a minimum of electrical connections fulfilled declared military needs. For integrated circuits to have an impact in the consumer market, however, they had to be economical. Economy was already inherent in the batch process of manufacture; all that remained was to find simple, universally applicable circuits that would warrant production in the tens and hundreds of thousands. Digital *gate* circuits provided this universality. Actuated by binary-equivalent electrical pulses, gate circuits use the basic mathematical functions of AND, OR, and NOT, plus the combined NOT-AND, or NAND, function to carry out all logical operations.

Manufacturers have utilized gate circuits to achieve standardization in a couple of ways. Dense chips have been fabricated with hundreds or thousands of unconnected digital gates that subsequently can be interconnected to a given customer's specifications. Alternatively, for sufficiently broad-based applications, pre-configured chips are practical.

Because of its fundamental simplicity and wide-ranging applicability, the chip has flourished. The realization that many mechanical functions are reducible to binary logic, and at a cost savings over equivalent mechanical parts, has resulted in the wholesale replacement in many products of gears, pulleys, and springs with digital chips. Examples range from calculators and clocks to an electronic sewing machine introduced by Singer in 1975.

The diffident debut of the microprocessor

Although anticipation of a "computer-on-a-chip" was in evidence as early as the mid-1960s, the first ones to emerge, sibling processors called the 4004 and 8008, elicited a mild startle response in their maker, Intel Corporation. Products of parallel, customer-sponsored development projects (the 4004 for a calculator and the 8008 for a video display terminal), the full market potential of the microprocessors only became apparent postpartum. From the former customer, driven by market forces to seek price reductions on its chip, Intel gained rights to sell to other customers for non-calculator applications. The latter customer cancelled its project, which Intel carried to completion on its own.

Yet, with its neonate microprocessors in hand, the then-small company, which had previously concentrated on implementing computer memories in large scale integrated circuits, was reticent to exercise its options. When Intel ultimately did decide to market the microprocessors, convinced from within that their potential was not as a replacement for minicomputers but as a way to insert intelligence into many products for the first time, it did so with vigour. An Intel advertisement in the November 15, 1971 issue of *Electronic News* announced "a micro-programmable computer on a chip" and heralded "a new era of integrated electronics," and the following year the firm initiated an ambitious program of seminars, customer training, and promotion.

A bevy of other semiconductor firms helped Intel to substantiate its portentous announcement. Two of the firms that had pioneered integrated circuit development — Fairchild and Texas Instruments — soon spawned their own microprocessors. Already in 1971, Texas Instruments had successfully fabricated all of the essential circuits for a complete microcomputer on a single chip. Fairchild developed an early two-chip microcomputer, called the F8, which enjoyed long and widespread application as a controller. By 1976, over fifty microprocessors were offered by an expanding vendor base that had come to include such companies as AMI, Mostek, Motorola, National Semiconductor, RCA, Rockwell International, Signetics, Teledyne Systems, and Toshiba. In addition, minicomputer manufacturers such as Data General, Digital Equipment Corporation, and General Automation, had begun to offer microprocessor-based boards.

By comparison with the literally hundreds of off-the-shelf, pre-assembled microcomputers that are today available, the first microcomputers, offered as kits, were primitive things. Wide-ranging variation in price, capability, and general sophistication have helped to make the microcomputer ubiquitous. Yet it is but one, albeit perhaps the most salient, application of the microprocessor. Chip-resident processors have revolutionized the toy and instrumentation industries and are making inroads in "white goods."

Chip to chore

Singer's electronic sewing machine, introduced five years ahead of any equivalent product, eliminated approximately three hundred and fifty precision-made parts found in comparable machines, and its twenty-four page instruction manual, roughly a third the number of pages in the average manual for a mechanical machine, was a testimony to the efficacy of the microprocessor as a means to simplify appliance operation.

Two years after the electronic sewing machine came the initial deluge of electronic games. Dedicated microcircuits enabled a host of traditional games to take on the modifier "electronic" and precipitated the development of many entirely new games specifically designed to exploit the microprocessor's capability to insure randomness of play, accommodate multiple skill levels, initiate novel audio and video effects, and even keep score. Player participation in such games is usually by means of a "joystick," a control stick such as would be found in an airplane cockpit (often with a "fire button," if the nature of the game warrants one), or a minimum-key pad, by which motion is controlled or directions input with a few keystrokes. At least in part, it is the simplicity of interacting with electronic games that accounts for the rapidity with which they have proliferated.

Less in the public awareness, perhaps, is the impact of the microprocessor on instrumentation. Instruments have variously become more accurate, more reliable, easier to use, and capable of self-diagnosis as a result of incorporating chip-resident microprocessors. The new generation of friendly, intelligent instruments is pervasive in its own right; some of its number may be found in automobile assembly plants and in the assembled automobiles, in hospitals and in hospital patients, in research laboratories and in laboratory animals. Advances in integrating microprocessors into sensors made of the same silicon material could further reduce the cost and increase the versatility of some instruments.

On the domestic scene, in addition to the home computer and the electronic calculator and sewing machine, the microprocessor has entered electric coffee makers, dryers, ovens (conventional and microwave), refrigerators, and washing machines. Incorporation of microprocessors is variously intended to make appliances easier to use, more efficient, or more reliable. To the extent that they do so, propagation of chips in appliances will undoubtedly increase adding economy to the foregoing list. A microprocessor can replace a set of controls that would otherwise have to be built component by component, and the functionality of microprocessor control can be altered or extended without any changes except to its programming.

Just how exotic a microprocessor-based kitchen appliance could be is illustrated by a prototype microwave oven demonstrated by Matsushita Electric Corporation in 1981. The oven — with a built-in six-inch television screen, a videotape library, and voice-recognition and -synthesis capabilities — can televise a dish's preparation *à la* Julia Child, automatically carry out the sequence of cooking steps in the recipe, announcing the completion of each, and plot cooking progress on a bar chart on the screen.

Where such a total system would find a niche isn't clear. To a home chef given to lingering over his or her creations, poking, smelling, touching, and tasting them at various stages, such a machine might be an anathema. One who cannot consistently properly prepare a TV dinner, however, while he or she might welcome an oven that takes its instructions from a computer, would probably be content to dispense with Julia Child and the bar chart.

Taken to an extreme, talking, programmed appliances might be deemed a trivialization of the deliberation, inspiration, and intuition that laid the foundation for the development of the microprocessors that make them possible. Some manufacturers have already exhibited a wariness of overindulging in the technology: a representative of a firm contemplating the development of a talking oven, reflecting on an image of a harried homemaker beset by a menagerie of babbling appliances, suggested that the product, if introduced, would very likely incorporate a "mute button" by which it could be shut-up if desired.

Nor does one have to look far for indisputably worthy applications of the chip. They are making cars safer and homes and businesses more energy efficient. They are helping children to learn more quickly and in new ways, and making valuable contributions in laboratories and research facilities.

Even so, the potential of the chip as we know it has hardly been tapped, and what might issue from it in the future could be as inconceivable as the the chip itself was only thirty to forty years ago.

Little more than half a century elapsed between science's first glimmer of understanding regarding the atomic structure of matter and the point at which it conceived the means to take a substance from common sand and transform it into a minute, but extraordinarily complex, electronic circuit capable of providing all of the necessary intelligence for a computer. The microprocessor in a chip manufactured by Motorola occupies only a quarter of its surface, circuits implemented on the remainder rendering the chip a complete, self-sufficient microcomputer. Four of these chips fit on the surface of dime.

"To see a microprocessor in a grain of sand,
And . . . hold a computer in the palm of your hand."

One can, today, read this paraphrase of lines from William Blake's *Auguries of Innocence* quite literally.

Making Semiconductors Conduct

In its purest, crystalline form a semiconductor will not readily conduct an electrical current. The nuclei of the atoms that comprise its crystals hold their electrons tightly. To induce these atoms to give up their electrons it is necessary to introduce an impurity into the crystal structure.

Pure semiconductor material is rare is nature. Semiconductor elements usually exist in combination with other elements. For example, silicon, the second most abundant material on earth and the principal semiconductor used in integrated circuit fabrication, is a constituent of rocks and ordinary beach sand. To be useful in integrated circuit fabrication, only impurities that will impart known electrical properties to the silicon can be used. Consequently, it is necessary to extract the silicon content from materials such as rock and sand and subject it to an exhaustive purification process. The resulting silicon is the purest industrial substance produced by man. To appreciate its impurity level of one part per billion, imagine that the entire population of the earth is blond. The introduction of two or three red-heads into this population would constitute an impurity on the order of that found in purified silicon.

Following its lengthy purification process, virgin silicon is once more made impure; but this time the impurities introduced into its crystalline structure are carefully controlled. The process of diffusing impurities into pure silicon is called *doping*. The impurity substance, called a *dopant*, is heated to a gaseous state, whereupon some of its atoms will seep into, and replace some of the atoms of, the silicon. Silicon that has been doped with a *donor* impurity, that is, one whose atoms have more valence electrons (the outermost electrons that form bonds with neighboring atoms) than it has, is called *n-type*. Silicon doped with an *acceptor* impurity, that is, one that has fewer valence electrons, is called *p-type*.

To understand how it is that an impurity substance can render a nonconductive substance conductive it is necessary to first recall that an electrical current is carried by the movement of electrons. The electrons in silicon, as noted earlier, are stable and not inclined to move. Only when atoms with either a surfeit or a deficit of electrons are introduced is the stability of the silicon's crystal structure disturbed.

Imagine a tank containing thousands of four-rayed starfish, all of which are holding rays. Each ray of each starfish is touched by a ray of another and each is touching another's ray. There is equilibrium in the resulting geometric arrangement of starfish. Now throw in a five-rayed starfish. To incorporate the newcomer into their pattern the indigenous starfish must adjust. To accommodate the extra appendage of the five-rayed starfish, another starfish, in order to take the newcomer's extra ray, must release the ray of some other starfish. The released ray must be taken by another starfish, which, to do so, must release yet another fish's ray, and so forth. The pattern is in a state of disequalibrium and a potential for motion is introduced.

Similarly, excess electrons in either dopant or semiconductor material will upset the electrical neutrality of the substance and provide charge carriers. When displaced from its proper position, one of these electrons can move through the crystal and carry current, leaving an unoccupied space where it used to be. While the space itself cannot carry a current, it affords nearby electrons the opportunity to move without having to be given enough energy to break out of their bonds. An electron that moves into the empty space will in turn leave a space which will be filled by another electron that will leave a space, and so on. This migrating space is called a *hole.*

Conceptually, then, conductivity in a semiconductor is achieved simply enough. Purified to a state of known non-conductivity, a piece of silicon is selectively tainted with specially selected impurity elements that impart to specific areas a potential for electron movement. By alternating and interconnecting these areas (which, because of the doping, will behave in a predictable manner when an electrical current is applied), the equivalent of multiple discrete electronic components electrically interconnected in a complete electronic circuit is produced within the solid substance.

What is more difficult to fully appreciate is the scale on which such

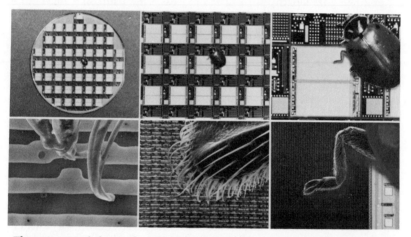

The sequence of photos above helps to illustrate the nature of dimensions on the order of one micron. The ladybug in the upper left photo is straddling a centrally located pair of 64K static RAM chips on a three inch slice of silicon. Under magnification in the photo next over, the ladybug's frontmost left leg becomes discernible. Though the ladybug appears quite large in the rightmost photo, the memory cells appear only as large white areas. Not until we can see, in the lower right photo, the fuzzy detail of the ladybug's leg do the individual memory cells begin to be visible, and only when magnified to the point that her foot dominates the frame (lower center photo) can we clearly see the features of the memory cells. The light lines in the lower left photo are the conductors, or "wires," that interconnect the memory cells. These are 2.7 microns (about one hundred millionth of one inch), the width of a hair on the ladybug's foot.

circuit fabrication takes place. The repeated doping that results in a piece of silicon becoming stratified in alternating layers of n-type and p-type material — as many as eighteen layers in some circuits — occurs in a slice of silicon that, to the human eye, has virtually no perceptible depth. The number of discrete components formed within an area of but one quarter of an inch square of such a sliver can number in the tens, and even hundreds, of thousands and the conductive strips — the "wires" that interconnect the components — are measured in microns, one micron being equivalent to approximately forty millionths of one inch. (See photos.) The manufacturing process by which such extraordinarily complex circuits are produced in such an infinitesimally small area is described in the "The making of a chip."

The Making of a Chip

An integrated circuit is a complete circuit, comprising components and connections, fabricated within a piece of solid material. While the term *solid state* accurately describes an integrated circuit, it was originated to describe a new approach to electronic component fabrication. It was discovered that by selectively introducing impurities into, or *doping*, a piece of pure semiconductor material, electrical fields could be created within the material that could be activated to achieve results similar to those obtained with vacuum tubes.

In a simple model of a vacuum tube, a voltage applied to a grid between a filament and a metal plate will cause a proportionally larger current to flow from the former to the latter. In a *transistor*, areas of n-type semiconductor material (roughly equivalent to the filament and plate in a vacuum tube) can be made to pass an amplified current between them in response to a lesser voltage applied to an intermediary layer of p-type material (equivalent to the grid in a vacuum tube).

The first solid state components were still discrete devices assembled into circuits with wires or printed circuit boards or both. Typically smaller than their vacuum tube counterparts, solid state components require less voltage and are hence intrinsically cooler in operation, as well. Thus, they can be placed closer together in circuits and the need for excess cabinet space for cooling is eliminated.

It was soon realized that if one transistor could be made in a piece of silicon, then multiple transistors connected within the silicon should be possible. With this realization, the era of the integrated circuit had arrived.

The process by which an integrated circuit is made using silicon diffusion is similar to the process employed in the making of a single transistor. Instead of the relatively simple masks used to control the doping of a piece of silicon to create one transistor, complex masks with entire circuit designs, which might include hundreds or thousands of individual transistors, as well as the minute conductors that interconnect them, are used.

Circuit designs still emanate from engineers, but, because of their incredible complexity, computer aided design (CAD) systems are often employed to simulate and evaluate circuit operation and to determine the correct size for each circuit component. Following computer analysis, a composite drawing is made in which schematic symbols are converted into actual shapes of circuit elements, and the drawing color-coded to distinguish among the many layers of interlaced n-type and p-type material that make up the circuit.

A variety of techniques exist for converting the composite drawing to a set of masks for controlling the doping of the silicon. Using optical lithographic methods, a drawing is reduced through a process similar to photo reduction. In x-ray and electron beam lithographic processes, drawings are first digitized, that is, converted into a form that can be processed by a computer, and then stored on magnetic tape. By reading the tape, an x-ray or electron beam system can cut a glass mask in the exact size of the finished circuit by focusing streams of x-rays or electrons on a glass plate. Actually, hundreds, or even thousands, of identical masks are cut into each plate, and a separate plate is cut for each circuit layer. Thus, one complete set of masking plates, laid successively over a single slice of silicon, produces many identical circuits that can subsequently be separated.

The raw material

Silicon as it is found in nature — largely in rocks and beach sand — is not suitable for producing solid state, integrated circuits. It must first be extracted from such materials and then purified. After being purified and then uniformly doped, say, with an impurity that renders it p-type, a single, monocrystalline ingot of silicon is grown. This is accomplished by lowering a seed crystal into a vat of the molten semiconductor material, and then slowly withdrawing it as crystallization occurs. A cylindrical contour is achieved by slowly rotating the ingot as it is withdrawn to prevent growth along the normal crystalline planes. The process somewhat resembles that by which an ordinary wax stick candle is produced. The term *monolithic* as used to modify "chip" refers to the fabrication of a circuit on a *monocrystalline*, or large single crystal surface.

A diamond saw divides the monocrystalline ingot into round, ultra-thin wafers, about three inches in diameter. After being polished to a perfect mirror finish, the wafers are ready to be used in circuit fabrication.

Fabricating the circuit

At this point, a repetitive process using the set of masks that has been produced by one of the lithographic techniques described above is begun. A uniformly doped silicon wafer is placed into a 1200° C furnace into which pure oxygen vapor is diffused to form a layer of silicon dioxide (an insulator) over the entire wafer surface. One side of the oxidized wafer is then covered with photoresist, a honey-like emulsion that hardens when exposed to ultraviolet light. The first mask is aligned to the wafer and, upon exposure to the ultraviolet light, the photoresist beneath the clear areas of the mask hardens while the remainder stays soft. The wafer is then washed in a solution that removes the soft photoresist exposing the oxide layer beneath it. An etching bath removes the exposed oxide uncovering a portion of the original silicon; there are now areas of oxide and silicon corresponding to the pattern of the first mask. The remaining photoresist is removed and the wafer is placed in a diffusion furnace in which impurity atoms of a substance that will create an n-type layer in the silicon will be allowed to penetrate the exposed area (that is, the area from which the silicon dioxide has been removed) to a prescribed depth. Now the remainder of the silicon dioxide is removed and a lightly doped layer of n-type material, through a process called *epitaxy*, is "grown" onto the wafer. This *epitaxial* layer replicates the crystal structure of the original silicon.

The masking process is repeated on the epitaxial layer, which is then subjected to a diffusion of p-type dopant. This pattern of masking and alternately diffusing the silicon with n-type and p-type dopants is repeated for each of the masks that comprise the circuit. The insulating coating of silicon dioxide applied after the last diffusion is masked for circuit contacts; all of this coating that is not etched away to expose contact points in the silicon beneath is left in place. A layer of metal, typically aluminum, evaporated over the surface of the wafer, dips down into the contact areas and touches the silicon. Most of this metal is then

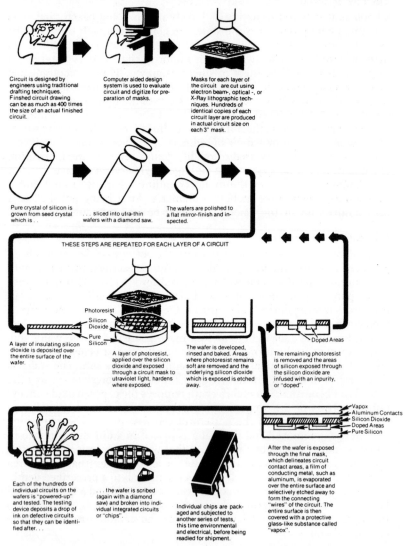

Circuit is designed by engineers using traditional drafting techniques. Finshed circuit drawing can be as much as 400 times the size of an actual finished circuit.

Computer aided design system is used to evaluate circuit and digitize for preparation of masks.

Masks for each layer of the circuit are cut using electron beam-, optical -, or X-Ray lithographic techniques. Hundreds of identical copies of each circuit layer are produced in actual circuit size on each 3" mask.

Pure crystal of silicon is grown from seed crystal which is . .

. . . sliced into utra-thin wafers with a diamond saw.

The wafers are polished to a flat mirror-finish and inspected.

THESE STEPS ARE REPEATED FOR EACH LAYER OF A CIRCUIT

Photoresist
Silicon Dioxide
Pure Silicon

A layer of insulating silicon dioxide is deposited over the entire surface of the wafer.

A layer of photoresist, applied over the silicon dioxide and exposed through a circuit mask to utraviolet light, hardens where exposed.

The wafer is developed, rinsed and baked. Areas where photoresist remains soft are removed and the underlying silicon dioxide which is exposed is etched away.

Doped Areas

The remaining photoresist is removed and the areas of silicon exposed through the silicon dioxide are infused with an inpurity, or "doped".

Vapox
Aluminum Contacts
Silicon Dioxide
Doped Areas
Pure Silicon

After the wafer is exposed through the final mask, which delineates circuit contact areas, a film of conducting metal, such as aluminum, is evaporated over the entire surface and to form the connecting "wires" of the circuit. The entire surface is then covered with a protective glass-like substance called "vapox".

Each of the hundreds of individual circuits on the wafers is "powered-up" and tested. The testing device deposits a drop of ink on defective circuits so that they can be identified after. . .

. . . the wafer is scribed (again with a diamond saw) and broken into individual integrated circuits or "chips".

Individual chips are packaged and subjected to another series of tests, this time environmental and electrical, before being readied for shipment.

etched away leaving an interconnection pattern among the circuit elements. Finally, a layer of vapor-deposited-oxide, or *vapox*, a glass-like material used to protect the circuit from contamination and damage, is deposited over the wafer and etched away only above the *bonding pads*, square aluminum areas to which wires will later be attached.

Remember that hundreds or thousands of identical circuits are being formed on the three-inch wafer simultaneously. These circuits are complete with the deposition and etching of the protective vapox layer, but they still remain part of a single wafer. Before being cut apart into individual circuits, or chips, they are subjected to the first of a series of computer-controlled tests. Each circuit is powered up and tested with fine needles that contact the bonding pad; substandard circuits are identified with a drop of ink left by the testing device.

After being separated, good chips are mounted in ceramic or metal packages and connected to metal leads on the package with minute wires. The packaged chips are then subjected to another series of environmental and electrical tests before being readied for shipment. Only through such exhaustive testing can faults on the order of those that can occur in these tiny chips be revealed. Imagine an aerial photograph of Manhattan Island lithographically reduced to the size of a typical chip, about a quarter of an inch square. Now imagine that in this photograph there is a crack in the pavement in the area of Sixth Avenue. In terms of chip integrity, this would constitute a defective circuit. To forestall defects caused by contamination, chip manufacture is carried out in rooms ten times cleaner than a hospital operating room and diffusion processes take place in as near-complete a vacuum as possible.

2

Everyman's Introduction to the Neurosystems of the Microcomputer

John Simon, 1983

There is a story about the president of a microchip manufacturing company who invited the firm's dog owners to enter their pets in a contest to determine which was smartest. The three finalists in the contest were a Poodle, a German Shepherd, and a Saint Bernard. For the final event, the president placed a personal computer on her desk. Alongside it she laid the relevant hardware and software manuals.

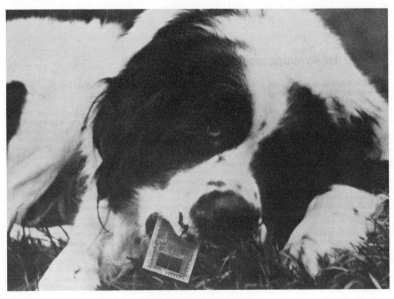

Ushered in first, the Poodle went directly to the back of the machine, grasped the power cord in his jaws, and plugged the unit into a wall outlet. He then jumped up onto the desk, pawed open a programming manual, and began keyboarding. Within ten minutes he had written and debugged a new general ledger system for the firm. "Remarkable," murmured the president, shifting her clipboard to make notes on the dog's performance.

The Shepherd was brought in next. She circled around the desk and retrieved a pocket screwdriver from one of the drawers. Then, jumping onto the desk with the screwdriver between her teeth, she pawed open a hardware manual and proceeded to disassemble the computer down to board level. She then reassembled and tested it, all within a span of ten minutes. "Truly impressive", said the president admiringly, making more notes.

Finally, it was the Saint Bernard's turn. No sooner had the door been opened than the big dog bounded into the room, leaped onto the desk, and knocked the personal computer to the floor. With a sweep of a massive paw he split open the cabinet and turned the devastated machine inside out. Then, very carefully with one nail, he nudged the microprocessor chip away from the rest of the rubble and promptly swallowed it. "Now there's a smart dog" exclaimed the president.

With the advent of the microprocessor chip has come the unbridled application of the adjective "smart" to anything that contains one. Today, one hears reference made to "smart" appliances, "smart" instruments, and "smart" terminals. This phraseology is akin to the more dated appellation, "electronic brain." Such terms are not terribly precise inasmuch as they imply intelligence in devices that are still fundamentally dumb. Computers possess no spontaneity of intellect; left entirely to themselves they will do absolutely nothing. They are dependent for their every "thought" upon the humans who build and use them.

The ability of computers to perform calculations at speeds faster than can be achieved by an unaided human brain is largely a function of the speed of electricity. The first computers to be built were designed to reduce complex mathematical calculations to simple, repetitive logic operations implemented in electrical switching circuits. Electro-mechanical circuits used in the earliest computers were later supplanted by more compact electronic circuitry. Concomitantly, techniques worked out for reducing the manipulation of words and pictures to the same kind of logical operations by which computers manipulate numbers vastly generalized the utility of the machines.

Computers can, in seconds, run through millions upon millions of logical operations that would take a human brain hours, or days, or even years to work through. Very likely, it was naive fascination with the raw processing speed of computers that led to their being regarded as electronic brains. Yet, the degree and extent of the supplemental "thinking" carried out by contemporary electronic brains for their human progenitors is incidental to the most instructive use of the analogy invoked by the term. For purposes of the following discussion, we are going to indulge in a stretch of the analogy and regard the stationary, occasionally semi-articulate boxes of today not just as electronic brains, but as "electronic beings."

The world that a human being thinks about is revealed largely through his or her senses. The basic "stuff" of thought is accumulated principally by hearing, seeing, smelling, tasting, and touching this world. The human brain organizes and consolidates these perceptions and often the being communicates observations or conclusions about them to other beings, through speech or writing, for example. A computer's world, though much more constrained, is perceived through a machine equivalent of the human senses, and it communicates to the external world through the equivalent of human communication organs. Through these "feelers," vast stores of data identified by humans can be translated into a form amenable to manipulation by a computer's internal processing machinery, and the consequences of its processing related to its human operators.

A computer's senses are called *input devices*. Keyboards, light pens, the rolling mouse, punched cards, scanners, sensors, and voice recognition devices are among their number. Its communication organs, called *output devices*, include such equipment as plotters, printers, video display tubes, and voice synthesizers. The dichotomy between input and output mechanisms in computers is not strict, however. Storage media such as cassette, disk, and tape possess a dual nature, inasmuch as a computer can be instructed to both "read" *input* from, or "write" *output* onto, their magnetic surfaces. Consequently, input and output media are usually lumped together and referred to simply as *I/O devices*.

Frequently used as a synonym for I/O device, the term *peripheral* derives from the physical relationship of such devices to a computer's other major components, its *central processing unit*, or CPU, and *memory*.

The computer's CPU is analogous to the human brain, the processing that takes place in it to human thought. Physically, the CPU is a mass of electronic circuitry incorporating many thousands of transistors and other semiconductor devices. These are used to implement electrical *gates* that enable the CPU to internally represent in a consistent fashion, using *binary logic*, data and instructions in the various forms in which they are accumulated by the computer's I/O devices.

Like the human brain, which occupies a relatively small area of the human body, sharing the head with some of the senses and communication organs, a personal computer's "brain" — realized in a tiny chip of silicon — occupies a very slight amount of space in a cabinet that may also house much of the machine's complement of I/O devices. Most contemporary microcomputers incorporate a video display tube in the same cabinet as the CPU. When also included in this cabinet, peripherals, such as disk drives and voice synthesis chips, are said to be *integral*.

The CPU that controls a computer's I/O devices and acts upon the data accumulated by them is, again like the human brain, made up of a number of interrelated segments. A typical CPU comprises three functionally distinct circuit areas.

Figure 1: The neurosystem of a microcomputer

... comprises a number of integrated circuit chips connected by a bus circuit, which is something like a beltway around a city, to one another and to external devices. All of a computer's internal memory can be implemented on only a couple of chips (RAM and ROM in the illustration), each of which might be only as large as a fingernail. Its microprocessor — which is further subdivided into an arithmetic/logic unit, *in which actual processing takes place,* registers, *which are temporary storage areas, and a* control unit, *which is the computer's traffic cop — likely inhabits another single small chip of semiconductor material. One or more chips, depending upon the number of I/O devices the machine will support, will variously enable the computer to interface with external devices such as display tubes, keyboards, and light pens. Because a microcomputer's bus is usually a two-way street, and the traffic an interminable stream of binary signals, timing is of the essence. A* clock circuit *generates millions of precisely timed pulses per second to help the control unit insure that the right binary signals arrive at the right locations at the right times.*

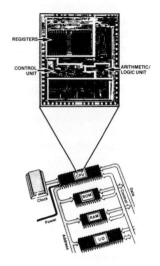

The processing done by a computer, that is, all of the arithmetic operations and logical comparisons performed on data, is carried out in an area called the *arithmetic/logic unit,* or ALU. Retrieval of instructions and data for the ALU is handled by the *control unit.* Sets of memory locations, called *registers,* serve as scratch pads for the control and arithmetic/logic units during operation.

Register memory has very specific storage assignments; various registers are used to store temporarily, small, transient parcels of information essential to current processing. More extensive memory, for storage of data and programs, is also required. Such memory is often provided in the form of separate, but closely allied, chips. Two basic kinds of memory are used. Although both are *random access memory,* or RAM, that term is commonly used to refer to the working memory in which a user can store active data and programs. Another type of memory, used exclusively for storing low-level programming instructions, is called *read-only memory,* or ROM. Programs loaded into ROM, typically during fabrication of the chip, provide the native intelligence for a computer. Generally, this kind of memory is not alterable by a user, although a variation, called *eraseable, programmable, read-only memory,* or EPROM, allows stored programming to be erased and new programming written by means of a special process involving exposing the memory circuits to ultraviolet light through a quartz window built into the chip. A *programmable, read-only memory,* or PROM, lacks the EPROM's re-programmability. Such chips are manufactured in a virgin state and can be programmed, one time only, to customer specifications. Once programmed, a PROM is functionally equivalent to a ROM and cannot be altered further.

As with humans, whose memory lies somewhere in the folds of their brains, a computer's memory chips are mounted in its cabinet. The RAM memory of modern microcomputers is impermanent, or *volatile,* meaning that its contents are not preserved indefinitely. The contents of RAM are effectively lost, for example, when power is turned off to the computer and, when power is on, can be rewritten at will. The contents of ROM, however, are fixed and permanent; a computer can be instructed to read from, but never to write to, ROM. RAM might be likened to a tape recording, the contents of which can be changed and/or erased, and ROM to a phonograph record which has a set store of sounds that can be played over and over but never altered.

Overall, a computer's memory is much less extensive than a human's, with the result that computers rely much more heavily on *mass storage devices.* When a computer "wakes up," it knows next to nothing. At best, the primitive intellect stored in ROM will be able to apprise you, with some defined signal or display, when it is "ready." If you then want to do some useful work, such as word processing, the computer will have to retrieve the "knowledge" of how to do word processing from the appropriate mass storage device and commit it to RAM for as long as it is needed.

Whatever the form of input used with a digital computer — whether keystrokes echoed as characters on a display screen or printer, scanned or digitized pages of printed characters or graphics, or spoken words — the internal representation of the data takes the form of a presence or absence of an electrical voltage at a number of circuit junctions. These electrical states (voltage/no-voltage) correspond to the 1s and 0s that are the basic expressions of the computer's binary logic.

The most elemental storage unit of a computer is called a *bit* (from binary digit). A bit equals a single value that can represent one or the other of two possible electrical states that can exist in a computer's circuits. A group of adjacent bits, usually eight, forms a *byte.* Bytes are used to represent characters, such as letters of the alphabet, punctuation marks, and special symbols. Bytes can also be used to represent instructions to the computer. For example, one byte might contain the instruction that tells a computer to add two numbers, another the instruction that tells it to move some data. Numerical values are represented by bytes lumped together into *words.* A computer's *word size,* measured in bits, determines the upper limit of the numerical values that can be processed by it.

As the early 4-bit microprocessors were rapidly supplanted by 8-bit processors with names like 6502 (manufactured by MOS Technology), 8080 (manufactured by Intel, Incorporated), and *Z80* (manufactured by Zilog, Incorporated), so these processors are being supplanted by 16-bit devices, such as Intel's 8086, Zilog's *Z8000,* and Motorola's MC68000.

Traditionally, if such a term may be used in this fast-paced technology, micro, mini, and mainframe computers have occupied distinct niches in terms of application. Microcomputers of the 8-bit variety have been best suited to single, simple tasks, such as word processing, spreadsheet analysis, and instrument monitoring and control. Minicomputers — by and large, 16-bit machines — have been an ideal choice for single complex tasks, such as computer aided design/computer aided manufacturing (CAD/CAM), or multiple simple tasks, such as supporting a variety of applications like word processing and statistical analysis in a time-sharing, or multi-user environment. The forte of mainframes, which are typically 32- or 36-bit machines, has been, and continues to be, supporting many complex tasks, and many users, simultaneously. Modelling activites in nuclear physics, for example, usually requires a high-end mini or a mainframe computer. At the same time that 16-bit and multi-processor microcomputers are making inroads into mini-territory, 32-bit super-minis are invading the mainframe domain.

As they are shuffled among a computer's major components — CPU, memory and I/O — data and instructions ride a *bus,* which is less analogous to the vehicle than to the paved path it traverses. Traffic flows along the bus in synchronization with precisely timed signals generated by a *clock circuit.*

A computer runs a program by *fetching* and *executing* the instructions that make it up, one at a time (because a computer can do only one thing at a time), interrupting the sequence whenever it is necessary to retrieve data. A typical computer program consists of a series of instructions intermixed with calls for data.

Like their larger siblings, microcomputers basically run two types of programs. *Applications* programs are those that provide a relatively high-level user service. Database management systems, electronic spread-sheets, and word processors are examples of applications. Such programs are like learned skills in a human. A human can learn mathematical skills, for example, from a textbook and apply these skills to the manipulation of data outside the textbook. A computer can "learn" how to do word processing from a program on a disk and through that ability allow you to create, store, and manipulate text in its circuits.

Your learning stays with you longer than that of most computers. You only have to return to a textbook if you forget a rule or two; (seldom would it be necessary for you to relearn, for example, all of your acquired mathematical skills). Because it has comparatively little internal memory, a computer cannot possibly store all at once all of the many programs it is capable of running. As a result, a computer relies heavily on external storage — predominantly disk and cassette — and refreshes its internal memory with specific applications as they are needed.

An *operating system* is a set of programs a computer uses to run itself. If we think of the computer's bus as a highway, then the operating system is its traffic cop, determining the "what" and "when" of traffic flow. It is because a computer has an operating system that you merely have to identify an application by name in order to run it. Identifying the addresses of the application's instructions on the external medium, selecting addresses in memory, and transferring to them a binary copy of these instructions are all processes handled by the computer's operating system. Similarly, when you want the application to process specific data, you simply identify a general location of the data by name and the operating system locates the actual memory addresses.

Earlier, we noted that you might forget a particular rule of mathematics and have to refresh your memory from a textbook. Getting the textbook, finding the page with the desired information, and reading it are all functions performed by your own equivalent of an operating system. Your conscious, offhand performance of this simple act offers no clue to the extensive neuro- and sensori-motor coordination it involves. The simple process of loading an application program and identifying a body of data, which seems to occur unremarkably enough, belies an equivalent underlying complexity of activity in a computer's circuits.

Some of the low-level programming that determines "specificities" for computers in order that interacting humans can deal in "generalities" is stored in ROM. A computer whose complete "subconscious" is not stored in ROM will require supplemental operating system software from an external source, such as cassette or disk. This software must be loaded into, and remain in, RAM for the duration of an operating session. As explained earlier, when an applications program is run the actual transfer of information from cassette or disk to memory is accomplished by the operating system. This being the case, how is the operating system, which contains the instructions for loading from device to memory, loaded? A *bootstrap loader,* or simply, *bootstrap,* is a simple instruction in ROM that the hardware is designed to jump to a soon as power is turned on or a reset switch is pressed. A bootstrap is often implemented in levels, an initial instruction reading additional instructions in from disk until the entire operating system is loaded into memory.

When you turn on, or *power up,* your computer and load its operating system you are enabling it to orient itself, much as you do when you first awake. The grandmotherly term for the human process is "clearing the cobwebs out of one's head." Nor are the manifestations of the process terribly different from humans to computers; the former yawn and sigh and blink their eyes, the latter whir and click and wink their lights.

To explain, conceptually, how the various components of the CPU function in relation to one another it will be helpful to interpolate a sub-analogy. Consider a simple manufacturing- transportation setting in which a factory is served by a railroad. Raw materials are received from distant ports, and products manufactured by the factory are shipped out by rail. A dispatcher controls the movement of all loads, both inbound and outbound.

In a microcomputer, the CPU is the factory and the bus the railroad tracks. The computer's I/O devices are like seaports or airports where incoming and outgoing materials are transferred from one mode of carriage to another. Data, the chief product of the factory, is manufactured out of instructions and possibly other data which together constitute the raw materials of the process. The computer's control unit assumes the role of dispatcher.

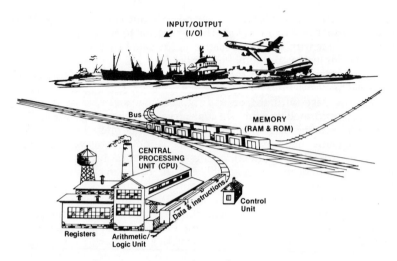

Figure 2: A manufacturing-transportation analogy

A typical factory comprises a manufacturing component, some capacity for temporary storage, and a dispatcher function for controlling traffic into and out of the various components of the facility. To a factory served by a railroad, air and seaports might represent both intermediate points of origin for raw materials and intermediate destinations for manufactured products. Changing the mode of carriage at a port does not substantively alter the cargo; a given cargo is the same whether it is contained by the walls of a railroad car or within the shell of an aircraft. Railroads store and sort cars that contain the freight entrusted to them in large yards from which individual cars strung together in trains are dispatched to appropriate destinations over the railroad's trackage. Like a factory's manufacturing component, a microcomputer's microprocessor, or CPU, has an area for processing, called the Arithmetic/Logic Unit, temporary storage areas, called Registers, and a dispatcher, called the Control Unit. Its I/O ports, like air and seaports, serve both as a source of input to and output from the multi-faceted CPU. A computer's memory serves the same store-and-forward function of a railroad yard, and its bus is the equivalent a railroad's trackage.

In a microcomputer, as on a railroad, controlling the movement of traffic is critical. With both, proper routing is essential to insure that collisions are avoided and that each discrete unit, be it a byte of data or a railway car, is delivered to the appropriate location at the appropriate time. The quandary of a CPU that receives data when it is expecting an instruction is not unlike that of a retailer of mattresses who has advertised a carload sale and discovers, upon breaking the seal on the delivered car, that it contains drums of lubricating oil. If the mattress merchant receives the car of lubricating oil days before the advertised sale there may still be time to locate and deliver the car of mattresses; however, if the discovery is made on the morning of the day the sale is to take place, recovery from the situation might be impossible. Similarly, an error in a CPU might disrupt processing momentarily or bring it to a standstill altogether.

One thing a microcomputer doesn't have to worry about that a railroad does is the damage threshold of the "freight" it moves about. The electrical states that migrate at incomprehensible speeds from location to location within the computer suffer no appreciable degradation as they do so. Compared to a computer's internal processing speed, speeds of peripheral devices are "clunky." Yet, even the clunkiest of a computer's peripherals, its printer, can out-type the most proficient human typist. Though they don't actually think, in light of the things they are capable of doing, and the speeds at which they are capable of doing them, regarding contemporary microcomputers as "smart" does not seem an unwarranted anthropomorphism.

Binary logic and gate circuits

Direct transfer of thoughts between brains is not the general order of interhuman communication. The external manifestations of thought that are the more common vehicles for communication — actions, speech, and writing — are translations of the chemical, electrical, and possibly holographic processes that constitute thought as it occurs within the brain. Regional and cultural distinctions among the human population account for a multiplicity of patterns — many quite different from one another — for translating thought into something that is externally perceptible.

How, and in precisely what form, thought occurs in the human brain is still a subject of research. How, and in what form, "thought" occurs in a digital computer is a *product* of research. Consequently, inasmuch as everything that takes place within computers does so (or is supposed to do so) by design, the anatomy of computer thought is a more tractable pursuit than the anatomy of human thought.

Despite the acknowledged disparity in our understanding of human and computer thought processes, certain analogies between the two will be helpful. A computer's *language*, for example, is constructed in much the same way as a human language. The elemental components that make up a human language are characters or letters, which, of themselves, carry little information. Combined into words, the letters acquire somewhat more meaning. Directions are often related in a few, or even a single, word: "Go," "Come here," "Leave that alone." Communication of thoughts of greater complexity can be accomplished by stringing words together into longer phrases and sentences.

Computer language follows a similar pattern. The computer's alphabet is simplicity itself, consisting of but two digits, a 1 and a 0. These equate to two possible states in a computer's circuits, 1) a presence of a voltage and, 2) an absence of a voltage; (which represents which is abitrary, a choice left to manufacturers). Of themselves, these *bits* carry little information. Like alphabetic characters, however, they can be used to construct *words* that can be strung together to convey instructions and data among a computer's memory and processing circuitry. Computers are usually designed so that simple instructions, like "add," can be represented by a single computer word.

Whereas in most human languages words can be constructed of any number of letters, words employed by a computer must all be of uniform length. Different word sizes are used by different computers, word-sizes of 8-, 16-, 32-, and 36-bits being common.

While bits and characters can be compared in a functional sense, as building blocks in their respective language systems, disparity begins to creep in even before one moves on to words. The extraordinary simplicity of the computer's two-state vocabulary is purchased at the expense of compactness. Clearly, if one attempted a one-to-one translation of the twenty-six letters of the English-language alphabet with but two digits, the supply of digits would be exhausted before the letter *C* was reached. In practice, letters, as well as decimal numbers and special characters, are represented by unique combinations of 1s and 0s. As a result, a single English-language word can comprise several computer words.

The *binary* number system — with its two digits, 0 and 1 — is ideally suited to specifying the logic states in computers. As in the perhaps more familiar *decimal* number system, the positional weights of numbers increase from right to left, in the decimal system by powers of ten (consider the respective values of the digit 2 in the decimal numbers 2 and 20. In the latter number, the 2 occupies the ten's position and has a value ten times greater than the 2 in the one's position. In the binary system, the positional weights of numbers increase by powers of two, as shown in the table below.

2^7	2^6	2^5	2^4	2^3	2^2	2^1	2^0
128	64	32	16	8	4	2	1

Added together, the decimal values of these eight bits is 255; thus, an 8-bit binary number can represent decimal numbers from 0-255. Rendered in binary, the number decimal 255 would contain a 1 in each of the eight bits and appear thus: 11111111. It might be enlightening to determine the binary form of another number, say decimal 99. By the table above, it is clear that the left-most position, which is greater than 99, will be coded as 0. The seventh position will be coded with a 1, as will the sixth position, since adding the two does not exceed the desired number (64 + 32 = 96). Positions five, four, and three, any one of which added to the subtotal would put it over 99, must all be coded as 0s. Finally, positions two and one, which together added to 96 will yield 99, are coded with 1s. Thus, decimal 99 in binary is 01100011.

Because translation of large numbers and text into binary produces long, unwieldy (for humans) strings of 1s and 0s, an intermediate representation is useful. This has been provided by both the *octal* and *hexadecimal* number systems. Three binary digits can be represented by one octal digit and four binary digits by one hexadecimal digit. The latter system is the one most commonly used with microprocessor-based computers. Octal (base 8) numbers can be represented with the digits 0-7. To represent hexadecimal (base 16) numbers, it is necessary to supplement the ten decimal numbers with the first six letters of the English alphabet. The letter *A* is assigned the value 10, the letter *B* the value 11, and so on, with the letter *F* having the value 15. It turns out that even large decimal numbers can be rendered in fewer digits in hexadecimal, making it a shorthand for decimal, as well as binary, representation. For example (and without any proof), decimal 255 equals hexadecimal FF.

The United States American Standard for Information Interchange, usually abbreviated, for obvious reasons, to ASCII (pronounce it "askey"), is a generally accepted coding scheme that provides binary and hexadecimal equivalents for every letter, character, and symbol, including the ten decimal numbers, in general use.

It is the function of I/O devices to make information intelligible to both humans and computers. When a human depresses a key on a computer keyboard, I/O circuitry sends the appropriate binary representation of the key to the computer in the form of electrical signals and the corresponding ASCII representation to the display screen.

If one could travel through a computer's complex neurosystem — through the incredibly intricate integrated circuit chips that constitute its brain parts and along its bus equivalent of a spinal cord to the I/O devices through which it interacts with the external world — what one would encounter would be a seemingly interminable succession of electrical states. Consider, for a moment, metropolitan Boston with its many parking lots and garages interconnected by criss-crossing streets and skirted by limited access highways. Imagine that each car represents the presence of an electrical voltage and the spaces between cars the absence of a voltage. In binary, the cars will be 1s and the spaces 0s. The parking lots and garages will be microprocessor and memory chips, the highway the computer's bus and the streets the circuit paths between elements. Like the contents of a computer's memory, some of the cars in the lots will be stationary for long periods of time, others will move quite frequently. Cars travelling along the highways will move onto the criss-crossing city streets and into various parking areas. In a crude sense, this activity can be compared to the electrical activity in a microcomputer's circuits.

Highways and parking areas are constructed of essentially the same materials — asphalt and concrete. The bulk of a microcomputer's circuits are realized in some solid semiconductor material, most commonly, silicon. Traffic flows from highway to streets and streets into garages through intersections. Electrical switches, called *gates*, are the circuit equivalents of intersections. Different gate structures enable a computer to variously store and forward the electrical states that are the basis of its language.

There are essentially three primitive kinds of gates, named for the logical operations they implement. Depending on its type, a gate may have one or more *inputs* which collectively will determine what it will *output*. The simplest of these is the NOT gate, or *inverter*, which simply reverses the value of its single input. Fed a 1, a NOT gate will output a 0, and vice-versa. An AND gate will output a 1 only if *all* of its multiple inputs are 1; otherwise it will output a 0. An OR gate will output a 1 if any *one* of its multiple inputs is 1. Only if all inputs are 0 will an OR gate output a 0. (More precisely, we are describing an *inclusive* OR, there being a variation called an *exclusive* OR that has a somewhat different set of conditions.)

All possible conditions at a particular gate type can be determined by constructing a *truth table* for it (see Figure 1). As is evident in the illustration, the truth tables for these gates are consistent with the general simplicity of the binary system.

NOT	
In	Out
1	0
0	1

AND		
In$_1$	In$_2$	Out
0	0	0
0	1	0
1	0	0
1	1	1

OR		
In$_1$	In$_2$	Out
0	0	0
0	1	1
1	0	1
1	1	1

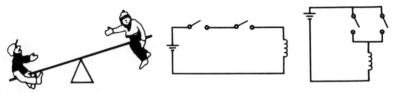

Figure 1: Truth tables

The associated truth tables show the logical outputs for all possible combinations of one or two logical inputs. Below the AND and OR tables are circuit diagrams for simple switches that can be used to demonstrate how the electrical events that correspond to the results in the tables are obtained. The switches correspond to the headings In$_1$ and In$_2$. A 0 input equals an open switch, a 1 input a closed switch. In the diagram below the AND table, the switches are wired in series. Simply closing one or the other of the switches will not permit a current to flow; both switches must be closed in order to pass a current, the electrical equivalent of obtaining a 1 output in the truth table. The switches in the diagram under the OR table, being wired in parallel, will pass a current if either or both are closed. The electrical function represented by the NOT table is that of an inverter; absence of a voltage input will yield a voltage at output, presence of a voltage at input will yield no voltage at output. This function can be illustrated by a seesaw; if one end is up (a 1 at input), the other end will be down (a 0 at output), and vice versa.

In actual system implementation, combinations of these elementary gate structures — the NAND (a NOT and an AND) and NOR (a NOT and an OR) gates — are most often used.

Gates provide two basic functions in a microcomputer; they regulate the passage of control signals and data and, suitably arranged, they can store data. The *Set Reset*, or *SR, flip-flop*, one of a number of types of flip-flops, is an arrangement that performs both functions. This device has two stable states, a 1 and a 0, and can be *set* to 1 and cleared, or *reset*, to 0 by inputting a control signal. Whichever state is set will be retained until a subsequent control signal is received to change it. Flip-flops used in this manner are called *latches*. Computer memory is made up of many latches, each of which can store one binary digit, or bit. Thus, eight latches will be required to store one byte of information. Since the latch structure incorporates several elementary gates, a one byte storage register will consist of many logic gates. In light of this, one can imagine the circuit complexity of even the most modest of microcomputers with a storage capacity of but a few thousand bytes.

Reduced to its ultimate conceptual simplicity, a computer is an extraordinarily complex network of electronic elements that are switched in a pattern determined by the bits in its instructions. Communication with the device is accomplished through I/O devices that translate what a human wants to do into a form the computer can understand. In a human being, an equivalent I/O mechanism in, say, the ocular system, converts visual input received by the eyes in the form of light rays into the electrical signals that are the "machine language" of the brain. Computer I/O devices take myriad forms, the keyboard, light pen, and mouse being common examples. In a typical human-computer exchange, thoughts in a human brain might be translated into a written-language form that can be typed on a computer's keyboard. Each typed character will be transformed by the computer's input device into a code that will signal specific electrical events to take place in the computer's memory or processor circuits. A computer "responds" through a reversal of this process, binary signals being converted by its output devices into an alphanumeric display on a page or a screen that can be perceived by the human eye and translated into the internal language of the human brain.

This is, of course, a great simplification of what actually takes place between communicating humans and computers, as was the foregoing explanation of the elementary facets of computer logic. Yet, the wonder of the internal workings of these machines, and of the man-machine interface, cannot help but be all the greater for realizing from what humble beginnings such capabilities arise.

3

Ringing in the New: What Digital Telephony and Divestiture Have Wrought

John Simon, 1984

During the past several decades, the respective evolutions of computing and telephony have become inextricably entwined. Through the agency of the computer, the telephone system has realized improvements in speed, efficiency, capacity, and range of services. Complementarily, the enhanced telephone system has provided improved communication services, not only among humans, but also among computers. The term that acknowledges this symbiosis, digital telephony, also has specific technical significance, which is discussed in the first part of the following article. The second part assesses a 1984 United States Department of Justice decree that shifted provision of the great bulk of telephone service from a single, regulated supplier, the American Telephone and Telegraph Company, to twenty-two separate entities organized into seven regional holding companies. Thus far, the cumulative effect of these technical and political changes has been largely "transparent to the users" as computer people are fond of saying; whether passed through analog or digital circuits, the voice at the other end of the telephone still sounds the same, and the traditional dial-tone that indicates that telephone service is present continues to be heard on lifting most any receiver.

Part I — Digital Telephony

L
ike water, the atmosphere is a fluid body. The incursion of a rock or a pebble into a body of still water will produce characteristic waves or ripples; a source of vibration in the atmosphere will produce in its substance alternating condensations and rarefactions that are wavelike in nature. If we think of the rarefactions as wave "troughs" and the condensations as wave "crests," the number of crest-to-crest cycles per unit of time will provide a useful measure of a vibration called *frequency.*

In human speech, buzz sounds that emanate from the vocal cords and hiss sounds that result from turbulence around constrictions in the vocal tract combine to produce in the atmosphere vibrations of continuously varying frequency. The loudness, or *amplitude,* of human speech is a measure of power, which also varies continuously with time and ranges from about one billionth of one watt for a whisper to one-thousandth of one watt for sounds spoken as loudly as possible. A one hundred watt lamp uses ten million times more power than the one-ten-thousandth of one watt associated with average human speech.

Speech consists in using the vocal apparatus to *modulate,* or impart some informational content to, air particles in the atmosphere. In converting thought patterns to sound waves, this apparatus acts as a *transducer,* a device that is activated by power in one system and supplies power in some other form to another system. The ear is a complementary transducer actuated by the power of speech. It *demodulates,* or extracts the information content of, sound waves. The action of the latter upon the tympanum, a drum-like membrane in the ear, stimulates tiny hair cells to produce electrical impulses that are transmitted over the auditory nerve to the brain. The brain presumably analyzes the impulses and thus do we derive intelligence from a movement of air particles.

The sounds we are capable of hearing over a distance of a mile or more, among them the shriek of a steam whistle, the blast of an air horn, and the roar of thunder and lions, convey little information beyond calling attention to the presence of their respective sources. Human speech, from which we might expect to derive the greatest intelligence, is audible over as great a distance as three hundred ninety-five feet in a quiet, rural setting, but can be heard only over a distance of about fifteen inches in a New York subway.

In 1831, Sir Charles Wheatstone demonstrated that sound waves could be conducted by a pine rod. Guests in Wheatstone's parlor were entertained by music produced on the sounding board of an unattended musical instrument connected by such a rod to the sounding board of a similar instrument that Wheatstone played in his basement. Extrapolating the technique to voice communication yielded the "lover's telegraph" or "string telephone," a device popular among children of another era in which vibrations produced in a tin can by the action of speaking into it are replicated in a taut cord and, ultimately, in another can.

Before telephony (from the Greek *tele*, meaning far, and *phone*, meaning voice) could become more than a parlor game, a way had to be found around constraints imposed by the nature of sound waves — the rapidity with which they weaken, their susceptibility to distortion, and the speed, a nominal one thousand seventy-five feet per second depending on altitude and atmospheric conditions, at which they travel. The way around proved to be electricity.

In 1837, Dr. C. G. Page, of Salem, Massachusetts, called attention to the fact that an electromagnet in an electric circuit will give off sound at the moment at which the circuit is closed or broken. It was in the process of trying to use this characteristic to increase the number of messages that could be simultaneously transmitted over a telegraph line that Alexander Graham Bell, a Boston University professor of physiology, struck upon a way to realize what he had earlier conjectured, that if he could "make a current of electricity vary in intensity precisely as the air varies in intensity during the production of sound, I should be able to transmit speech..."

Electrical transmission of speech was proposed some twenty years before Bell invented the telephone by Charles Bourseul in an article in the August, 1854 issue of *L'Illustration*, a Paris periodical. What M. Bourseul conjectured, Philippe Reis, of Friedrichdorf, was the first to realize. Inasmuch as he invented what is probably the first operational telephone capable of both transmitting and receiving sound, it is perhaps appropriate that Reis, in a lecture delivered to the Physical Society of Frankfort in 1861, was also the first to use the term *telephony*. Reis's telephone, which reproduced vowel sounds only poorly, was used primarily for transmitting music. In operation, a membrane, made to vibrate by the sounds that impinged upon it, opened and closed an electrical circuit with each vibration, thus transmitting as many electrical pulses as there were vibrations in the sound. The pulses acted on an electromagnet at the receiving station causing it to give out a sound of a pitch corresponding to the number of times it was magnetized or de-magnetized.

In the telephone Bell later invented, the strength of an electrical current was varied as a consequence of modulating, by means of spoken sounds, the pressure on an iron diaphragm. Bell's telephone transmitted electrical waves that were an "analog" of the sound waves that struck the diaphragm. Conducted over wires, these electrical waves are reconstituted as sound waves in the instrument at the receiving end. The process of conversion, transmission, and reconstitution occur at such speed as to seem instantaneous, providing the equivalent of face-to-face communication, sans the visual component, between conversants physically removed from one another.

Though Bell's early telephone predominated, other designs were introduced, a telephone utilizing friction principles having been patented by Elisha Gray, also of Boston, Massachusetts, hours before Bell's. Thomas A. Edison also invented a friction telephone and A. E. Dolbear, a professor at Tufts University, produced a telephone that utilized electrostatic phenomena.

To understand how the telephone works, how it functions in a network, and what is meant by analog and digital switching and transmission, it will be helpful to return briefly to the string telephone described earlier. Let us construct, with only string and tin cans, a telephone system that can serve multiple subscribers over long distances.

As was the case with the earliest electrical telephones, each tin can will serve as both transmitter and receiver. These will be the transducers that will convert sound waves into mechanical energy in a transmission medium, in this case, string, and vice versa. Energy loss is characteristic of all transmission media; that is, the amount of power output by a medium is less by some amount than the amount of power input to it. In a mechanical system utilizing string for transmission, the inhibiting force is called *inertia;* in an electrical transmission medium it is called *inductance.* Transmitted energy that has had information impressed upon it is called a *signal.* Loss in, or weakening of, a signal is called *attenuation.* Transmitted signals are also subject to *distortion.* Atmospheric disturbances can induce non information-bearing vibrations in a string transmission line that can adversely affect the message-bearing vibrations. Similarly, in wire or microwave radio transmission, transmitted signals are subject to interference from atmospheric conditions and from competing signals on neighboring media.

The effects of attenuation and distortion can be overcome by periodically relaying, or *repeating,* a signal. An obvious way to do this in our mechanical system is to terminate a given piece of string at a point at which a spoken message can still be heard clearly. If we terminate the string in a can, and supply another can connected either to another relay or to the junction of subscriber lines that we will describe in a moment, we can station an individual between them whose job it will be to repeat everything heard in one can more loudly into the other. Unless we are able to employ exclusively highly-skilled mimics, however, our system already has a significant defect in that the voices heard at either end of a connection will not be those of the actual subscribers.

Switching is a method whereby the need for every subscriber to have a direct line to every other subscriber is eliminated. To cross connect even one hundred telephones, a number to which we will restrict our hypothetical system in the interest of simplicity, we would have to string four thousand, nine hundred and fifty separate lines. By terminating all subscriber lines at a central location so arranged that we can interconnect any two, we can service the entire subscriber base with but one hundred lines.

The nature of our system will dictate that each line terminate in a numbered can, and we will also require the services of fifty individuals to serve as "connectors." (In fact, their job will be functionally the same as that of the "repeaters.") We also need a switcher, or *operator,* to service requests for interconnection.

Consider the network in operation. A subscriber who wants to call another subscriber must first get the attention of the switching center. Let us say he does so by shouting into his can the word "Operator" followed by the number of the can that belongs to the subscriber he wants to communicate with. This message will be repeated at each relay between his can and the switching center. The operator, upon hearing the message, will "ring" the subscriber to whom that can belongs. Again, at each relay, an individual will repeat the word "ring" until the voice of the last repeater in the line is heard from the can in the home of the subscriber. If the called party is at home and hears her can, the operator, upon acknowledgement of the fact (the called party saying "hello," for example), will place in the hands of one of the connectors both the can that originated the call and the can that answered. The connector will provide a unique path for the call, and will repeat, as appropriate, whatever is heard from one can into the other. Given conversants who are patient and willing to speak in turn, it is possible to imagine successful two-way communication taking place over this *switched network*. It is not possible to imagine a practical telephone system constructed in this manner.

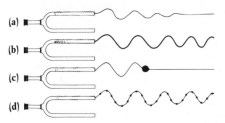

Figure 1: Loading in telephone transmission lines — a mechanical analogy

The analog and digital switching techniques employed by contemporary telephone systems grew out of the limitations that make the system described above impractical. We noted earlier that sound waves travel at a speed of one thousand seventy-five feet per second. A pair of wires of zero resistance, in free space, separated from all other conductors and without leakage, would transmit electrical waves at the speed of light, which is one hundred eighty-six thousand miles per second. Conditions are seldom perfect, however, and wave speeds are almost invariably retarded. Nevertheless, the magnitude of the speed differential between sound and electrical waves is significant.

But for all of their extraordinary speed, electrical waves, like sound waves, are susceptible to attentuation and distortion. To account for attenuation of the sound waves in our string telephone system we employed repeaters. Using heavier string, though it would not have eliminated the need for repeaters, would have enabled us to space them further apart. Similarly, telephone engineers found that the range of early transmission lines could be extended by increasing the *gauge*, or thickness, of the wire used. Heavier wire is more expensive, though, and over very long distances, such as on an early link to Denver, Colorado, the "wires" took on the proportions of small bars.

An alternative technique, called *loading*, provided a means to get equivalent range from smaller gauge wire. Loading may be understood by means of a mechanical analogy constructed by attaching to a tuning fork one end of a stretched string (see Figure 1). If the fork is vibrated, a mechanical wave will be propagated for a short distance along the string and then die out (a). Substitution of a heavier string results in the wave travelling further before dying out (b), a consequence of inertia, which is analogous to inductance in an electrical conductor. To discover whether propagation might be assisted by adding inertia at some one point we will again use a lighter string, this one bisected by a single heavy weight. What we discover is that the wave starts out as in (a) but, upon reaching the weight, dies out altogether (c). If we use a few scattered, lighter weights, the wave will not pass the first. However, if many tiny weights are equally spaced with several in each wave length (d), the result is the same as with the heavier string in (b). In analog telephony, loading takes the form of coils that provide "lumps" of inductance at equal intervals along a wire transmission line.

To appreciate the degree of attentuation that would take place in a transmission line that employed no means for boosting transmitted signals, the following illustration is cited:

> The loss of a 19-gage H-44 side cable circuit 1000 miles long is approximately 480 db (decibels). If we attempted to transmit energy over such a circuit without any means of boosting the transmitted power along the line, an input power of one milliwatt at the sending end would be attenuated to 10^{-51} watt at the receiving end. This reduction is so great that if one milliampere of current, which is 6.28×10^{15} electrons per second, was sent into this line, the current at the receiving end would be approximately one electron every 10^{14} million years. (American Telephone and Telegraph Company 1938, 239)

As with loading, but for a somewhat different reason, boosting, or amplification, of telephone signals is accomplished by many, fairly evenly spaced devices. To obtain, in the above example, the same strength signal at the receiving end as was transmitted from the sending end would require an amplifier of impractical proportions; even distributing the amplification over several devices would not be feasible. Consequently, telephone signals transmitted over wire cable are amplified about every fifty miles.

The devices that perform such amplification, designated *repeaters* in telephone work, are the progeny of Harold D. Arnold of the Bell Telephone System, and Irving Langmuir of the General Electric Laboratories, who independently, in 1912, converted the three-element electron tube invented by Dr. Lee de Forest six years earlier into a high vacuum electron tube that could be used to amplify electrical signals. The first repeaters to be used in a commercial telephone circuit were installed in Philadelphia on the New York to Baltimore line in 1913. Within two years, the use of repeaters had made possible coast-to-coast telephone communication. With the advent of repeaters, loading, because it was found to increase rather than reduce attenuation in open wires during damp weather, was removed from all open wire telephone transmission facilities.

Implemented as proposed in our string model, switching would be a chaotic affair. Even the most primitive switching methods employed in electrical telephony are a picture or orderliness and compactness by comparison. A manual switching center, or *exchange*, for an electrical telephone system substitutes an electrical panel with numbered sockets for the numbered cans in our earlier example and jumper wires for the human "connectors."

Consider, in light of the sequence of events suggested for placing a call in the string system, the equivalent activity as it occurred in early manual systems. A telephone system is essentially an extraordinarily complex electrical circuit. All lines that emanate from an exchange are supplied with a constant low voltage; local batteries associated with each telephone instrument in early systems were supplanted in later systems by a central battery that supplied all of the lines for a particular exchange. The contacts held down by the pressure of the receiver on its cradle or hook produce the effect of an open switch, which keeps the telephone instrument, except for the bell, out of the circuit. When the receiver is lifted, the contacts make and a lamp over the socket associated with that telephone at the central exchange is made to glow, signalling the operator that a caller is waiting. By plugging her own headset into the socket she can communicate with the caller regarding the number of the telephone that is to be called. She then connects the socket associated with the called party's telephone with a socket connected to a ringing circuit. This causes the lamp over the called party's socket to glow. When the called party lifts her receiver from its hook, the light goes out, signalling the operator to move the end of the cord in the ringing socket to the caller's socket. This done, both lights go out. When the caller hangs up both lights again glow, signalling the operator to disconnect both. Thus, glowing lights signal attention: over an open socket, that a line is to be answered; over a cord, that a line is being rung; over two cords, that the parties are to be disconnected.

As the telephone became more popular and the volume of calls increased, successive techniques for automating calling and switching activities were devised. Though obscured by mechanical detail, logic and memory functions were incorporated in an early, dial-actuated, step-by-step switch invented in 1889 by Almon B. Strowger, a midwestern school-teacher and undertaker. In the Strowger switch, an advancing arm is moved by a rotary mechanism one step for each pulse that results from a dialed digit. Any one of one hundred contacts, arranged in ten levels of ten positions around a circular switch, is capable of being contacted by the arm.

The Strowger switch was followed, in 1915, by the Western Electric Company's panel switch. This switch stores dialed digits in registers whose numerical contents are converted by a "decoder" into a form that a "sender" can use to control the switching that will establish actual electrical connections between telephones. With the control and switching functions separated, only the switch itself is tied up for the duration of a call, the registers, decoders, and senders being released after the connection is made to handle other calls. Thus, control becomes a "common," or shared function, whereas in the step-by-step switch control was "distributed" in the sense that it was directly associated with the physical switch that established an electrical connection. In the late 1930s, an improved form of common control electromechanical switching was realized in the crossbar switch, a fast, compact arrangement of horizontal and vertical bars that tilt and pivot under the action of electromagnetic relays.

The age of solid state electronics, which so transformed the early relay operated computer over a span of but of few decades, worked a similar metamorphosis in telephone switching. The transistor, invented in the Bell Telephone Laboratories in 1947, together with other solid state devices that followed, made possible electronic systems capable of performing switching, or changing circuit conditions, at speeds of a few nanoseconds (billionths of a second) under the control of stored, computer-like programs. By contrast, the fastest relay operation achieved in electromechanical systems is on the order of milliseconds (thousandths of a second).

The first commercial electronic switching system installed by the Bell System was the No. 1 E.S.S., which went into service in Succasunna, New Jersey, in May, 1965. This switch, and its contemporaries, such as the GTE Automatic Electric Company's No. 1 and No. 2 EAX (electronic automatic exchange), and successors, the No. 2, No. 3, and No. 4 E.S.S., are essentially electronic computers. As noted earlier in reference to step-by-step and panel switches, telephone switching comprises two functions: (1) control, which is the process of interpreting and carrying out instructions, and (2) switching, which is the act of establishing physical electrical connections on the basis of such instructions. Although stored programming in an electronic computer supplies the control function in the No. 1 E.S.S., switching is accomplished by means of contact switches that pass analog electrical signals. Thus, the term "digital" is not appropriately applied to the switching function of a switch such as the No. 1 E.S.S., but only to the control function as it is carried out by a computer that is "digital" in that its repertoire of logical operations consists entirely in manipulating the bi-stable states of memory locations that can be completely represented by the binary digits, 0 and 1.

Advances in semiconductor technology saw the contact switches employed in early electronic switches supplanted by *gate circuits* in later, truly digital, switches. The gates are formed — together with transistors, diodes, capacitors, resistors, and other circuit elements — in a solid piece of semiconductor material collectively termed an *integrated circuit*. The presence of special control signals at these gates controls the passage of information-bearing signals through them.

With the advent of electronic switching systems, the default for a telephone call became no-operator. Virtually all connections, whether local or long-distance, could be established, all supervisory functions, such as provision of dial-tone and ringing, provided, and all call accounting information necessary for billing recorded without the intervention of an operator. The human telephone operator is by no means extinct — AT&T retained forty thousand after divestiture — but their services generally are no longer required for routine tenor eleven-digit calls or for interconnection with other carriers.

The simple fact is that the present traffic in communications that daily passes over the network could not be handled by electromechanical switching apparatus regardless of how many operators were employed. The digital computer has provided the necessary speed, capacity, and flexibility to do so, and it contributes compactness into the bargain. The speed of electronic switching systems is such that, although a system performs all call processing and automatic maintenance functions serially, the results of much of the activity seem to occur simultaneously. A given subscriber will perceive that he or she has the system's complete and undivided attention from lifting the receiver through completion of a call, yet the switch is scanning each of thousands of subscribers' lines for an off-hook condition five or more times per second even as it processes calling information for, and establishes circuit connections among, a multiplicity of callers.

In terms of capacity, analog switches use several stages of 8×8 or 10×10 switch arrays. With digital designs, fewer stages of 100×100 arrays are more usual. With larger arrays, the likelihood of *blocking*, that is, of a call not finding an open path, is reduced as is, to some extent, the need for costly rearrangements to balance traffic loads among different sections of a network. Because it has the inherent information processing capabilities of a computer, which, after all, it is, an electronic switch can record, process, and bill, automatically, for all services that pass through its circuits.

The traffic on the circuits switched by the earliest electronic switches was still entirely analog. The analog signals that made up this traffic were produced in much the same way as they were in the first telephones and, in fact, are still produced today. The resistance in loosely packed carbon granules in the telephone receiver is varied by the action of sound waves on a thin metal diaphragm; the flow of electrons among the granules becomes freer when the diaphragm is compressing them, and vice versa. The steady-state current in the transmission line is modulated by these variations. At the other end of the line, the receiver in another telephone handset, by passing the varying current through an electromagnet, modulates a diaphragm in such a way as to produce in it the same vibrations as were induced in the transmitting diaphragm by the speaker's voice. Circuitry in the telephone handset prevents the speaker's voice from echoing back through his or her own receiver.

The transmission medium that connects a telephone subscriber to a local switching center, or *central office*, is called a *twisted pair*. The name derives from the twisting together of two wood pulp or plastic insulated, high-purity copper wires. By varying the twist length, or pitch, of neighboring pairs, they can be grouped into cables of from six to twenty-seven hundred pairs with a minimum of interference, or *crosstalk*, among the separate pairs, each of which can carry voice signals simultaneously in both directions.

Simultaneous, bi-directional transmissions over twisted pair wiring cannot be amplified, however. Consequently, before a call gets too far in the network, it encounters a device called a *hybrid* that transforms the two-wire circuit to a four-wire circuit in which one pair is used exclusively for outgoing signals and the other exclusively for incoming signals. One-way amplifiers, or repeaters, can be used on these circuits. A complementary hybrid that recombines the incoming and outgoing signals on a single twisted pair will be encountered before the call reaches its destination.

The inherent limitations in sending each voice message over a separate wire circuit, or channel, began to be in evidence early. *Space division routing* is a fancy name for the technique that yielded such unsightly urban wirescapes as that depicted in the accompanying photograph.

Multiplexing, or simultaneously transmitting multiple signals over the same medium, was to transmission what crossbar and electronic switches would be to switching. Fundamental to multiplexing is the *carrier* principle, which term derives from the use of alternating currents of selected higher frequencies to "carry" messages in the voice frequency range of from 200 to 3,500 cycles per second. This measure of frequency is usually indicated by some number *hertz*, (or simply *hz*), one hertz being equal to a frequency of one cycle per second. A frequency band 4000 hz wide is usually employed for voice transmission. The resulting *guard band* — of a couple of hundred hertz at each end of the voice spectrum — provides a margin against interference among separate carrier frequencies. As long as the width of the transmission band is maintained, it is possible to shift a given telephone message to a higher set of frequencies; for example, voice signals on a twisted pair cable with a frequency range of 0-4,000 hz can be shifted by a modulator at the central office to a frequency range of 10,000,000 to 10,004,000 hz. If we then shift the respective frequency ranges of eleven more 0-4,000 hz messages up to eleven consecutive 4,000 hz slots from 1,004,000-1,048,000 hz we can transmit the lot of them over one channel as a single, complex 10,000,000-10,048,000 hz signal. Called *frequency division multiplexing*, this technique can be used to transmit as many as 10,800 separate voice channels over a single coaxial or microwave circuit (see Figure 2).

A coaxial conductor consists of a central conducting wire separated from an outer conducting cylinder by insulating discs spaced at approx-

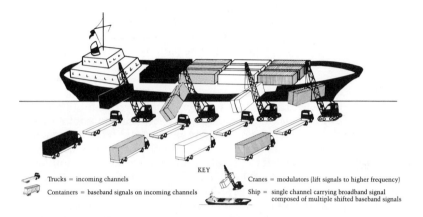

KEY

Trucks = incoming channels

Containers = baseband signals on incoming channels

Cranes = modulators (lift signals to higher frequency)

Ship = single channel carrying broadband signal composed of multiple shifted baseband signals

Figure 2: Frequency division multiplexing

A navigation company with a brisk business in container cargo does not put each container trucked into port onto a different ship for the ocean-going part of its voyage, but rather loads into the hold of a single ship many such trailers, each with its respective cargo separate and intact. At the port of destination, individual containers are transferred from the single ship to many waiting trucks, each of which will pull its particular container over a route specific to its destination. Like the containers that begin their journeys behind separate tractors, signals originated by different instruments in a telephone network begin their journeys over separate paths, or channels. *These signals are of the form of electrical waves, the frequency of which can vary over a broad spectrum. The number of waves, or* cycles, *per second can be rendered as some number* hertz, *(e.g., 3,000 hertz equals 3,000 wave cycles per second). A continuously-varying wave can have many different frequencies, the highest and lowest of which will determine its range, or* bandwidth. *A bandwidth of from 0-4,000 hertz, which is adequate for maintaining the intelligibility of human speech, as well as for providing a margin against interference from competing signals, is usually allocated to voice signals at their point of origin. If one maintains this bandwidth, but at a much higher frequency, one can combine, or* multiplex, *many* baseband *voice signals, arriving on as many separate channels, into a single, complex* broadband *signal that can be transmitted over a single channel. At the other end of such a channel, as at the port of destination for the container ship, the component parts of the multiplexed signal can be separated and routed once more over unique paths to their individual destinations. This process of dividing a high-frequency signal with a broad bandwidth into many individual signals each of a relatively narrow bandwidth is called* frequency division multiplexing. *One might think of the greater bandwidth availability at higher frequencies in terms of equivalent percentages of given* carrier frequencies, *that is, higher frequencies upon which lower-frequency baseband signals are impressed through a process called* modulation. *For example, 10% of a carrier frequency of 1,000 hertz (1 Kilohertz) is only 100 hertz, whereas the same percentage of a carrier frequency of 1,000,000 hertz (1 Megahertz) is 100,000 hertz.*

imately one inch intervals. Signal-bearing electromagnetic waves are guided through the space between these conductors. Coaxial conductors are frequently grouped in cables, or *pipes* in telephone parlance, often with twisted pairs included for passing control and alarm signals. In microwave transmission, electromagnetic waves are beamed with a very narrow focus over a line-of-sight path between two towers. Tower spacing in open country is typically twenty to forty miles. Facing antennas can both transmit and receive over the same path by assigning different frequency ranges to incoming and outgoing groups of signals.

The term *modulation,* which we used earlier to describe the process of creating analog signals in a telephone handset, also describes the process by which some characteristic of a carrier signal is varied by a characteristic of a message signal. The three wave characteristics most often varied are amplitude (or height), frequency, and phase. Amplitude and frequency modulation are well-known (as AM and FM), though not necessarily understood, techniques for enabling a multiplicity of radio stations to broadcast in a given geographical area. In both, one characteristic of a high-frequency carrier signal is varied in relation to one characteristic of a *baseband* signal, that is, a signal in its original frequency spectrum.

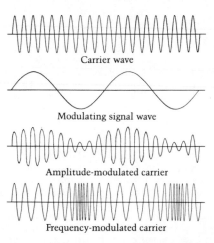

Carrier wave

Modulating signal wave

Amplitude-modulated carrier

Frequency-modulated carrier

Figure 3: Amplitude and frequency modulation

Amplitude modulation is the process of varying the amplitude of the carrier signal in relation to the amplitude of the message signal. Frequency modulation consists in varying the frequency of the carrier signal in relation to the amplitude of the message signal (see Figure 3). Insofar as an available bandwidth is apportioned such that multiple messages can be transmitted at specific ranges within it, frequency division multiplexing in telephone transmission might be compared to FM broadcasting in radio. In radio, however, each station operates its own transmitter by which message-bearing signals at an assigned frequency are propagated at a specified power in all directions simultaneously. Telephony uses frequency division multiplexing to transmit an entire bandwidth (all of the radio stations together) over a single, narrow transmission path.

It is also necessary, of course, to be able to separate the modulated signals at the receiving end of the line and, ultimately, to return them to their original voice frequencies. The former is accomplished by means of a special kind of electrical circuit invented in 1915 by George A. Campbell, a research mathematician employed by the American Telephone and Telegraph Company. Called *electrical wave filters,* such circuits, which are usually constructed of crystalline quartz, are designed to pass only selected frequencies. Quartz crystals are possessed of natural frequencies, or periods of vibration, determined by their dimensions, density, and elasticity. When the frequency of an applied alternating electrical voltage is the same as the natural period of vibration of a crystal, the intensity of the vibration of the crystal will reach a sharp "resonant" quality. Thus, crystals of selected frequencies can be used to pick out and pass along only certain bands of a broad band of carrier frequencies. The selected frequencies can then be converted back to their original voice frequencies for delivery over separate channels to the receiving telephones through a process called *demodulation.*

As it has been for more than a century, voice communication continues to be served admirably by analog techniques. Nevertheless, changes effected in telephone switching by the debut of the electronic digital computer were complemented by the development of digitally-oriented modulation techniques for transmission.

By mid-century, the computer had become a commonplace in business and education. Concomitant with the proliferation of, and increasing reliance upon, computers came a need to extend access to them and also to share information, or data, among physically separated machines. Inasmuch as electricity is the native language of computers and wires are a natural conduit for electricity, the existing telephone network could provide both an expedient alternative to such slow and cumbersome transfer media as punched cards and magnetic tapes and a logical extension to the wires that connect local terminals to large timesharing computers.

Electricity is propagated through a computer's circuits as discrete pulses, which are the electrical manifestation of the binary, or two-state, logic that is the basis of all of its operations. An electrical pulse signals one of these states, the absence of a pulse the other. Strung together, in the manner of the dots and dashes of the Morse Code, these states, or *bits,* can be used to store, process, and communicate information.

The concept of interleaving multiple messages on a single circuit harks back to the Baudot telegraph system, which predates the invention of the telephone. The generic term for the process is *time division multiplexing,* that is, the separation of messages in time rather than in space or frequency (see Figure 4). A telegraph transmits electrical pulses rather than continuous analog signals. Received pulses are decoded to obtain the transmitted message. Similarly, the presence or absence of an electrical voltage at millions upon millions of discrete locations in a computer's circuits constitutes a great store of coded information that can be decoded and made intelligible to a human on demand.

A coding scheme that can represent all possible information by means of combinations of only two physical states possesses a stability born of its simplicity. If these states are the presence or absence of an electrical

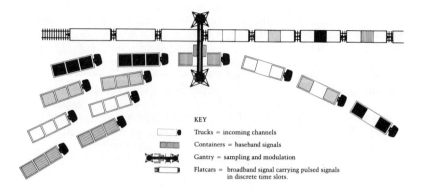

Figure 4: Time division multiplexing

Unlike such cargo shipped by sea, container cargo shipped by rail moves toward its destination not altogether on an expansive deck, but rather serially, one container behind another, on the beds of railroad flatcars. In the world of trucks and trains, because cargoes are identified by markings on the containers and not by the relative positions of the containers on a string of flatcars, the transshipment process needn't be so orderly as that depicted in the illustration above. We have rendered it so because it makes an analogy to time division multiplexing *easier. Let us pretend that each of four large shippers is sending a number of containers to a different destination. Although we have shaded the arriving tractor trailer configurations differently to indicate the various originating shippers, let us further pretend that they all appear identical to the terminal personnel. If we transfer from truck to rail one container from each shipper in turn and follow the same sequence for the rail to truck transfer at the other end of the line, we should end up with each container behind the appropriate shipper's tractors. Time division multiplexing consists in transmitting in turn — as broadband signals on a single channel — baseband signals arriving on many individual channels. In time division multiplexing, each signal uses the entire bandwidth of the broadband channel, but only at regularly recurring intervals. One might think of the flatcars in the illustration as a high-frequency carrier signal divided into individual time slots and the railroad track as the broadband channel. Another characteristic of time division multiplexing, explained by means of another liberty taken with the illustration, is that of* sampling. *Note that only one of several containers on each truckbed is being transferred. Continuously-varying voice signals, in order to be transmitted piecemeal over time, are converted into pulses that correspond to a subset of the amplitude values of the original signal. When decoded, this subset of values is used to generate a new wave that is a close enough approximation of the original to be indistinguishable from it for purposes of voice reproduction.*

pulse, to receive a string of code one needs only to be able to detect a pulse, failure to do so constituting receipt of the other state. This is precisely the form in which coded information stored in a computer is exchanged among machines that are directly wired together. Transmission requirements for information in this form turn out to be much less rigorous than for information in a continuously varying, or analog, form.

Since the information content of a pulse lies in its presence (or absence), and not in the precise amplitude of the pulse, it is not lost if the latter is distorted by extraneous electrical signals, called *noise*, that originate in all conductors and as a consequence of the close proximity of multiple conductors. So long as a pulse is not attenuated beyond detection, a new, perfect pulse can be regenerated at intervals as required (see Figure 5). Thus, using *pulse-regenerator circuits* of a much lesser complexity than the repeaters used in analog circuits, signals of the same strength as those transmitted can be delivered to a receiver.

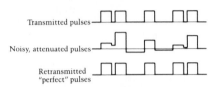

Transmitted pulses

Noisy, attenuated pulses

Retransmitted "perfect" pulses

Figure 5: Pulse regeneration in digital transmission lines

Since human speech is an analog process, in order to transmit it over digital circuits it is necessary to code it and to use the code to modulate a carrier signal such that it pulses. A commonly used technique, called *pulse code modulation*, entails several steps. Since it is impossible to code a continuously varying wave, some set of discrete values of the wave sufficient to later reconstruct it must first be derived. Through a process called *quantizing* a continuous wave is transformed into a step-like pattern, each step of which has a discrete set of values associated with it. Because all attempts to quantize a continuously varying function at a given instance in time must be approximations, however close, some error is inherent in the process. Called *quantizing error*, it can be held to a minimum by choosing sufficiently small steps, or intervals, and is usually not objectionable. A quantized signal is *sampled* to obtain a subset of these values. It has been determined that sampling the amplitude of a quantized wave at a rate of twice its bandwidth per second will permit an adequate reconstruction. Thus, voice signals in the frequency range of 0-4,000 hz must be amplitude-sampled at least eight thousand times per second. If the quantization intervals are numbered, then it is only necessary to transmit a sequence of numbers corresponding to the sequence of sample values. In order for these numbers to be transmitted as pulses, they are translated into their binary equivalents (see Figure 6). At the receiving end of the circuit, a decoder reconstructs the quantized signal, which is restored to its original continuous wave form by passing it through a *low-pass filter*.

One can think of the quantizing/sampling process in the following manner. *Pitch* in the human voice is analogous to frequency in an electromagnetic wave; both are measures of cycles per unit of time. The human voice can change pitch in a continuous manner, whereas a piano creates pitch in discrete units. If we sample at prescribed intervals the notes in a tune hummed by a human voice we will accumulate a sequence of discrete notes that can be played on a piano keyboard. Given a sufficiently large sample, missing notes can be inferred from the location of the sampled notes on the scale and a continuous tone reproduction of the original sound can be produced.

When pulse code modulation is wed to time division multiplexing, the multiplexing functions become so intimately integrated with switching as to preclude delineation of boundaries between them. Microprocessor-based multiplexer/switchers quantize, sample, and code incoming signals from many lines and put them, a sample at a time, on a common circuit, or *bus*. Each of the channels gets a piece of the bus eight thousand times per second. One such device is capable of multiplexing the signals from ninety-six incoming lines onto low capacitance, twisted pair cable for transmission over short distances. Because each sample is represented by an eight-bit code and each of the ninety-six channels is sampled eight thousand times per second, a transmission speed of $8 \times 96 \times 8,000$, or 6,344,000 bits per second (6.3 Megabits/second) is required to interleave the pulses.

Computers are, by design, digital creatures. Human beings, by nature, are predominantly analog creatures; our senses respond to continuously varying conditions in our environment. Because the existing telephone network mixes and, if it is to continue to serve both people and machines, must continue to mix analog and digital techniques, a considerable amount of transformation and retransformation must take place.

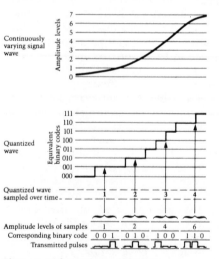

Figure 6: Pulse code modulation

A computer or computer terminal required to pass data over twisted pair wire such as connects most households with the network must be able to convert its native bit stream into analog signals compatible with the bi-directional medium. Conversely, it must be able to translate signals returned from the communicating computer, which perforce must adopt an analog form for arrival at the local telephone handset, into bit-pulses the local computer or computer terminal can understand. The facilitating device that makes such two-way translation possible is called a modulator-demodulator, or *modem*. The function of a modem is essentially the same as that of the equipment used in telephone networks to modify signal-bearing waves for transmission among different media and for combining multiple signals for transmission over single channels. Thus, a modem uses the pulsed signals from a computer terminal to modulate an outgoing voice frequency carrier and intercepts and converts to pulsed signals incoming voice-frequency signals.

The mix of analog and digital communications and equipment yields some interesting sequences of translation. With hundreds of millions of route miles of digital transmission facilities in place, most non-local .

voice calls are converted to digital at some point in their travels and then back again to analog for delivery to receiving telephones. Digital traffic originated by a computer typically undergoes a conversion to analog by a modem at the originating station, is converted back to digital for transmission over digital long-distance circuits, and then back to analog for delivery to the receiving station where another modem converts it back to digital for the receiving computer. In both cases, the information-bearing signals may be shifted up and down in frequency and be modulated and demodulated many times and in various ways, travel alone or in the company of as many as ten thousand other signals from which they must ultimately be separated, and traverse aerial and buried twisted pair wires, tunnel through coaxial cable, streak through the air between microwave towers, or leave the atmosphere altogether in order to rendevous with, and be beamed back by, a satellite more than twenty-two thousand miles away, and yet arrive at the receiving terminal with sufficient integrity that, upon undergoing a final demodulation, they are rendered either an identifiable voice or a processable bit stream.

Part II — Divestiture

U niversal telephone service, as it is enjoyed in the United States, is a legacy of the Bell System, which formerly comprised the American Telephone and Telegraph Company, the Bell Telephone Laboratories, the Bell operating companies, and Western Electric Corporation. The roots of this system reached all the way back to the invention of the telephone and to the inventor of the most successful of the earliest telephones, Alexander Graham Bell. Thomas Sanders and Gardiner Hubbard, who shared the financial support for the perfection and patenting of Bell's telephone, also participated in the germ that would eventually become the American Telephone and Telegraph Company. The Bell Patent Association came into existence on February 27th, 1875, by written agreement between Bell and Messrs. Sanders and Hubbard. Mechanical assistance with the experiments Bell was carrying on at this time in a workroom in a Boston boardinghouse was provided by a machinist named Thomas A. Watson.

In 1877, after failing to interest the Western Union Company in acquiring the Bell patents, the members of the Bell Patent Association, together with Mr. Watson and others, formed the Bell Telephone Company. The company's success in selling the idea of telephone communication to a skeptical public aroused interest in other quarters. The Western Union Company somewhat belatedly purchased the telephone patents of other inventors such as Amos E. Dolbear, Thomas A. Edison, and Elisha Gray and organized the American Speaking Telephone Company. To fortify itself against competition from this then-forty million dollar concern, the fledgling Bell Telephone Company secured additional capital and reorganized as the New England Telephone Company. Four months later, a new Bell Telephone Company was formed to handle business outside of the territory served by the New England Telephone Company.

Already, the pattern of manufacturing and leasing telephone instruments to licensed operating companies had been established, with the Bell Company manufacturing and leasing telephones to licensees outside of New England and selling telephones to New England Telephone for lease to New England licensees.

The formation of the second Bell Telephone Company brought in the single individual who was to be most instrumental in laying the foundations of the latter-day telephone giant. Prior to accepting the position of general manager of the new Bell Telephone Company, Theodore N. Vail, over a period of fourteen years, had risen from a drug store clerk to general superintendent of the railway postal service. As a railway postal clerk in Omaha, in 1869, Vail revolutionized the railway postal service by initiating the practice of pre-sorting the mail that was loaded onto railway cars. Prior to this, mail ricocheted back and forth across the continent as mail clerks extracted only letters destined for their stations and forwarded the remainder unsorted to the next station.

Vail continued as general manager when a subsequent infusion of funds brought new interests into control of the Bell Company and resulted in the consolidation of that company with New England Telephone in 1879. During the one-year existence of the resulting National Bell Telephone Company, Vail introduced telephone service throughout the United States and in several foreign countries. It was also with National Bell that Western Union reached a settlement whereby the two companies agreed to restrict their activites to telephony and telegraphy, respectively.

In 1880, with a virtual monopoly on telephone patents and yet another infusion of capital to finance further expansion, the company once again reorganized, this time as the American Bell Telephone Company.

Vail's interest in interconnecting the many telephones of the proliferating operating companies by means of long-distance lines led to the formation, in 1885, of the American Telephone and Telegraph Company, a subsidiary of the American Bell Telephone Company. Vail resigned as general manager of the latter in order to assume the presidency of the new company. With American Telephone and Telegraph providing for interconnection of the local exchanges of licensed Bell operating companies and for private lines for long-distance communication, American Bell became primarily a holding company, engaged in licensing and investing in operating companies, owning telephone instruments, and maintaining the commercial viability of the overall enterprise.

Provision and repair of telephone instruments for the succession of Bell companies was originally accomplished by the Boston electrical shop of Charles Williams and by a gradual conversion of independently-owned telegraphic instrument shops into telephone manufacturing facilities. By 1881, American Bell had acquired a controlling interest in the Western Electric Company, which, as the supplier of all of the electrical apparatus for the Western Union company and its subsidiary, the American Speaking Telephone Company, had become the largest and best-equipped U.S. producer of telegraph and telephone equipment.

Over a span of about seven years, Vail had assembled the organizational components that would characterize the Bell company and enable it to dominate telephone communication for more than a century: local exchange services provided through licensed operating companies; unified long-distance interconnection provided by the subsidiary American Telephone and Telegraph Company (later the Long Lines division); large-scale manufacturing and research capability provided by Western Electric (and, with its creation in 1924, the Bell Laboratories). Two years after assuming the presidency of the long-distance arm of American Bell, Vail resigned the position in poor health.

While they were in force, American Bell defended its patents vigorously, initiating some six hundred patent infringement suits between 1879 and the expiration of the basic Bell patents in 1893 and 1894. Subsequently, independent companies flourished. Within ten years after the expiration of the Bell patents, the number of independently-owned stations had come to nearly equal the number of Bell-owned stations. An attempt to consolidate the growing number of independent companies

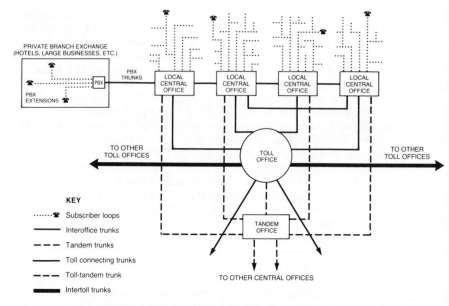

PRIVATE BRANCH EXCHANGE
(HOTELS, LARGE BUSINESSES, ETC.)

PBX
TRUNKS

PBX
EXTENSIONS

LOCAL CENTRAL OFFICE

TO OTHER TOLL OFFICES

TOLL OFFICE

TO OTHER TOLL OFFICES

TANDEM OFFICE

TO OTHER CENTRAL OFFICES

KEY

·······☎ Subscriber loops

——— Interoffice trunks

— — — Tandem trunks

——— Toll connecting trunks

— — — Toll-tandem trunk

▬▬▬ Intertoll trunks

Figure 1: Local and toll switching — a study in line conservation

In a television commercial that aired in 1984, a pair of telephones belonging to the respective occupants of two igloos were connected by a wire strung between two poles, one in front of each igloo. To incorporate a telephone in a third igloo into a system such as this it would be necessary not only to string more lines (three would be required), but also to install a two-position switch in each telephone. Four phones would require six lines and three-position telephone switches, five phones, ten lines and four-position switches, and six phones, fifteen lines and five-position switches. If this arctic population of telephone owners were to grow to one hundred and we wished to continue to provide direct interconnection

into a single organization that would be national in scope and would provide long-distance service independently of American Bell failed with the collapse of financial support for the Telephone, Telegraph and Cable Company, which was organized in New Jersey in 1899. Nevertheless, the collective development of the independents, which kept pace with that of American Bell through about 1907, helped to further popularize the telephone, spur technical developments in it, stimulate long-distance and promote rural services, and generally drive down rates. It also, however, led to the expensive and inefficient duplication of exchange facilities.

By 1910, duplication of local exchange facilities had reached such uneconomical proportions that American Telephone and Telegraph, in a report to its stockholders for that year, espoused government control over a continuation of the existing state of affairs. This was not inconsistent with Vail's vision of national telephone service reflected in the "one system, one policy, universal service" philosophy he propounded in public lectures. His belief that telephony was a service that could be provided *among all of them we would have to string four thousand, nine hundred and fifty lines and each phone would have to incorporate a ninety-nine position switch. Each successive change in this primitive system would entail considerable changes in physical plant and necessitate hardware changes in each participating telephone. The impracticality of such a system was recognized early and addressed by centralized switching. If we were to connect each of the the one hundred telphones in the community described above to a single large switch in a central location, we would not only reduce the overall number of lines required, but would limit hardware changes necessitated by future expansion to a single device. The advent of electronic switching and stored program control eliminated much of the manual activity associated with accommodating changes in sub-scriber populations. The* local central office *of a telephone operating company is such a switch and the subscribers whose lines terminate at it constitute an* exchange. *We can grow such a system by adding additional exchanges to the central office and by adding additional central offices to support still more exchanges. As we increase the number of central offices, as is often necessary in large metropolitan areas, we can realize the same economy of lines as we did when we centralized switching activity earlier by introducing a* tandem office. *The tandem office is to local central offices what the local central office is to the individual subscribers in one or more exchanges. While there are tandem offices that have no other function, in fact, any central office capable of interconnecting two other central offices can be said to be functioning as a tandem office. The lines between central offices and between central and tandem offices are called* trunks. *A technique called* multiplexing *(sending multiple signals over a single line simultaneously) enables single trunks to operate as if they were the functional equivalent of many hundreds or thousands of individual subscriber lines. A* toll office *is a gateway to long-distance, or* intertoll, *trunks, which provide access to subscribers in exchanges served by geographically remote central offices. Before it was split up, the Bell System comprised hundreds of toll offices and more than twenty-five thousand central offices. In addition, more than fifteen thousand central offices operated by previously independent operating companies participate in the U.S. telephone network. In general, the central offices of the Bell System went to divested operating companies and the toll offices to AT&T Communications (formerly the Long Lines Division of the Bell System), although apportioning was by no means so simple.*

best by a monopoly regulated by government agencies in lieu of competition was evolved publicly in the annual reports to the stockholders from 1907 to 1910.

American Bell had been consolidated with the American Telephone and Telegraph Company in 1900 at which time the location of the corporate offices was changed to New York. In 1907, banking interests assumed control of the organization and Vail, restored in health and shed of some of the intervening interests that had preoccupied him during his twenty-year absence, accepted a second invitation to resume the presidency of the now-parent American Telephone and Telegraph Company. There followed a shift from meeting competition from independents by means of rapid expansion to doing so by absorbing and purchasing them. Western Union was acquired by American Telephone and Telegraph in 1909. Simultaneously serving as president of both companies, Vail rehabilitated the former while continuing the expansion of the latter, achieving transcontinental telephone service in 1915.

Alleged violations of the Sherman Antitrust Law led, toward the close of 1913, to the Kingsbury Agreement between the American Telephone and Telegraph Company and the United States Department of Justice. Under the terms of this agreement, the former disposed of its interest in Western Union and agreed not to acquire control over any other operating companies while opening its own system to interconnection with those of independent companies that met the physical equipment requirements of the Bell System. With prospects for a competing national system grown exceedingly dim, many owners of independent systems who sought to dispose of their properties were precluded by this agreement from dealing with the single company that could potentially offer the best price. Consequently, the Willis-Graham Act was passed in 1921 permitting, on approval of State authorities and the Interstate Commerce Commission, the consolidation and merger of competing telephone companies.

American Telephone and Telegraph had amended its contract with Western Electric in 1908 in order to allow the latter to sell equipment to non-licensee operating companies, thereby further expanding the company's market and resulting eventually in an increase in the amount of work it contracted to smaller independent manufacturers and suppliers. After 1922, recognizing that both the telephone industry in general, and its own interests in particular, would be best served by such a tack, AT&T adopted an increasingly cooperative attitude toward the remaining independents.

Between 1907 and the mid-1930s, all but three States established commissions that exercised regulatory authority over intrastate telephone matters. Their jurisdiction was complicated, however, by the local companies' participation in the national toll system of AT&T. The regulation of interstate telephone service, invested in the Interstate Commerce Commission in 1910, was shifted to the Federal Communications Commission with the creation of that agency by the passage of the Communications Act of 1934.

The United States has been very nearly alone in providing national telephone service through a privately-owned, government-regulated monopoly; in most countries such services are operated as a department of government or as a public corporation. Some of the larger independent U.S. telephone companies, such as the General Telephone and Electronics Corporation and the International Telephone and Telegraph Company, have long provided service in international markets, often under contract to the local government. In some countries, international connections are provided separately from domestic telephone service.

With national telephone service mostly to itself in return for submitting its rates to federal and state regulatory authorities — the Federal Communications Commission (FCC) and public utilities commissions, respectively — for approval, the Bell System systematically set about to encourage as near universal use of the telephone as possible. Though it cost more to provide service to rural areas than to cities and towns, residential rates were made comparable in all areas and subsidized by charging a premium for long-distance service. This approach profited independent telephone companies, which derived revenues from long-distance calls made from their areas, as well as Bell. Although transmission costs are greater over routes with light traffic and those that traverse difficult terrain, in the interest of convenience for both telephone companies and subscribers, lines were leased for a uniform charge per mile. The Bell System owned, operated, and maintained all of the sprawling network it had spawned — exchanges, transmission facilities, and all of the equipment that interconnected with them.

The concurrent metamorphoses of the computer and communications industries worked by solid state electronics was a harbinger of equally significant changes in the manner of providing telephone service. Radical change was only part of the process, though. As they converged on emerging microprocessor technology, computers and communications became inextricably intertwined. The computer became absolutely requisite to the further expansion of the telephone system and the switched network — the millions upon millions of miles of extant wire and radio transmission facilities — became vital to the proliferation of the computer. Each provided a market for the other's product. Each was also, however, a potential marketer of the other's product.

By the end of the 1960s, two small, but signal firsts had occurred: (1) a non-Bell device called a Carterfone had won the right to connect with AT&T lines, and (2) certain non-Bell forms of long-distance telecommunication had been allowed. Then in 1974, the Justice Department filed suit to separate AT&T from its manufacturing facility, Western Electric Corporation. Seven years later, in 1981, the trial finally began. In 1982, the two parties agreed on a plan for breaking up the Bell System. Less than two years later, a modified divestiture plan won final approval and, on January 1, 1984, put asunder what Bell had joined together some hundred years before.

While AT&T and the Justice Department were attempting to come to terms, the Federal Communications Commission was further opening the communications market to competition. Greater latitude was provided for connecting non-Bell equipment into the network. A host of new common-carrier communications services, using partly private and partly leased Bell facilities, emerged.

With divestiture, communications became essentially a new game. It never was a simple game, but for the better part of a century it had been made to seem a relatively routine one.

Like the home team that elicits widespread interest only when it makes the playoffs, AT&T's attention-grabbing had been limited to the introduction of radically new services, such as Direct Distance Dialing, and products, such as Touchtone® and Picturephone®. The underlying research activites and technological advances that made such products and services possible — like the practices, trades, and acquisitions that contribute to a team's performance — went largely unremarked. For most of those who daily pick up one of the hundred million or so telephones that plug into the network, it remained service as usual. The incredible complexity of the switching and transmission facilities and support services that make near-global communication possible at practically any time of the day or night is nowhere in evidence in the ease of use of the telephone handset.

The playing field — post-divestiture

There were independent telephone companies in the United States before divestiture; large independent companies operate in Alaska, Hawaii, New York, and Ohio, and a host of "Mom and Pop" companies provide service in remote and rural areas. With divestiture, the number of independents increased by twenty-two, the number of operating companies through which the American Telephone and Telegraph Company formerly provided local service. The twenty-two newly independent telephone companies were organized into seven regional holding companies having roughly equal numbers of telephones and profit potential. With the exception of the equipment that was formerly rented to subscribers (what AT&T calls *customer premises equipment)*, the companies own essentially what they operated before — the local central and tandem offices; local transmission facilities, including the wires into subscribers' premises; and the local Yellow Pages.

AT&T retained ownership of its customer premises equipment and of the long distance communication services — including Dataphone Digital Service (high-speed data circuits), Wide Area Telephone Service (WATS) and 800 Area Code calling — formerly provided by the Bell System Long Lines Division. Though other firms, like MCI Communications, General Telephone and Electronics (Sprint), International Telephone and Telegraph (Longer Distance), and hundreds of smaller firms that resell network facilities leased from the larger common carriers are carving out portions of the long-distance communications business, probably three-quarters of all long-distance traffic is still provided by AT&T, whose transmission plant includes a billion and one-half miles of microwave radio and coaxial cable circuits and more than ten thousand satellite circuits.

Although the original Justice Department suit sought to divest AT&T of its manufacturing facility, Western Electric, though no longer by that name, remains a part of the parent company.

In the wake of divestiture, AT&T is endeavouring to reenter the international communications market from which it withdrew in the mid-1920s in order to concentrate on domestic service. In this arena, it is competing not only with companies already there, such as GTE and ITT, but also with a host of U.S. firms that are responding to an increasing shift toward de-regulation of public communications services in other countries.

The growing need of multinational businesses for reliable, versatile, and economical international communications, together with the potential erosion of protected national markets, has led a number of European firms to enter into relationships with U.S. suppliers. With the intention of supplying satellite and cable television hardware to European markets, the Plessey firm, one of three principal suppliers to the significantly deregulated British Telecom, joined hands with the American firm, Scientific Atlanta, while Siemens of West Germany undertook a joint venture with U.S.-based Corning Glass to supply optical fiber for West Germany's government-run communications service, the Deutsche Bundespost and, hopefully, to commercial markets elsewhere in Europe. AT&T's feelers reached out and touched both N. V. Philips' Gloeilampenfabrieken, a giant electrical manufacturing firm in the Netherlands with which it hopes to market electronic switching systems internationally, and a British consortium organized around the budding cellular radio market there.

Rules of play

Although it is generally the case that local telephone service to a given geographical area is provided by the same local operating company (whether formerly or newly independent) that provided it before, the new rules governing provision of communications services do not preclude multiple providers of local telephone service in the same area. Further, except for being restricted from engaging in certain information processing activities and the manufacture of telephones, the new companies, like the independents before them, can provide whatever services, and enter into whatever nonregulated businesses, they choose.

Local operating companies are constrained to provide services only within designated Local Access and Transport Areas (LATAs) worked out by the Department of Justice and the Bell System prior to divestiture. Although in the New England states, LATA boundaries conform pretty much to Area Code boundaries, in most of the rest of the country they are related to statistical metropolitan areas. Traffic between LATAs, that is, inter-LATA traffic, must be transported by a Federal Communications Commission-licensed, long-distance common carrier.

AT&T Communications remains the most dominant presence among long-distance common carriers and, for a time, was the default carrier for toll calls that did not specifically seek another carrier, a situation that is changing as steps are taken to comply with a Federal Communications Commission ruling that calls for all long-distance carriers to be provided equal access to the network. Among other things, "equal access" implies that users of alternative services should not have to dial up to twenty-two digits in order to complete a long-distance call.

Dialing parity is expected to be accompanied by parity in the prices interexchange carriers must pay for access to the local operating company's lines, termed the *local loop*. Because of dialing *dis* parity, and sometimes inferior connections, access rates for non-AT&T carriers have been significantly discounted.

Connection to the local loop has been billed under what are called Exchange Network Facilities for Interstate Access, or *Enfia*, tariffs. The new nomenclature for usage fees differentiates among several carrier access elements. A *carrier common access line charge* is assessed on a per-minute basis for use of the local loop at each end of an inter-LATA call. *End office charges* include fees assessed by the local operating companies for line termination, local switching, and intercept services. *Transport charges* cover the cost of delivering an inter-LATA call from the rate center in which a customer is located to the rate center in which the interexchange carrier's closest point of presence is located.

As with local and long-distance telephone service, as long as there have been telephones there have been alternative manufacturers of telephones. Until 1968, however, it was not legal to connect any of their equipment to Bell System lines. Now, the local lines belong to the new operating companies whose business is the marketing of networks, not telephones, and subscribers are free to buy their equipment from whomever they choose. In addition to AT&T and other long-time vendors of telephone equipment, such as GTE and ITT, one can now buy telephones from a variety of sources including mail order houses and discount department stores. With this change, however, comes a change in equipment maintenance, primary responsibility for which has shifted to the owner of the equipment. Subscribers who retained rented or leased AT&T equipment presently obtain service directly from AT&T, while those who purchased their AT&T equipment, or purchased equipment from any other source, must seek service as directed by the manufacturer or seller.

With the shift toward digital technology in communications equipment and a blurring of the distinction between computers and specialty devices like high-speed electronic switching systems, many traditional "computer" companies entered the communications market. As it does from such established suppliers as GTE, ITT, and Northern Telecom, AT&T faces strong competition from these newer entries, but it also now has the latitude to market its own computer expertise in the form of consumer products, something it was prohibited from doing as a regulated monopoly.

Adding to the burden on the regulators were essentially new services, such as cellular radio, which made its debut in Chicago and the Baltimore-Washington, D.C. area in 1977, six years after the technical aspects of the system had been detailed in a Bell Laboratories filing with the Federal Communications Commission.

Traditional mobile radio service, designated Improved Mobile Telephone Service (IMTS), has used forty-four VHF radio frequencies and omnidirectional broadcasting to connect wireless telephones to wireline telephone services within a seventy-five mile radius. The system suffers from poor signal quality, poor economics, and limited capacity. New York Telephone's metropolitan area IMTS service, for example, has a capacity of twenty-three simultaneous calls.

Cellular radio overcomes capacity and signal quality problems by subdividing an area of coverage into *cells*, and broadcasting independently over each cell at a lower power. Frequency ranges in a 40 MegaHertz spectrum (formerly used for UHF television channels 70 to 83) can be apportioned to the various cells. Because non-adjacent cells can operate on identical frequencies, the potential range and capacity of a system is limited only by the capacity of its central switch. The switch is analogous to a wireline company's local central office switch; it interconnects the various base-station transmitter/receivers and controls the passing of signal handling from station to station as an active phone crosses cell boundaries in a moving vehicle.

A nationwide allocation scheme for cellular radio systems was established by the Federal Communications Commission in 1981. It divides the nation into Metropolitan Statistical Areas (MSAs) in each of which two, 20 MegaHertz cellular systems will be licensed. FCC regulations call for one license to be reserved for a local wireline company, the other for a non-wireline company, and mandate that the former provide the latter with equal access to the local telephone exchange. Both licensees are required to provide access to resellers who want to market their own hardware and services via the network.

Notwithstanding the apparent widespread interest in cellular radio, it is an analog technology with mobile delivery of voice communication as its principal service offering. This characteristic could put it at a disadvantage with respect to paging services that variously offer tone, voice, numeric, and alphanumeric devices. Recently-introduced pagers capable of receiving one thousand alphanumeric characters, and the promise of associated printing capabilities, suggest the possibility of digital pagers functioning as electronic mail terminals. Cellular radio could provide data services in the manner in which traditional analog communications systems have provided them — utilizing modems — or by incorporating codec chips (processor chips that code analog, and decode digital, signals in a telephone handset), but even without such enhanced capability, cellular phones, at more than two thousand dollars, are expensive.

Under the complex cross-subsidization scheme of the regulated Bell System, construction costs associated with extending cable into lightly populated rural areas were borne by the entire subscriber base. With this form of subsidization terminated by divestiture, there will be an increasing emphasis on pricing services to reflect actual costs. In this situation, cellular radio might provide a competitive alternative for providing telephone service to remote areas that are not already "wired."

Cellular radio could also be a contender in the so-called *bypass technologies* market. "Bypass" simply refers to avoiding telephone company charges by avoiding telephone company services. It entails substituting one's own transmission facilities for some segment of the telephone company's circuits.

One way of defining bypass is in terms of which portions of the network are to be bypassed. One can, for example, completely avoid the local operating company by directly linking together two or more high-density traffic locations, such as office buildings. This entails creating what is essentially a mini-telephone company. The function of the local central office must be provided at each location, usually by a private branch exchange (PBX), to handle intra-location switching as well as to establish connections between locations. The inter-location portion of the system, which corresponds to a telephone company's *trunk* circuits, can utilize any viable transport medium, twisted-pair or coaxial cable, optical fiber, microwave, or even satellite links. Implemented as described, this bypass approach results in an isolated network. Both Boeing Corporation, in the Seattle area, and Westinghouse Electric Corporation, in Pittsburgh, use microwave radio systems to support inter-facility telephone communications independently of local operating company services. Though they have realized significant savings from the arrangements, both maintain links with their respective local operating companies to accommodate traffic that originates in the world outside the corporate network. A need to provide data communication at speeds that cannot presently be achieved over the voice network has motivated some businesses, notably in the Manhattan area, to opt for bypass over coaxial cable such as that of Manhattan Cable TV.

It is also possible to secure access to a long-distance carrier without going through the local central office of an operating company. The Federal government and some state governments are already using private lines, variously owned or leased from local operating companies, to interconnect with long-distance services. One can avoid both local and long-distance carriers by buying or renting transponder space on a satellite and either building, or buying time on, satellite transmission and receiving facilities.

Bypass is an expensive proposition, entailing purchase of terminal equipment, construction of transmission facilities, and provision of maintenance and backup services. But to the extent that business finds bypass a viable alternative to commercial network services, it will deprive the latter of potential revenue.

Competition among long distance vendors in the wake of divestiture, insofar as it leads to rates reflecting the actual cost of providing long distance services, will likely drive up the residential rates they have traditionally subsidized. If residential rates were to increase too much, however, there would be those who would no longer be able to afford having a phone and the country's near-universal telephone service would become less near. Preservation of some level of subsidization of residential rates will most likely be accomplished through legislation.

A more exciting game for the fans

Not too many years ago, subscriber options were pretty much limited to the selection of one of a handful of rotary or pushbutton handsets. With the opening of its lines to foreign equipment, AT&T met a market influx of high-tech and designer telephones with a battery of its own new products.

With cordless phones in the vanguard, a host of new products have appeared, including telephones with varying levels of intelligence and with memories capable of storing from a few randomly ordered numbers to alphabetized directories of upwards of one hundred names and numbers. Some display date and time of day, or a called number, in a calculator style window, while others possess call forwarding and restricting capabilities. Yet others will — on the basis of input from sensors that monitor room temperatures, sound levels, and electrical systems, or detect smoke — dial an appropriate emergency number and play a stored message.

Rolm Corporation, which since 1975 has made a transition from a manufacturer of military computers to the number two manufacturer of private branch exchanges, introduced a combination electronic telephone and intelligent terminal that incorporates a variety of personal service features, including message and reminder facilities, a stored telephone list, and calculator functionality.

Those who cannot afford personal telephones of an exotic nature are being afforded an opportunity to interact with such devices as a new breed of public telephone debuts. Initially being placed in airport and hotel lobbies, smart phones from AT&T and MCI incorporate charge card readers. The AT&T phones will read magnetically coded data from AT&T Calling Cards and provide operating instructions on a seven-inch, black-and-white screen capable of displaying sixteen, thirty-two character lines. The MCI phones will accept calls placed via Visa and Mastercard without regard to whether the card-holder is an MCI subscriber.

Videotext (or *videotex*) is the generic name for the technology that uses telephone lines and video display tubes (in the form of either video display terminals or ordinary television receivers) to connect subscribers with database-related services resident on a remote computer. The technology is being actively exploited in-house by at least two computer firms, DEC and IBM, and one automobile manufacturer, Buick, but has met with limited commercial success to date. Business uses of videotext have been concentrated in areas such as employee training, remote document retrieval, and inter-office electronic mail, although IBM's SVS/1 system, which is capable of controlled simultaneous display of an identical frame on up to thirty-two terminals, has been successfully employed in teleconferencing applications. The consumer market for videotext services, though it has been tapped only experimentally in this country, and has not proved strong in England, where the largest commercial vendor of videotext, British Telecom's Prestel, is turning its attention increasingly to business users, is not without potential. Banking and shopping are ideal candidates for videotext and, insofar as telephone operating company revenues are related to the amount of traffic that passes over their lines, it would seem reasonable to expect encouragement of such services from that sector.

For those with complex communication needs — high-speed, high-volume, inter-office data and video transmission, for example — a host of new alliances promises increased capability and compatibility in and among electronic switching and communications gear. Rolm, in 1983, accepted IBM's hand in a partnership to link computers with telephones in the office.Other computer firms that have tied knots of one sort or another with communications firms include: Data General Corporation with Northern Telecom; Digital Equipment Corporation with Northern Telecom; Hewlett-Packard Company with Rolm Corporation, Northern Telecom, and Intercom, Incorporated; Honeywell Corporation with Swedish-owned Ericsson Information Systems; Wang Laboratories, Incorporated with Northern Telecom.

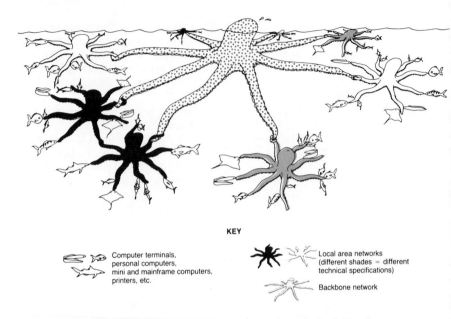

KEY

⮑ ⮑ Computer terminals,
personal computers,
mini and mainframe computers,
printers, etc.

🕷 ⁕ Local area networks
(different shades = different
technical specifications)

Backbone network

Figure 2: Networking local area networks — a view through the fish tank

Local area networking, that is, providing a communications link among personal computers in fairly close physical proximity, is typically accomplished through the medium of a hardware and software combination that is highly vendor-specific. The hardware can be coaxial or fiber optic cable or radio frequency devices;

Although cable television and alternative long-distance companies are stringing coaxial and fiber optic cable with the same fervor with which the early telephone companies strung twisted-pair cable, direct broadcast satellites powerful enough to be picked up by small-diameter, home dish antennas will provide yet another avenue for routing video signals into homes.

On both the Atlantic and Pacific coasts, a new species of communications center is growing. Called *teleports*, the facilities under construction will include satellite earth stations capable of providing access to two dozen or so domestic and international communication satellites. Laser-powered, fiber optic cables will link the teleports with metropolitan areas and local telephone operating companies. The facilities will also provide secure, environmentally-controlled shelter for teleport and customer communications equipment.

Construction of the Atlantic-coast specimen, succinctly named The Teleport, is a joint venture involving the City of New York, the Port Authority, Merrill Lynch and Company, and Western Union Corporation. When completed, in five to eight years, the two hundred and ten acre Staten Island facility is expected to incorporate approximately one million square feet of office space and provide a centrally-located hub for a the software is frequently vendor-developed and product specific. The result is usually incompatibility among different local area networking schemes. The situation can be illustrated by analogy to a very large fish tank. Imagine a population of fishes in which communication is exclusively tactile; to communicate with another fish a fish must swim over and touch it. In any population, individuals who have more in common or share particular interests tend to group together and communicate with one another more frequently. Intra-group communication within our imagined fish population will entail a great deal of moving about as well as a considerable amount of lost time as fishes desiring to contact engaged fishes wait their turns. Now imagine that these fishes discover that by clustering around an octopus and each tapping in through a tentacle they can communicate with one another at will, the octopus taking all of their messages simultaneously and forwarding each to its designated recipient. It soon occurs to the fishes that by reserving one of their octopus's tentacles for another octopus they should be able to communicate not only with one another but also with the cluster of fishes associated with the connected octopus. Unfortunately, they discover that not all of the octopuses are disposed to communicate with one another. Two white octopuses who are close enough to touch will do so readily enough, as will two gray or two black octopuses. None, however, will take the tentacle of an octopus of a different color. Then the fishes discover the speckled octopus, a creature so communal that it will hold tentacles with any octopus, regardless of shading, and they quickly realize that if each of their individual octopuses holds tentacles with this creature fishes connected to a particular octopus will be able to communicate with fishes connected to any other octopus as readily as they will with those connected to their own. If one reads through this fish story again making the substitutions indicated in the key (and making generous allowances for deficiencies in the analogy), one should arrive at an elementary understanding of the way in which a number of local area networks, most of them incompatible with one another, can be interconnected by building into each compatibility with a single backbone network, such as the national telephone system.

wide range of communications and networking services. The Teleport's counterpart, being constructed by Harbor Bay Isle Associates on San Francisco Bay near the Oakland Airport in Alameda, is expected to occupy one thousand acres and incorporate six million square feet of office space and more than three thousand residential units. In addition to a host of satellite and cable links, a central branch exchange that will support intrafacility switching and database retrieval is planned. All office and residential units are expected to have access to a coaxial and fiber optic cable system that will support local area networking of installed personal computers and word processors and provide premises security monitoring, temperature control, and other automated services.

Evolved from more modest, commercial facilities operated by firms such as International Telephone and Telegraph, Radio Corporation of America, and Cable and Wireless Limited (the latter's facility in Hong Kong, which has been in operation for more than twenty years, has the distinction of being the oldest commercial teleport), contemporary municipal teleports currently under construction and consideration may one day be regarded as the pyramids of the present era of communications.

4

From the Earth to Geostationary Orbit — the Up- and Down-Side of Satellite Communications

John Simon, 1983

Communication satellites today constitute an integral part of radio, telephone, and television circuits. Evolved from earlier relay satellites, like Telstar, that had to be tracked by large, expensive antennas as they made their way around the earth a relatively scant thirty-eight hundred miles from the surface, modern communication satellites, like Westar, routinely broadcast from seemingly stationary orbits more than five times distant to small dish antennas of fifteen feet and less in diameter.

Soon after its first orbit, Telstar, a one hundred seventy pound, thirty-four and one half inch diameter satellite launched by the American Telephone and Telegraph Company in 1962, successfully relayed live television programming across the Atlantic. Before Van Allen Belt radiation damaged some of Telstar's one thousand transistors, cutting short its useful broadcast life, overseas telephone communications also passed through its circuits.

A cone-shaped vehicle named SCORE, launched in 1958 by the National Aeronautics and Space Administration (NASA), is generally regarded as the first true communication satellite. It broadcast to earth an on-board tape recording of President Eisenhower's Christmas message. Two years later, another NASA satellite, a one hundred thirty pound aluminized plastic balloon named Echo I, passively reflected back to earth signals bounced off its ten story high, five one-thousandths of one inch thick "skin." Another satellite launched in 1960, the Department of

Defense Courier, received, stored, and, further along its orbit, rebroadcast signals received from earth.

Although distinguished from earlier communication satellites by its ability to transmit and receive simultaneously, Telstar shared its predecessors' orbital characteristics. Most early satellites were placed into elliptical orbits at speeds — necessary to compensate for earth's gravitational pull — that carried them completely around the earth in from one to four hours. A given earth station can only "see" a satellite in such an orbit for brief intervals during which it must "track," or move its antenna to point at, the target satellite. Telstar's orbital distance from earth varied between 600 miles at *perigee* (the point of an orbit at which an object is closest to earth) to 3800 hundred miles at *apogee* (the point of an orbit at which an object is furthest from earth). Because a satellite can be seen for longer periods of time, and by more stations, the further it is from earth, it is desirable that the apogee of a satellite's orbit be over its designated earth stations.

Well beyond the apogee of Telstar's orbit, at 22,300 miles from earth, is an orbit with very special characteristics. A satellite placed into a circular orbit over the equator at this altitude will circle around the earth in twenty-four hours, exactly the time it takes the earth to complete one rotation on its axis. To earth stations communicating with it, such a satellite will appear to "hover" permanently in precisely the same place in the sky.

Figure 1: The global communications satellite system

(A) As envisioned by Arthur Clarke in 1945

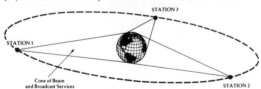

STATION 3

STATION 1

Cone of Beam
and Broadcast Services

STATION 2

(B) As realized by Intelsat in 1970

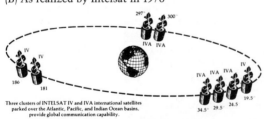

297°   300°

IVA   IVA

IV
IV

IVA   IVA   IVA   IV

186
181

19.5°

34.5°   29.5°   24.5°

Three clusters of INTELSAT IV and IVA international satellites
parked over the Atlantic, Pacific, and Indian Ocean basins,
provide global communication capability.

The uniqueness of this *geostationary* orbit was recognized as early as 1945 by Arthur C. Clarke, a British postal clerk turned science writer. Clarke (1945, 305) suggested that if three satellites were equidistantly spaced in geostationary orbit, at least one of the three could be seen at all times from any point on earth, save the extreme polar regions (Figure 1a).

In 1964, two years after the launch of Telstar, NASA placed Syncom 3 into geostationary orbit. The difference between its apogee and perigee was a mere two hundred nineteen yards. Three months after its launch, Syncom 3 transmitted live television coverage of the Tokyo Olympics from Japan to Point Mugu, California over its single communications channel.

A year later, in 1965, an eighty-five inch diameter satellite capable of relaying voice signals over two hundred forty two-way circuits, or video signals over a single, two-way television channel, was launched by the Communication Satellite Corporation (Comsat). Their Early Bird was the first commercial communication satellite.

Roughly twenty-five years after Clarke postulated global telecommunications with three geostationary satellites, three clusters of satellites positioned over the Atlantic, Pacific, and Indian Ocean basins actually provided it (Figure 1b). The satellites were operated by the International Telecommunications Satellite Consortium (Intelsat), an organization that grew from fourteen to more than ninety-three members and was responsible for producing and operating five generations of satellites, in a span of eighteen years.

Three Intelsat II series satellites, launched in 1967 to extend telephone and television coverage being provided by Early Bird, were placed into geostationary orbits over the Atlantic and Pacific Oceans. Of five Intelsat III series satellites launched between the end of 1968 and the spring of 1970, three were placed into geostationary orbit over the Altantic Ocean, one over the Pacific Ocean, and one over the Indian Ocean. Thus was global communication similar to that envisioned by Clarke achieved.

Intelsat II satellites incorporated the same number of voice circuits per vehicle as Early Bird. Intelsat III satellites, at more than the combined weight of Early Bird and an Intelsat II vehicle, provided twelve hundred voice circuits or four television channels per satellite, more than four times the capacity of the earlier vehicles.

Beginning in 1971, Intelsat IV and IVA satellites, each weighing in excess of fifteen hundred pounds and equipped with between four and six thousand telephone circuits, began to replace the earlier Intelsat vehicles. Like Syncom 3 and Early Bird, the Intelsat II and III series satellites were used occasionally for experimental purposes as they continued to orbit after retirement from active service.

The transition from elliptical to geostationary orbits for communication satellites significantly affected the nature of ground transmitting and receiving stations. Larger, more powerful "stationary" satellites didn't require broad, moveable antennas, like the eighty-five foot, three hundred and eighty ton steerable horn erected under an eighteen story dome in Andover, Maine for use with Telstar. Much simpler, parabolic dishes began to predominate, and it became possible, once they were fixed on the desired satellite, for receive-only stations to be unmanned.

Domestic satellites are fully as powerful as international satellites but employ directional transmitting antennas to concentrate their signals over a particular geographic area rather than spread the signals over the fullest extent of the earth's surface (roughly 40%) that they can see from their geostationary orbit. Vehicles in this category include Radio Corporation of America's Satcom, Western Union's Westar, American Telephone and Telegraph's Comstar, and Telesat of Canada's Anik satellites. Reception of these satellites within their intended service areas is possible with dish diameters ranging from twenty feet down to ten feet and less, depending upon the location of the receiving station.

Use of the word "powerful" in reference to communication satellites warrants qualification. Currently, a "powerful" communication satellite is one that transmits, from all of its twenty-three thousand miles away, at about five watts. Compare this to the one-half to one megawatt (one megawatt is one million watts) output a typical terrestrial transmission facility broadcasts over its local coverage area. With roughly the equivalent output power of a Citizens Band radio, a communication satellite distributes its signal over a greater area than an earthbound transmitter one hundred thousand times more powerful. Although conventional household television antennas cannot pick up these signals, small household dish antennas will be able to capture signals from *direct broadcast satellites,* whose broadcasts, at from one to two hundred watts, will still be only one-thousandth the power of earth transmitters.

Coupled with microprocessor control and motorized mounts, smaller dishes could take on something of a life of their own, alternating among satellites on the basis of programmed schedules relayed from microcomputers. One can imagine such a station, programmed to record late-night programming on videotape for next-day or later use, suddenly coming alive in response to instructions from an unattended microcomputer somewhere, and the pitched electrical pulse of the motor and concomitant slow movement of the ghostly dish combining to cause a patrolling security officer a moment of discomposure or induce palpitations of another sort in the hearts of a couple keeping tryst beneath it.

Communication Satellites: the "Uplink"

A rtificial satellites (the qualifier distinguishes between man-made objects put into orbit from those, like the moon, placed there by nature) have been put to a variety of uses since the first one, Sputnik I, was orbited by the Soviet Union in 1957. Current satellite missions include scientific research, weather forecasting, navigation, photographic and electronic reconnaisance, and communication. The latter represents the first commercial application of satellite technology.

Satellite construction varies with mission. Some of the components common to communication satellites are shown in Figure 1.

An artificial satellite must employ a framework substantial enough to protect its mission-specific hardware from the violent shaking it endures in the cargo hold of its launch vehicle. To loft a several thousand pound satellite into orbit, nothing short of a fire-belching, earth-shaking behemoth will do. Domestic satellites have relied heavily upon the Thor Delta, while the later international communication satellites have required the greater payload capacity of the Atlas Centaur and Titan III rockets to achieve orbit. More recently, the space shuttles, led by Columbia, have not only successfully ferried satellites into orbit, but have retrieved vehicles that have failed to achieve proper orbits and effected repairs to malfunctioning satellites.

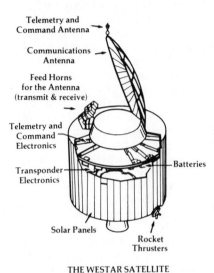

Telemetry and Command Antenna

Communications Antenna

Feed Horns for the Antenna (transmit & receive)

Telemetry and Command Electronics

Transponder Electronics

Batteries

Solar Panels

Rocket Thrusters

THE WESTAR SATELLITE

Figure 1: Components of a typical communications satellite

Since 1965, all communication satellites have been designed to be placed in *geostationary orbit,* a specific, circular orbit over the equator, 22,300 miles distant, in which a satellite's movement is in synchronization with the earth's rotation. Because it essentially "tracks" the earth, a satellite in geostationary orbit is always over the same geographic area.

Figure 2 shows the stages to geostationary orbit. A launch vehicle carries a communication satellite from the earth's surface (indicated by the first rocket firing) into a low orbit. A second firing at *perigee* (the point of the orbit closest to earth's surface) puts the satellite into an elliptical *transfer orbit.* The *apogee* (the point of the orbit furthest from earth's surface) of the transfer orbit is at roughly 22,300 miles, the distance to geostationary orbit. A third firing, at apogee, kicks the satellite into geostationary orbit. Great precision of location and timing is necessary at each firing point.

A number of forces affects the orbit of a satellite, changes in the gravitational pulls of sun, moon, and earth, and pressure from solar winds, among them. To compensate for orbital drift induced by these forces, satellites are fitted with sets of small rocket thrusters that can be fired remotely by a flight controller on earth.

Satellites are monitored constantly for position, status of mission systems, and general condition by on-board telemetry systems that communicate data, via telemetry and command antennas, to a flight controller's computer. Earth to satellite instructions — as for positioning the communication antenna, firing the rocket thrusters, or switching a satellite's systems on or off — are beamed to the satellite's telemetry and command antenna by the earth station's transmitting antenna.

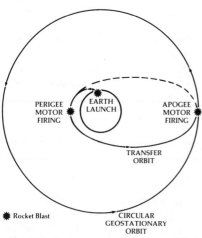

PERIGEE MOTOR FIRING

EARTH LAUNCH

APOGEE MOTOR FIRING

TRANSFER ORBIT

✷ Rocket Blast

CIRCULAR GEOSTATIONARY ORBIT

Figure 2: Stages to geostationary orbit

Like the telemetry and command antenna, the larger communication antenna both receives and transmits. To avoid interference between the weak incoming signals received from earth and the strong, boosted signals it beams back, a communication satellite must have a means of changing signal frequencies. A set of frequency converters accomplishes this, altering the frequency of the signals it conducts from its communication antenna to its radio/television receivers. The new frequency signals are passed to a set of on-board transmitters, or *transponders*, that boost the strength of the signal for the trip back to earth.

Power for a satellite's on-board systems is provided by a system of solar panels or cells and storage batteries, the latter supplying power during the occasional periods when a satellite's exposure to the sun is blocked by earth.

Functionally, these compact parcels of orbiting communications gear are equivalent to terrestrial microwave relay stations that forward signals from point of origin to point(s) of destination. Early communication satellites like Telstar (1962) were very much relay satellites — Telstar relayed its first transmissions, beamed to it from Andover, Maine, to only three locations, two in the United States and one in France. From these receiving stations, the signals were distributed in the usual manner, over terrestrial microwave and cable services. Actually, Telstar only did from space what the transatlantic cable has been doing for years under water — it provided a communication link between North America and Europe. Unlike the suboceanic cable, however, Telstar wasn't always in position.

Its fast, elliptical orbit periodically carried it beyond the tracking range of its transmitting and receiving stations.

When Syncom II was placed into geostationary orbit, it resolved the "now you see it, now you don't" aspect of its predecessors and eliminated the need for earth antennas to track, a function purchased at considerable expense and complexity. Large and powerful transmitting antennas are still necessary to get signals to satellites, but because satellites in geostationary orbit "hover" in the same place all the time, earth receiving antennas need possess only a modicum of steerability. Once "locked on" to a satellite, an antenna needs to be moved only if the satellite's orbit is intentionally shifted, or if it is desired to change satellites. More powerful transponders and larger communication antennas incorporated by later satellites have made possible a reduction in the diameter of earth antennas as well.

The increasing power of the satellites being placed into orbit and the increasing economy of earth receiving stations has led to the evolution of the *distribution satellite*. Unlike relay satellites, which bounce signals among a handful of large and expensive transmitting and receiving antennas, distribution satellites transmit to a broad area with a signal sufficiently strong to be picked up by increasing numbers of relatively small antennas.

With the advent of distribution satellites, antennas of twenty feet and less in diameter began to blossom on the rooftops and in the parking lots of corporate headquarters, printing and publishing houses, cable television operations, and hospitals and educational institutions.

Communication satellites are currently being used to distribute radio, telephone, facsimile, and data, as well as television programming. Through an agreement with the National Aeronautics and Space Administration, the University of Hawaii has used the ATS 1 satellite to interconnect computers and terminals on the various islands using its so-called "ALOHA" packet broadcast system.

With distribution and direct-broadcast satellites, the latter powerful enough to be picked up by small home antennas, the analogy of the microwave relay station gives way to that of a 22,300 mile high television transmission tower.

Commercial communication satellite service began in 1965 with a vehicle called Early Bird. Less than two decades later, North America was being served by fifteen domestic satellites, twenty-three more were proposed, and transponder space was at once at a premium and becoming increasingly economical, a situation that spawned "brokers" in that commodity. These agencies assist clients in locating transponder space, in the desired capacity, among the proliferation of orbiting satellites.

Meanwhile, geostationary orbit "real estate" is filling up. As of October, 1982, approximately ninety active communication satellites orbited the earth and as many as one hundred more "birds" were planned for launch in the coming decade, making it entirely conceivable that geostationary orbit may one day become effectively "full."

Satellite Earth Terminals: the "Downlink"

Most commercial satellite antennas are parabolic, fiberglass "dishes" (see photo) with a supporting structure that enables them to be angled upwards to "catch" incoming signals beamed down over the entire continent (and beyond) from orbiting satellites. The dish surface bounces the signals onto the reflective surface of a smaller antenna (inset photo) that acts as a collector. Called a *feedhorn*, or simply *feed*, antenna, this mini-antenna, usually mounted at the focus of the parabaloidal main antenna, funnels the aggregate signals to a signal "booster."

Surface accuracy and rigidity are important dish attributes. Deviations across the surface of an antenna are measured in thousandths of an inch, installed commercial antennas usually having surface deviations of less than plus or minus fifty one-thousandths. In order to maintain such surface accuracy, antennas must be sufficiently rigid to withstand the effects of high winds and solar heating without experiencing distortion.

Site selection and pad preparation are important logistic considerations related to antenna selection. An antenna must be mounted in such a way that it can be aimed at the point in the sky from which the target satellite is transmitting. This is called having the proper *view angle*. Because it will be capturing signals that are weak as they reach the culmination of their 22,300 mile journey (most satellite transponders have a five watt output power rating), the antenna should also be located in an area of relatively low interference. Finding a site that meets these requirements and encounters no neighborhood objections, unfriendly local ordinances, or future building plans can constitute a formidable preface to site preparation.

Antenna support is typically provided by concrete piers or a concrete pad. Mounts on building roofs are not unheard of, but most roofs are not designed to contest the wind for possession of a large, bowl-shaped structure. Wind forces of sixty-five miles per hour for operation, and one hundred and twenty-five miles per hour for structural integrity, must be allowed for. Parking lots and the roofs of parking garages are frequent candidates for satellite earth terminals.

In order to receive signals from a satellite, an antenna must be able to "see" it. The view angle referenced above is the corollary of a satellite's *look angle,* that is, the angle at which the satellite "looks at" the earth. Two adjustments are required to point an antenna at a satellite, a horizontal plane adjustment for the *azimuth* or *bearing* of the satellite, and a vertical plane adjustment for the *elevation* of the satellite.

The most rudimentary antenna mount is an azimuth-elevation, or AZ-El, mount. The simplest to construct, this type of mount requires that two adjustments, the horizontal adjustment for azimuth, and the vertical adjustment for elevation, be made each time the antenna is pointed at a different satellite. A *polar* mount requires greater precision in installation, but eliminates the need to make a separate elevation adjustment when changing satellites. Properly installed, with a true north orientation, a polar mounted antenna can be positioned to see any domestic satellite in geostationary orbit by means of a single adjustment; as the antenna is moved on the horizontal plane, a mechanical linkage simultaneously effects the proper vertical dish orientation.

Having identified a site, constructed a pad, and decided on type of mount, arrangements must be made to receive the antenna. The cost of shipping and/or storing a crated antenna can be considerable. A convenient approach is to have the antenna delivered to, and installed by, a local rigger, since a crane will probably be called for anyway. Before the rigger arrives, azimuth and elevation angles and electrical power should be available, the necessary coaxial cable laid, and the other components of the earth station in place.

The dish is only the most prominent feature of a Television Receive Only satellite earth terminal, or TVRO. Just as terrestrially originated signals received by a satellite are weak and must be boosted before being transmitted back to earth, so signals received from a satellite by an earth station are weak and must be boosted before being passed through the local distribution medium. Boosting at the satellite end is done by a *transponder,* which is like a combination receiver and transmitter; the TVRO component that boosts the signal captured by its antenna is the *Low Noise Amplifier,* or *LNA.* The weakness of the captured signal is such that the LNA, a sophisticated, and consequently expensive, piece of electronic hardware, must be located as close as possible to the antenna. Typically, it is bolted right to the antenna structure at the prime focus point.

Inherent in the signal boosting process is the generation of "noise," an undesirable characteristic which must be kept to a minimum. LNA noise is measured in degrees Kelvin, with a range typically from one hundred to two hundred degrees. Lower noise levels are reflected by higher component prices.

There is a relationship between antenna size and LNA quality. As explained earlier, a satellite antenna receives signals over its entire surface and reflects them into a smaller, feedhorn antenna that funnels them to

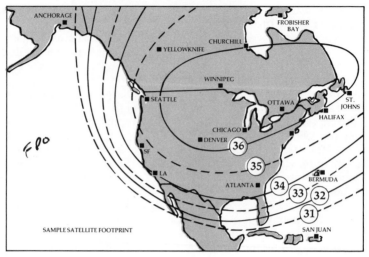

Figure 1: Footprint map with sample satellite footprint

Signal strengths of satellites are measured in units of decibels referenced to one watt, represented as some number dBw. The numbers are associated with a series of ellipses that describe a satellite's coverage pattern. The central ellipse is the area where signal strength is strongest, typically 36 dBw. Each successively outlying ellipse receives a slightly diminished signal indicated by a decrement in the dBw number. Maps on which the ellipses, or footprints, of various satellites are plotted are useful for determining the necessary equipment characteristics for a particular receiving location.

the LNA. A larger dish will deliver a stronger signal to the LNA. As dish size decreases, a higher-quality, more expensive LNA will be required to boost signals while keeping noise levels acceptable.

Determining an antenna-LNA combination that will yield adequate results most economically involves careful analysis. *Footprint maps* plot signal strengths for satellites as series of concentric ellipses over their entire coverage area (see Figure 1). Signal strength is greatest in the area of coverage within the central elliptical region, and decreases progressively within the successively outlying ellipses.

An amplified signal from an LNA is still at microwave frequency (in the range of 4000 megahertz), and requires a special, and hence expensive, type of low loss coaxial cable to convey it to the next component of the system, a microwave receiver. The microwave receiver and certain other associated equipment detect, amplify, and down-convert the transponder signals to their original video and audio frequencies. Receivers are either of the manually tuneable variety, or "agile," meaning they have crystal controlled, switchable frequency selection. Signals received by the microwave receiver are remodulated so that they are compatible with ordinary television sets to which they can be transmitted over more or less conventional coaxial cable.

5

The Observation and Nature of Electrostatic Charge and the Evolution of the Xerographic Process

John Simon, 1983

The earliest practical application of electrostatic charge may have been made by women of ancient Greece who used the attracting power exhibited by a piece of rubbed amber to lift feathers and small hairs from garments. From lint removal to image recording by electrostatic charge is a story that spans more than five thousand years and, consequently, is related only selectively in the following article.

Electrostatic charge, or static electricity, was known by its effects to the ancient Greeks who observed that a piece of amber, when rubbed, will attract hairs of fur and small objects. Used variously as a jewel and for ornamentation, amber was called *elektron* by the Greeks, who considered its pale-yellow hue to be reminiscent of the color of sunlight. The first recorded observation of amber's power of attraction was made by Plato in the fourth century B.C. in his dialogue, *Timeaus,* wherein he refers to "the wonderful attracting power of amber and the Heraclean stone [lodestone]."

That Plato mentions both substances in the same passage is significant, for nearly half a century would elapse before a fundamental distinction between the attracting power of amber (which is electrostatic) and that of lodestone (which is magnetic) would begin to emerge.

The earliest attempts to explain these phenomena were anthropomorphic in nature; the attraction was usually described in terms of one object having a "longing" or "need" for another. Alexander of Aphrodiseus

(A.D. 3rd century), for example, held that a magnet "eats and feeds on iron."

But even in Plato's time, there were attempts to find nonanthropomorphic explanations for the amber and lodestone effects. Explanations involving air held sway for many centuries. Plutarch, for example, suggested that air was pushed away by exhalations from the amber or lodestone and then circled round and returned to the evacuated place pushing the other substance before it.

Perhaps the earliest record of differences in the attracting powers of lodestone and amber was also made by Plutarch. Although he contrasted the exclusivity of lodestone's attraction, which was for iron only, with the democratic attracting power of amber, which, when rubbed, draws all manner of small objects to it, the impact of his observation was slight.

Probably the first hypothesis to posit the attracting powers of amber and lodestone as distinct phenomena was put forth by a sixteenth century mathematician and physician, Jerome Cardan, who summarized differences observed by many earlier scientists thus:

(i) Amber draws everything that is light; the magnet, iron only.

(ii) Amber does not move chaff toward itself when something is interposed; the attraction of the magnet for iron is not similarly hindered;

(iii) Amber is not attracted by the chaff; the magnet is drawn by the iron.

(iv) Amber does not attract at the end; the magnet attracts iron sometimes at the North, sometimes at the South. [A piece of amber, even when rubbed, does not exhibit poles, whereas a lodestone has permanent poles.]

(v) The attraction of amber is increased by friction [rubbing] and heat; that of the magnet, by cleaning the attracting part [thus removing foreign matter and scale].

As is evident from this list, a theory of magnetism had by this time been arrived at that included recognition of the polarity of magnetic substances and the disposition of a magnetized needle to orient itself in a North-South direction. The mariner's compass had already been invented. Cardan's hypothesis, directed at separating the "amber effect" from a general magnetic theory with which it was in many ways at variance, held that rubbed amber emits a "fatty and glutinous humor [liquid]" which, in being consumed by a nearby substance, draws it toward the amber.

In the following century, William Gilbert, a royal physician, fabricated what is very likely the first electrical instrument, a thin needle balanced lightly on a point of support in the manner of a compass that would move when an electrically charged object was brought near it. He called this instrument a *versorium*. With the aid of this device, which was, in fact, the prototype *electroscope*, he was able to identify a great many more substances whose powers of attraction were too feeble to overcome surface friction to move an object. He gave to these substances collectively the name "electrics" from the Greek word for amber.

Gilbert also substituted for Cardan's "humor" a material "effluvium" that spreads in all directions from an excited (rubbed) electric and draws nearby objects to it.

In 1675, Robert Boyle, in a treatise devoted exclusively to the subject of electricity, suggested strongly that the effluvium must be some kind of matter, such as particles or atoms.

It was during this period of experimentation that the word *electricity*, having for its meaning "a power to attract straws or light bodies," came into use in the English language.

About the turn of the century, Francis Hauksbee, of whom little is known beyond his prolific experimentation under the aegis of the Royal Society of London and his authorship of many papers collected, in 1709, into a book entitled *Physico-mechanical experiments on various subjects*, used Boyle's work as a springboard to many new observations about the properties of electricity. He observed, for example: that the interposition of a fine piece of muslin between two electrics, one of which has been excited, will inhibit attraction between them; that moisture, specifically humidity, hinders experiments of an electrical nature; that an excited electric brought into proximity to the face exerts a force like a faint wind. This latter force, known today to be a stream of charged particles, is called an *electric wind*.

Hauksbee also found an alternative to the time-honored technique of exciting an electric by holding it stationary and rubbing it by hand. In contriving a mechanism composed of a spinning glass vessel that could be excited by merely resting one's hands upon it as it revolved, Hauksbee realized the "frictional electric," or "triboelectric," generator. Although he subsequently witnessed, in the temporary excitation of a glass tube brought into proximity to his spinning glass globe, the phenomenon of *electrification by influence*, the discovery was lost in his attempt to explain it within the context of existing theory; (Hauksbee ingeniously credited effluvia from the spinning globe with "rubbing" the tube and thereby electrifying it).

Stephen Gray, another member of the Royal Society, followed with a demonstration that the "electric virtue" of a rubbed glass tube can be transmitted to other bodies with which it is brought into contact. Using first sticks, and then a sturdy twine called packthread, he demonstrated that electrification can occur through intervening bodies. Further, in noting that the packthread would conduct when supported by silk, but not when supported by wire, Gray had distinguished between *conductors* and *non-conductors*, or *insulators*, the latter being Gilbert's *electrics*. Equally interesting is that Gray demonstrated electrical conductivity, and erected what constitutes the first aerial transmission line on poles, with six hundred and fifty feet of packthread, a relatively poor conductor. Gray later successfully transmitted the electric virtue over three lines simultaneously, and further observed that a communication line electrified by influence, that is, by proximity to another electrified line, could in turn induce electrification in yet another parallel line as much as a foot away.

In the middle of the eighteenth century, Christian August Hausen, a lecturer at the Leipzig Academy, and Georg Matthias Bose, then at the University of Leipzig, independently demonstrated that a human body charged by conduction by a triboelectric generator (Gilbert's spinning glass globe) would retain the charge until some uncharged conductor was brought close to it. Bose dramatized the effect by concealing the generator with which he charged the body of a young woman whom he then invited a member of his audience to kiss, an experience that shocked, quite literally, the obliging individual.

A Pomeranian clergyman and amateur experimenter, Ewald Georg Von Kleist, in 1745, attempted to discover if the "evaporation" of the "electric fluid" that always occurs when an electrically charged body is in the open air could be reduced by enclosing the charged body. His attempt to "bottle" an electrical charge took the form of charging by conduction through a nail inserted in the narrow neck of a glass bottle some water contained therein. Holding the bottle in one hand and bringing the other into contact with the nail, Von Kleist discharged the bottle, receiving a severe shock in the process. He discovered that the water would retain its charge for several hours if no object were brought close to the nail for that period of time. Von Kleist could not explain, however, why he could obtain neither shock nor spark from the electrified bottle if he touched it while it was supported by a wooden table rather than held in his other hand.

In an experiment similar in all respects to that of Von Kleist except that a metal support underlay the bottle on the table, Pieter von Musschenbroek, a teacher and physical experimentalist at the University of Leiden, was able to produce a spark and a "great shock" by touching the metal support with one hand while bringing just the tip of a finger of the other hand into contact with the end of the nail. Musschenbroek's *condenser* came to be known as the *Leiden* (or *Leyden) jar*, for the University where he carried out his experiments.

The first recording process to employ electrostatic phenomena was conceived by George Christoph Lichtenberg, a professor of physics at Göttingen University. Professor Lichtenberg noticed that dust that settled onto a charged cake of resin formed starlike patterns that could be developed with a powder. In 1788, a few years after Lichtenberg created the temporary images that today bear his name, Villarsy contrived a two-component powder mixture that could reveal the polarity of charge of *Lichtenberg figures*. Sprinkled through the meshes of a muslin bag, the sulphur component of the mixture adheres to positively charged lines making them appear yellow, while the minium (red lead) component adheres to negatively charged lines turning them red.

During the early part of the nineteenth century, Lichtenberg's discovery was put to work in a device contrived by Ronalds for recording changes in atmospheric electricity. Ronalds' *electrograph* consisted of a lightning rod connected to a contact that was moved by clockwork in a spiral path over a resinous surface. Later sprinkled with powder, the surface would exhibit configurations varying in shape and breadth with the intensity and nature of the electricity imparted to it by the moving contact.

A method of producing powder images of objects, such as a T-punch, was conceived by P. T. Reiss. The technique consisted of touching an object laid on a pitch plate with the contact of a Leyden jar, and then removing it with an insulated handle and dusting the plate surface. Around the turn of the century, K. Bürker produced a three component powder mixture that improved the clarity and distinctiveness of Lichtenberg and other powder images and Walter König devised an electrostatic recorder for measuring the period of duration of alternating currents.

With the exception of the Ronalds and König recorders, the earliest applications of electrostatic recording to image production were, like the early Greeks' use of amber, of an ornamental nature. Lichtenberg figures, for example, were regarded for their aesthetically pleasing appearance.

Experimenters seeking practical applications of electrostatic phenomena embarked on a number of divergent paths during the early part of the twentieth century, at which point it becomes necessary to focus on the route that leads to the development of "electrophotography," a term that describes the process by which image formation takes place in most commercial copiers and modern laser printers.

In the early 1930s, a Belgian engineer, M. De Meulenaere, used a selenium plate and a Leyden jar to form an image as a powder pattern on another plate placed close to the selenium surface of the first. Patented in 1932, his invention, which was never developed into a practical process, nevertheless came close to anticipating the work of the acknowledged inventor of xerography, Chester A. Carlson, which would begin in earnest a few years later.

While in public school, and throughout his attendance at Riverside Junior College and the California Institute of Technology, where he majored in physics, Carlson worked to support his invalid father. Later, he would work while he invented. Shortly after joining the Bell Telephone Laboratories, Carlson transferred into patent work, an occupation that led him to recognize the utility of document copying. With the idea of developing a technically simple, easy-to-operate copying device for general office use, Carlson began to spend much of his time in the New York Public Library.

Conceptually, what Carlson aimed at was a conjoint application of electrostatics and conductivity, the novelty of which is reflected in a characterization of the period by John Dessauer and Harold Clark:

> Electrostatics was a subject serving only as an academic introduction to electricity and field theory; photoconductivity was the least studied or practically useful form of photoelectric phenomena; highly insulating photoconductors in particular had never been studied seriously; triboelectrification was a forgotten curiosity; corona emission held slight interest to science or technology; and finally, new reproduction processes attracted no attention from academic and industrial research laboratories. (1965, 11)

Carlson reasoned that a thin layer of photoconductive material might serve as a kind of photographic plate in which electric currents could be controlled by a light pattern or image, and, in 1937, filed a preliminary patent application for an invention based on this principle. In 1938, he employed Otto Kornei, a German refugee physicist, to conduct laboratory experiments aimed at reducing his invention to practice. Kornei produced a sulphur-coated zinc plate that could be charged sufficiently by rubbing with a handkerchief or piece of fur and, together with Carlson, succeeded in copying an image on October 22nd of that year, the image being that of the date (10-22-38) and place (Astoria) of the successful experiment. Carlson had, according to Dessauer and Clark, "...synthesized a method of photo-reproduction which invoked for the purpose obscure phenomena, neglected separately, and never conceived of as capable of functioning usefully in the forms or combinations he proposed."

Subsequently, working once again on his own, Carlson designed a nearly-automatic machine, a working model of which was eventually built and tested, and later patented. He also obtained the basic electrophotography patent.

Unable to interest a manufacturer in his invention, Carlson, in 1944, entered into an agreement with the Battelle Memorial Institute, a Columbus, Ohio research organization. Battelle undertook further development work on the invention in its Graphic Arts Recorder Division under Dr. Roland M. Schaffert. Three years later, the Haloid Company of Rochester, New York (now Xerox Corporation) acquired a license and began supporting research at Battelle. Exactly ten years from the day on which Carlson and Kornei made their first xerographic print, at a meeting of the Optical Society of America in Detroit, Michigan, Battelle and Haloid publicly announced and demonstrated the xerographic process. The term *xerography*, derived from the Greek *xeros* meaning dry and *graphos* meaning writing, emphasizes the process's fundamental difference from wet (chemical) photographic methods.

As demonstrated, the process evidenced numerous refinements of Carlson's early techniques. The work of L. E. Walkup and E. N. Wise resulted in a new development process using a two-component developer made up of materials of opposing triboelectric properties, a fine pigmented powder (toner) being charged by contact with larger (carrier) granules, such as plastic-coated glass beads or round sand. Tumbled, or *cascaded*, over a xerographic plate, some of the toner clinging to carrier beads by electrostatic attraction is transferred to an electrostatic image on a plate or drum. The process is called *cascade development*.

In their early experiments, Carlson and Kornei employed rubbing, and later a Leyden jar, to charge their xerographic plates prior to exposing them. Walkup devised a screen-controlled corona charging unit that reduced the likelihood of overcharging and concomitant damage to plates and resulting images.

Schaffert conceived an electrostatic transfer method in which a corona discharge having an electrical polarity opposite to that of the charged powder particles in the developer is sprayed over the back of a transfer sheet that has been laid over the powder-developed image. The sheet can then be peeled away from the plate with the powder image adhering to it.

W. S. Bixby's discovery that amorphous or vitreous selenium were photoconductive insulators with a much greater sensitivity to light than the sulphur and anthracene used by Carlson and Kornei, together with

C. D. Oughton's development of a technique by which these materials could be evaporated onto an aluminum or brass plate in a high vacuum, resulted in a new process for producing xerographic plates.

Incorporating all of these refinements, the Xerox Copier was introduced by the Haloid Company in 1950. This first commercial xerographic copying machine comprised three discrete components: a plate charging and developing unit; a camera for exposing the plates; a heat-fixing unit for making the powder images permanent. The process of making a copy with this early equipment is described in Figure 1.

An automatic copier introduced by Xerox in 1954 for producing paper copies of microfilm input substituted a selenium-coated revolving drum for the flat plates of the original copier and performed the xerographic process steps concurrently at various stations around the drum. By 1959, Xerox had incorporated these features in a high-volume office document copier. Placing documents on the stationary exposure platen, which facilitated the copying of bound materials and paste-ups, was the only manual operation associated with the Xerox 914 Copier. A counter enabled an operator to produce up to fifteen copies per document automatically at a speed of thirty seconds for the first copy and six copies per minute thereafter. A tinting screen could be placed between document and scanning glass to improve the reproduction quality for large solid black areas and halftones.

In the late 1950s and early 1960s, Xerox products were joined by those of American Photocopy Equipment Company, Charles Bruning Company (later a subsidiary of Addressograph-Multigraph Corporation), Dennison Manufacturing Company, Minnesota Mining and Manufacturing Company, Plastic Coating Corporation, Poly Repro International, Limited, Robertson Photo-Mechanix Company, Savin Business Machines Corporation, and SCM Corporation, among others.

By 1965, one could find both desktop xerographic copiers and floor models capable of producing up to twenty-four hundred copies per hour.

A variety of tangential developments were also taking place. Though from its invention, the principal emphasis of xerography, and the application with which it has become synonymous, has been the photocopying of printed materials, many other uses of the xerographic process, in the graphic arts as well as in other fields, exist.

Production of paper masters for offset, spirit, and diazo duplicating machines constituted one of the earliest commercial applications of xerographic copiers. Paper offset plates produced on Electrofax-type paper are suitable for short-run (around ten thousand impressions) lithographic printing. Xerographic processes also found early application in producing hard copy from microfilm and, later, in both the production and reproduction of other microimage storage media. Decoration of ceramic tiles and photoengraving techniques for preparing surfaces such as those of printed circuit boards for chemical etching have also employed xerographic processes. The early discovery that the surface charge on a photoconductive insulator could be dissipated by x-rays, as well as by light, led to the development of a process called xeroradiography, which has

been used, for example, in the non-destructive inspection of metal castings and welds.

Intercedent processes utilizing logic circuitry for sorting out image bits, and a synchronizing scanning mechanism to locate the bits at their proper places in a picture, enable high-speed xerographic printers to dispense with paper originals and produce hard copy directly from electrical signals or digitized elements stored on magnetic tape or other computer storage media. Such electronic images can be obtained originally from hard copy documents by using an optical scanning device to produce a digitized form of the optical image, or may be generated directly within a computer as a digitized form of patterns, designs, or alphanumeric characters.

Xerographic machines used primarily for computer output printing usually replace the optical system with a scanning laser beam, being in other respects similar to conventional, high-speed xerographic copying machines. In so called *laser printers*, a beam, typically from a helium-neon laser, scans the photoconductive surface of a revolving drum or moving belt or web, thereby exposing it. The beam is directed at the photoconductive surface by a multi-faceted mirror that rotates, in the IBM 6670 laser printer, for example, at eight thousand revolutions per

Figure 1: Early, hand-operated Xerox copier

In the earliest xerographic equipment, flat plates with photoconductive surfaces were exposed, developed, and cleaned, and the resulting copy image fused, in separate units. The process of making a copy with this type equipment is described by Schaffert:

> The selenium plate was mounted in a plate holder with a removable opaque shield. . . . The plate, with the shield removed, was first placed in the charging device. A switch operated a corona unit which traveled forward and then back across the plate. After charging, the opaque shield was inserted, and the plate was removed from the charging station and placed in the camera unit. The document to be copied was then inserted in the camera. After the opaque shield was removed, the plate was exposed by operating a timer switch. The shield was then replaced, and the plate placed face down on a light-tight developing tray. The shield was again removed, and the developing tray was flipped over and rocked several times to cascade the developer over the plate surface. Transfer of the developed image to paper was accomplished by placing a sheet of paper over the plate surface and re-inserting the plate in the charging station. After transfer the paper was peeled from the plate and placed in the fixing unit. Prior to re-use the residual powder was removed from the plate by wiping with cotton. (1965, 126-127)

Although the process described took about two minutes, much of the time was consumed by the manual activities associated with it. Charging, developing, and exposing the plates, and transferring and fixing the image, actually required only a few seconds per process.

second. Beam intensity is varied by a light modulator in the beam path.

In the Xerox 9700 laser printer a mirrored beam exposes a photoconductive belt a line at a time, much as an electron gun writes on the surface of a cathode ray tube, on the basis of a stored dot-matrix pattern consisting of fourteen thousand pixels, or bits of picture information, per square centimeter. As in traditional xerographic processes, the charge on the photoconductive surface is freed wherever it is struck by light; hence, the beam actually exposes the background of an image, being deflected from actual image areas by the rotating mirror and thus leaving the charge in these areas intact. Although this process takes place on a pixel-by-pixel basis, the Xerox 9700 can process as many as seventy-two hundred pages per hour.

A non-laser electronic xerographic printer, Wang Laboratories Intelligent Image Printer, utilizes a twenty-five centimeter wide by five centimeter high raster-scan cathode ray tube covered by a fiber optic face plate formed of millions of optic fibers cemented side by side. Picture information stored, as in the Xerox 9700, in a fourteen thousand pixel per square centimeter dot-matrix is carried to a photoconductive belt a line at a time by the cathode ray tube.

The utility of non-impact electronic printers is vast. Such devices are capable of operating at speeds far in excess of those that can be achieved by impact devices, and the size and cost of such printers is coming down as their producers make greater use of semiconductor technology in their manufacture. There is, not surprisingly, a laser on a chip — the semiconductor junction laser used in the Canon, Incorporated Model LPB-10 printer.

Together with the host of amenities derived from years of enhancement of conventional xerographic photocopying machines — switchable paper stocks, automatic assemblers incorporating collators, stitchers, and punches, image enlargement and reduction, and video display operator consoles — electronic xerographic printers also provide such capabilities as accommodation of digitized images conveyed over voice-grade telephone lines or bounced off satellites, and elimination of the need for printed forms (a form image can be stored digitally by a computer and printed by a xerographic printer at the same time as the information that will complete it).

Notwithstanding such sophisticated applications, the basic mechanism by which image recording and transfer is accomplished in contemporary laser printers is the same as that by which Chester Carlson, in 1938, produced the first xerographic image using a force of attraction that had been observed, pondered, and studied for over five thousand years.

How Xerography Works

A xerographically produced copy of an image consists of many millions of carefully arranged bits of pigmented plastic or powder fused, or in some other manner bonded to, a piece of paper or some other surface. The agent responsible for the careful arrangement of toner particles is electrostatic charge, the phenomenon by which oppositely charged objects are attracted to one another. The process of xerography consists in creating, on a uniformly-charged, highly-insulating, photoconductive surface, a faithful electrostatic replica of an image to be copied, developing this image, transferring the developed image to a manipulatable surface, such as a piece of paper, and permanently fixing the image thereon.

An appreciation of the essential characteristics of a xerographic plate is fundamental to an understanding of the xerographic process. Like cheese and crackers, a xerographic plate consists of a thin layer of a photoconductive material with a low-conductivity (the cheese) deposited onto a conductive substrate (the cracker), often by evaporation in a vacuum. Early xerographic plates were just that, flat, rectangular plates, but most contemporary xerographic devices employ a revolving drum or, in most high-speed machines, a moving belt or web.

Except for exposure of the plate, all of the steps to the production of a xerographic copy are carried out in the dark. Chester Carlson, the inventor of xerography, charged the plate on which he formed his first xerographic image by rubbing it. Most contemporary xerographic devices employ a *corona charging unit*, which consists of a fine wire or wires drawn taut in an insulating frame spaced close to the photosensitive surface of the plate, drum, or web to distribute a uniform, intense field over its surface. Operated at a high electrical potential, the wire ionizes the air around it and the ions are driven onto the photoconductor by electrical forces that exist between the wire and the plate.

The image to be copied is then illuminated or reflected onto this charged surface. This step is equivalent to exposing the film at the back of a conventional camera. The nature of a photoconductive surface is such that electrical charge retained by the surface is given up to photon carriers. Thus, only surface areas corresponding to dark areas of an image, such as printed material, will retain a charge after exposure, the charge on surface areas flooded by light having been surrendered to the photon carriers. What remains of the charge on the plate surface after exposure is an electrostatic replica of the dark areas of the image. That this charge remains stable during development and transfer is a function of the insulating nature of the photoconductive surface, which prevents lateral leakage of the charge across it.

In a modified form of xerography, called Electrofax by the Radio Corporation of America, which pioneered the process in the early 1950s, the charged plate serves also as the copy after being developed and fixed. Electrofax employs a zinc-oxide pigment in a resin binder bonded to a

Figure 1: Steps in the xerographic process

This sequence illustrates six steps in the xerographic process. (a) A corona charging unit, a fine wire that ionizes the air around it, distributes a uniform electrical charge over the photoconductive surface of a xerographic plate. (b) Exposed to an illuminated image, the photoconductive strata surrenders its surface charge to photon carriers in areas struck by light, i.e., areas not masked by the image. The charge remaining on the plate mirrors the image to which it was exposed. (c) The exposed plate is developed. The illustration suggests the cascade method, in which a two-component developer is "cascaded" over the photoconductive surface. Charged toner particles are attracted away from the carrier beads that transport them by an opposing charge on the plate surface. Other development techniques include fur- and magnetic-brush development, which are similar in principle to cascade development, and liquid-suspension and powder-cloud development. (d) Applying a corona charge to a conductive surface in close proximity to the plate causes the toner image to be transferred. The illustration looks through the back of a piece of paper being charged. Toner has been attracted to the underside of the paper where the corona wire has passed over it leaving residual toner particles on the plate. Beneath that part of the paper that has not yet received a corona charge the toner remains on the plate. (e) Following transfer, paper and plate part company. The paper moves on to a fixing station, where the image is made permanent. The illustration suggests heat fusing. Techniques involving pressure, adhesion, and solvent, employed singly or in combination, are also used. (f) While the toner image is being fixed on the paper, the photoconductive surface of the xerographic plate is cleaned in preparation for another machine cycle, beginning with recharging, or sensitizing. The illustration suggests a brush technique. Vacuum, blade, and cascade "anti-development" methods are also employed. Most contemporary machines would substitute a photoconductive belt, drum, or web for the flat plate shown. Substrate-to-surface proportions of plates and plate-to-paper distances are exaggerated for clarity.

paper backing. In this process, the photoconductive plate is the consumable item, whereas in the perhaps more familiar xerographic process the consumables are ordinary paper and developer, the photoconductive plate being reusable.

Developing an electrostatic image consists in supplying quantities of a pigment with a charge opposite to that of the latent image on the plate surface; electrostatic attraction does the rest. Typically, the pigment is supplied in the form of a two-component developer consisting of a very fine pigmented powder or plastic, called *toner*, which is charged triboelectrically (frictionally) by contact with, and clings to, larger granules of sand or plastic called *carrier beads*. When developer is allowed to tumble over the electrostatic image (in a process appropriately called *cascade development*) the charged areas of the plate surface attract toner particles from the carrier beads.

Alternative techniques for charging and delivering toner to an electrostatic image include so-called *fur-brush* and *magnetic-brush* development. In the former process, a continuous supply of toner is charged by contact with, and adheres to, the bristles of an oscillating brush made of a soft fur, such as beaver. Toner is attracted from the bristles as the brush is swept over an electrostatic image on a charged plate. The magnetic-brush technique is similar, except that iron filings clinging to a magnet

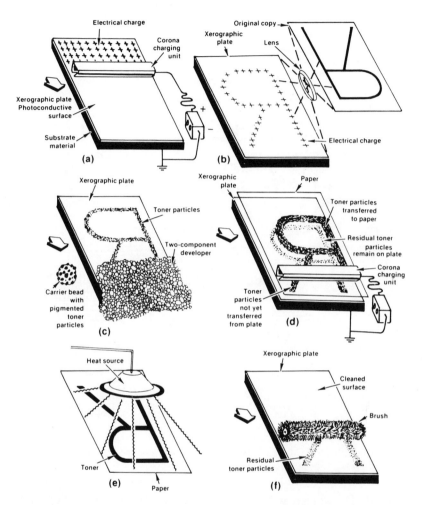

take the place of the bristles in the fur-brush technique, or the carrier beads in cascade development. Other techniques involve air-spraying toner in a fine powder cloud or mist and deposition of toner particles suspended in a liquid. A high-speed development technique employing mohair and velvet covered rollers to charge and distribute toner particles was developed at the Endicott, New York laboratories of International Business Machines Corporation.

With development, an electrostatic image on the surface of a xerographic plate becomes a toner image. In most high-volume xerographic processes, this toner image is transferred to another medium, most commonly, paper. Electrostatics is often employed in this transfer, as well. A piece of paper to which has been applied an electrical potential opposite that of the toner particles, when brought into contact with, or very close

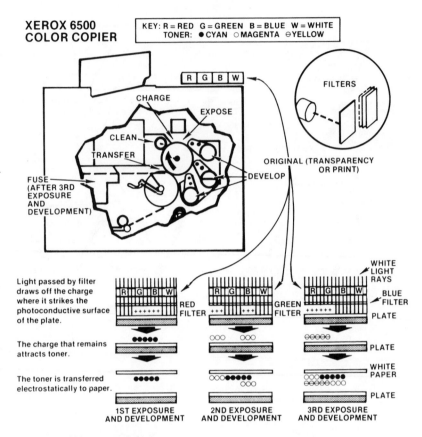

Figure 2: Color xerography

As early as 1947, R. M. Schaffert xerographically produced color prints from a Kodachrome® transparency. The process he employed consisted in successively

to, a developed plate will draw the particles from its surface. Typically, the electrical potential is imparted to the paper, as it is to the plate, by a corona charging unit. An alternative method of image transfer involves the use of an adhesive sheet that simply picks the toner off the plate when brought into intimate contact with it.

Because toner is attracted most strongly to those areas where a greater field intensity, or sharp voltage contrast, is present, large black areas might be expected to be solid only at the edges. The contrasty or washed-out appearance that would result from this tendency is avoided by the *development electrode*. A simple form of the development electrode is a metallic sheet positioned close to, and parallel with, the surface of a xerographic plate. An electrical potential applied to this sheet electrode changes the field configuration of the electrostatic image, increasing the field in the space above the large solid areas of charge. The development *exposing the surface of a photoconductive plate to a transparency through red, green, and blue filters. The plate was charged before, and the electrostatic image developed and transferred to paper after, each exposure. Finally, the multiple transferred images were fused to the paper. It was necessary to maintain precise registration of the images throughout the multiple exposure process, and the amount of exposure and development for each color had to be carefully controlled. An inherent advantage of the xerographic process is that once the proper exposure and development times have been determined, the photoconductive materials can be used repeatedly with consistent results. Because he lacked a photoconductive surface that was adequately sensitive to all three of the primary colors represented by the filters he used, Schaffert employed two plates, one with an anthracene surface for green and blue exposures, and one with a selenium-sulfur surface for red exposures. Today, photoreceptors with panchromatic response, that is, sensitivity in the blue, green, and red areas of the color spectrum, are used. Schaffert used three developers. The toner colors he selected — cyan, magenta, and yellow — are the complementaries of the three primary colors. The charge pattern remaining on the photoconductive plate surface after being exposed to the transparency through a red filter corresponded to image areas where cyan toner was to be attracted. Similarly, the charge pattern remaining after exposure through a green filter attracted magenta toner, and that remaining after exposure through a blue filter, yellow toner. By 1960, the Radio Corporation of America, under contract to the United States Government, had produced a xerographic color map-printer capable of printing in registration, in successive passes, as many as five colors. The device employed roller applicators and a liquid development technique and could produce five-color maps at a rate of sixteen inches per second. A similar multi-color xerographic printer was produced by the Harris Intertype Corporation, also for United States Government applications. Contemporary commercial three-color xerographic copiers process prints in a manner remarkably similar to that originated by Schaffert, save for automation of the various process steps. In the Xerox 6500, for example, a scanning exposure system, operated with three filters, produces successive electrostatic images on the photoconductive surface of a drum. Following exposure through each filter, one of three separate developing stations is brought into contact with the drum and the image is developed with a color complementary to that of the filter that produced it. Developed images are transferred to a piece of paper that, to maintain registration, is held stationary on a transfer cylinder until the final transfer is complete. The paper is then released and passed to a fuser that fixes the three color components simultaneously by heating.*

electrode is essential to high-quality, continuous-tone development and to the reproduction of solid blacks.

The next step in the xerographic process is that of fixing the image. There are several techniques for accomplishing this; toner can be variously melted onto paper by heating, fused into paper by application of a solvent vapor, or forced into the paper surface by compression. Some development processes involve a combination of these techniques. A typical method consists in passing a sheet containing unfixed toner between a heated roller coated with silicone rubber and a non-resilient backing roller. In the case of adhesive transfer, toner becomes embedded in the adhesive material and becomes permanently fixed with the drying of the adhesive coating. Certain toners deposited out of a liquid suspension become permanent upon drying and do not require further fixing.

Some of the toner that forms the developed image on a photoconductive surface usually remains on that surface after the transfer step is completed; transfer is seldom total. The final step in xerographic processes that do not use a consumable plate is cleaning such residual toner from the plate and resensitizing the photoconductive surface. This, too, is an end for which a variety of means exist. For particularly non-tacky toners, a cascade "anti-development" approach has been used; particles bearing a charge opposite to that of the toner are cascaded over the plate, usually several times, drawing the residual toner away by triboelectric attraction. Most high-speed machines employ a blade or brush in combination with vacuum suction to remove residual toner. The photoconductive materials used in xerographic plate-making are sufficiently durable to withstand the mildly abrasive actions of such devices. Transfer and removal is sometimes abetted by adding very small concentrations of "dry lubricants" to the toner.

After cleaning, the photoconductive surface is ready to receive another uniform charge from the corona discharge unit preparatory to a repetition of the entire process. The photoconductive plates used in xerographic processes can be reused many thousands of times.

6

The Author-Computer-Typesetter Interface

John Simon, 1983

Like computers, and in part because of them, machines that set type are becoming increasingly smaller and more interactive. Contemporary digital and photo-mechanical typesetters can readily accept manuscripts stored in electronic form on a variety of media and employ coding conventions that make pre-coding of manuscripts by authors increasingly practicable.

Although there were antecedent efforts in the development of single, movable types among the Chinese (in the eleventh century) and the Koreans (in the fifteenth century), it was techniques devised by Johann Gutenberg in the mid-fifteenth century that revolutionized the mechanization of manuscript reproduction. Gutenberg's methods for casting precision metal types in quantity and expediting the hand-setting process by rendering the types movable were to prove extremely durable; in the wake of his inventions, typesetting technology settled into a slow evolutionary track that saw no significant changes in fundamental processes for nearly four centuries.

Inventions of typesetting machines intended to eliminate hand-setting proliferated throughout the 1800s. More than two hundred inventions, in appearance resembling everything from looms to pianos, and employing an equal gamut of operating techniques, were introduced during that century. A machine patented in England in 1822 by Dr. William Church of Vershire, Vermont, established working principles incorporated in many subsequent inventions and is generally regarded as the parent of typesetting machines, but it took nearly half a century of refinement before a typesetting machine sufficiently practical for commercial purposes was developed.

In 1885 Ottmar Mergenthaler, a one time apprentice to a watchmaker, introduced a typesetting machine of which two hundred were eventually built. The first Mergenthaler Linotype was installed in the composing room of the New York *Tribune* in 1886. The machine used matrices (a printer's matrix is a die with a character recessed into its surface) to cast *slugs*, or one-piece, fully spaced lines of type, from a pot of molten metal. Upon completion of a job, the *slugs* were melted down and the metal reused.

Contemporary with the Mergenthaler machine, and the only other major kind of hot-metal typesetting machine to achieve lasting success, the Monotype, which set a single character, rather than a line, of type at a time, was invented by Tolbert Lanston, of Troy, Ohio, in 1887.

As mechanical typesetting machines impacted hand-setting, so the adaptation of photographic techniques to typesetting impacted hot-metal typesetting. Processes that sought to dispense with metal type actually pre-dated introduction of the first commercially viable metal type-casting machines, but they were rudimentary and limited in application. An example is a machine, patented in 1876 by Michael Alisoff, that printed musical scores on transparent sheets. The sheets were photographed and plates made from the negatives.

The early 1920s saw a number of attempts to convert hot-metal typesetters to photo-typesetters. R. J. Smothers, of Holyoke, Massachusetts, who collected eleven patents related to photo-typesetting during the decade, in 1925 replaced the hot-metal mechanisms in a line-casting machine with a camera and film-controlling unit. The first commercially significant adaptation, the Intertype Fotosetter, made its debut more than two and one half decades later. Introduced in 1949, the Fotosetter produced justified type (type with a straight, rather than a ragged, right margin) directly on photographic film or paper in *galley* form (originally a long tray on which compositors arranged lines of type that were to be tied up into pages, galley today refers to the typeset copy delivered by the printer). Operationally, type was fed from a magazine and formed into lines just as in a hot-metal machine, but the lines were then photographed rather than cast. As many as eight lenses were employed to provide a range of character point sizes.

Among the first photo-typesetters to employ a design that was not an adaptation of a hot-metal machine was the Linofilm. Introduced by the Mergenthaler Linotype Company in the mid 1950s, the Linofilm consisted of a keyboard, used to record characters of text and typesetting instructions as sequences of perforations in a paper tape, and a photographic unit that was driven by the tape. The photographic unit used a xenon light source to completely expose one of eighteen character grids selected from a turret according to instructions on the perforated paper tape. Operation of an eight leaf shutter permitted only one character at a time to enter the optical path — which consisted of a complex lens arrangement and a mirror — and be recorded on film.

Developing alongside the early photo-typesetters was the neonate computer. By the mid 1950s, the calculating engines of two decades earlier had been succeeded by high-speed, general-purpose computers capable of manipulating text as well as numbers. When Mergenthaler enhanced the versatility of the Linofilm by computerizing some of its functions, including certain keyboard operations and paper tape correction, the company also provided a means for transferring textual materials stored on computer magnetic tape onto perforated paper tape that could be used as input to the machine.

In 1961, Professor Michael Barnett, then at the Massachusetts Institute of Technology, used a large International Business Machines, Incorporated computer to drive a Photon 500 series photo-typesetter. Developed by Photon, Incorporated, of Wilmington, Massachusetts, from the inventions of two Parisians, René Higonnet and Louis Moyroud, the Photon 500 exposed characters on a rotating plastic disc by means of a stroboscopic flash.

Later in the decade, the Mergenthaler Company introduced a typesetter that was fundamentally a slave device, relying for its input and instructions on a formatted tape produced on a general-purpose computer. Though it used a character storage technique similar to that of the earlier Linofilm, the Linotron 505 packed nearly three times the number of characters onto each grid. Illumination of a character grid in the 505 transferred the entire set of character images onto a photo cathode at the back of a character generator tube that converted the light energy of the images into electron energy. The electron images of the characters were conducted through focus coils in the character generator tube onto the back of an aperture plate. An array of selection grids in front of the aperture plate electronically controlled which electron images were passed through it. Those permitted to pass were converted into television signals, which generated single lines, or *rasters*, on the screen. Character images were built up on film as a result of successive rasters being passed through a lens onto film. Electronic circuitry determined the size of the characters formed by the rasters.

The Mergenthaler Company had experimented with cathode ray tubes as a means for generating characters as early as 1946, but the resolution of the tubes of that time was inadequate to produce well-defined characters of graphic arts quality, and their illumination levels were too low to properly expose photographic materials. While waiting for video technology to mature, Mergenthaler explored alternative schemes.

The photo-mechanical process by which character generation is accomplished in Mergenthaler's V-I-P photo-typesetter is contrasted with that employed by the later Linotron 202N digital typesetter in Figure 1.

Digital typesetters differ from earlier cathode ray tube typesetters in that fonts (a font is a complete set of type in one size and one face) are pre-recorded in digital form rather than being converted while typesetting is in progress, as was done by the Linotron 505. The pre-recorded fonts are stored on an integral disk.

The precise nature of the digital form in which type font masters are stored varies among manufacturers, but patterns of vertical lines, or *strokes*, are most common. Character sizing is achieved by expanding or condensing stroke lengths and interstroke spacing. Degradation of letter forms, which could result from overextension or overcontraction of

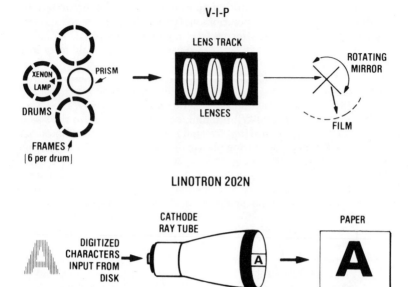

Figure 1: Photo-mechanical and digital typesetters compared

An elementary understanding of the differences between photo-mechanical and digital typesetters may be had by examining the internal mechanisms by which characters are exposed to photographic paper in each of two typesetters — the V-I-P and the 202N — manufactured by Merganthaler Linotype. Character fonts for the V-I-P, the older of the two machines, are stored on small film strips. Each font, which is a complete set of type in a single size and face, occupies one film strip. A set of three drums serves as a mounting receptacle for these strips. Six strips can be inserted into each drum, giving the V-I-P access to eighteen fonts at any one time. Within each drum is a stationary xenon light source. When a particular character is called for, the drum holding the film strip that contains that character rotates to bring it into position before the xenon lamp. The lamp flashes through the character, projecting it onto a prism, which, in turn, reflects it through a zoom lens assembly into a rotating mirror. Photographic paper is exposed to the mirrored image, the size of which is determined by the position of the lens along a track at the instant the lamp is flashed. The Linotron 202N dispenses with film strips, drums, prisms, and mirrors in favor of computer disk storage and a cathode ray tube. Character fonts are stored digitally on an integral disk. The disk contains the digitized characters of one hundred and sixty fonts — more than nineteen thousand characters. What is actually digitized are character outlines. Internal circuitry in the Linotron calculates on the fly, for each character retrieved from disk, the appropriate stroking pattern, or series of overlapping vertical lines, required to form the character in the desired size. The stroking pattern is executed by a writing beam on the cathode ray tube screen. Photographic paper is exposed to the succesive strokes of light drawn by the writing beam.

stroking patterns, is avoided by providing multiple masters for each font, the stroking patterns contained on each master being appropriate for a specific range of point sizes.

The Linotron 202N uses a different technique to insure the preservation of letterforms; it stores characters in outline form and utilizes internal circuitry to dynamically determine the appropriate stroking pattern for a given size in a wide range of sizes.

A typical output medium for the 202N is resin-coated photographic paper, which yields a positive image when developed. The exposed and developed paper constitutes the galleys, photo-copies of which can be provided to authors for proofing. Output resolution of the 202N is nine hundred and seventy-five lines per inch, as compared to three hundred lines per inch for fine half-tone reproduction.

Though both are computer-driven, the 202N is significantly faster than the V-I-P, the latter being constrained by its photo-mechanical processes. The 202N also operates more quietly than its predecessor since almost all of what takes place within its smaller frame occurs electronically. Two rollers in the film transport, the disk drives, the film advance trip counter, and a cooling fan are the 202N's only moving parts.

The author-computer-typesetter interface

Before computers and typesetters got together, the author-publisher interface with a typesetting vendor was rather narrowly defined; an author had few alternatives to supplying the typesetting house with marked-up manuscript in the form of a sheaf of pages, waiting a prescribed length of time, and paying the bill. The transfer of text and typesetting instructions from paper to perforated paper tape was done by staff of the typesetting house on special keyboards. The paper tape was fed into a reader and the instructions encoded in it drove the internal mechanisms of the typesetting machine to format the accompanying encoded text on whatever output medium was being used.

Modern typesetting machines still interpret coded text and instructions in order to set type, but perforated paper tape is no longer the exclusive, nor even a frequent, coding medium. Early in the relationship between computers and typesetters, routines were devised for transferring manuscripts stored on computer magnetic tape to perforated paper tape. Advances in computer technology, which have radically altered so many interfaces, soon eliminated the need for conversion by expanding the repertoire of input devices that could directly feed the typesetter. Interactive editing terminals, by which typed manuscripts could be entered into computer storage, largely supplanted the paper tape perforating keyboards, and telecommunications opened the door for direct computer-to-computer transfer of manuscripts.

Inherent in all of this, of course, is a fundamental change in the form of the manuscript. Not too many years ago, electronic storage of manuscripts was available only to those who enjoyed accounts on a computer, usually belonging to some central service organization. As computers became at once smaller, more powerful, and less expensive, they proliferated. Many of these smaller computers, by allowing for the electronic composition, storage, and transfer of manuscripts, are today providing an alternative author-typesetter interface. By enabling authors to take a step or two in the typesetting process, these systems are making possible savings in time or money or both.

The steps an author may take are actually incremental. An author who supplies a typesetting vendor with an electronic version of the text of a manuscript — whether on magnetic tape, floppy disk, or through a modem and over telephone lines — can expect to save some time and little money. As might be expected, more time and more money can be saved by taking a further step, in this case, pre-coding the manuscript for the vendor's typesetting system.

The burden shifts from author to typesetter over a variety of approaches to pre-coding, authors who elect to learn thoroughly the coding conventions of a particular typesetting system and laboriously type into their text all of the necessary codes encumbering the greatest burden. Often, it is possible to automate the coding to some degree, and reduce the need to have a working knowledge of the coding conventions, by using *macros*, abbreviated codes that identify, and automatically call, sets of codes assembled to achieve particular formatting objectives. Alternatively, one can develop a *generalized markup language*, a set of generic formatting tags that can be translated differently according to the typesetting system to be employed. Authors will encumber the least effort who can identify vendors that possess, or are willing to develop, the necessary conversion tables to transform whatever coding is employed by their own word processing programs into corresponding typesetting codes.

Compatible electronic manuscripts

The compatibility requirements for transporting text to a typesetting computer from another computer are not nearly so rigorous as they are for transporting, for example, programs or data from one computer to another.

Authors who have access to an appropriately equipped computer can make use of the convenient medium of magnetic tape. Computer magnetic tape tends to be very versatile and magnetic tape drives are a common component of electronic typesetting systems.

Telecommunications is to tape transfer as making a telephone call is to mailing a letter; it is faster inasmuch as it eliminates the need for hand delivery. The *tele* in telecommunications derives from the medium over which *communication* takes place, that being telephone lines. Special instructions, called *protocols*, control the flow of information telecommunicated between computers.

The technology that has engendered what constitutes the greatest revolution in the mechanization of manuscript reproduction since Gutenberg has a remarkably practical bent; at the same time that it has provided computer-based systems to speed up our compositional activities and provided means for carrying forward to other devices (read "typesetter") the textual fruits of our computer-assisted efforts, it has also so speeded up the "other" devices to such an extent that no matter how collectively prolific we might become, we couldn't possibly overwhelm them.

7

The Record With a View — Videodisc

Madeleine Butler, 1983

A videodisc looks like an extraordinarily shiny phonograph record. The most exotic videodisc player, superabundantly supplied with control knobs, push buttons, and even, perhaps, a detachable keypad, is not particularly distinguishable from an expensive stereo component system. But similarity between videodiscs and players and their look-alike audio counterparts ends with appearances. The following article explains the principal distinctions among contemporary videodisc systems, surveys some of the more remarkable applications of videodisc, and discusses the medium's potential role in education.

The Sears, Roebuck Catalog is on one. On another, Pierre Franey demonstrates how to chop an onion, with optional commentary by Craig Claiborne. You can use one to perform a diagnostic exercise in gastroenterology or learn about diabetes or hematology. Others will take you on a simulated drive through Aspen, Colorado, a bicycle ride on a roller coaster, or a field maneuver through the woods in a tank. You can see them at Walt Disney's Epcot Center or your local car dealer, in law schools and physics classes, and in private homes. For adults and children alike, the videodisc is one of the newest and most exciting developments in video technology.

In its most basic form, a videodisc may be likened to a long-playing record designed to hold pictures as well as sound. Visual and auditory information, traditionally recorded in a motion picture medium, like videotape, is instead recorded in a special way on a disc. The stored images and sound track are "read" by a player that spins the disc much as a turntable spins a record.

Videodisc technology has followed two principal divergent routes. The *capacitance* type of videodisc most closely mimics a record in that the disc has grooves that are tracked by a stylus. The *capacitance electronic disc* (CED) was developed by Radio Corporation of America (RCA) as a consumer device. To date, the format is capable only of linear play, such as a traditional videotape recorder provides. Later models of CED players included stereo audio. The advantage of the capacitance format is its low cost, which makes it a popular choice for viewing movies at home. Because discs are purchased pre-recorded, like records, the format is not suited to recording television programs off the air or creating home movies.

The other principal videodisc format, the *laser-optical*, was developed with both consumer and industrial/educational markets in mind. A radical departure from the RCA stylus-in-groove approach, the laser/optical disc provides superior picture quality and greater durability, and possesses capabilities that have led to its being described as the marriage of video and computers.

Information on a laser videodisc is recorded in the form of a continuous spiral of microscopic pits on the surface of the disc, as many as fourteen billion pits per thirty minute side. A reflective medium underlies the pitted surface. The tracks of the disc are read from the center outward by a low-power laser focused to a spot of light one thirty-thousandth of one inch in diameter (about one-millionth of one meter, or one *micron*). In the reading process, the pattern of pits interrupts the reflected beam and the interruptions are translated into electronic pulses that can be decoded to produce television audio and video signals. Because they operate on the principle of reflected light, laser discs are sometimes referred to as reflective discs.

Since playing a laser disc does not involve physical contact with its surface, playing life is practically unlimited. A durable, clear plastic coating enables the disc to be handled without ill effect. Accumulated fingerprints sufficient to impair the laser's ability to read the pits can be cleaned away with a soft cloth and a little window-cleaning fluid without harm to the surface.

The pits on the disc surface spiral outward from the center in fifty-four thousand discrete tracks. Each track, which is formed by one 360° rotation of the spiral, contains the information for one video frame, analogous to a frame of motion picture film. The laser disc player is designed to read frames continuously at thirty frames per second, the standard television rate for linear play. It is also capable of reading the same track repeatedly, thereby continuously playing the same frame to achieve the production of a still, or *freeze frame*. Because frames are consecutively numbered in the laser system, individual frames can be selected by calling for the corresponding frame number. A videodisc player can find and display any one of fifty-four thousand frames in a few seconds. Highly sophisticated players are capable of finding some frames in less than one second. This random access of frames is a slower, video equivalent of the random access of information contained on a computer disk.

To appreciate the implications of having fifty-four thousand still frames, one might consider how many slide trays would be required to contain fifty-four thousand images and how hard it would be to organize them in such a way as to provide immediate access to any one. Videodisc has a distinct advantage over traditional motion picture media in the method by which it plays still images. Using standard film or television production methods, an image that is to be held is shot for the number of linear seconds the producer assumes is necessary to make the desired point. Single images on a videodisc may be recorded as single frames, stored at a density of thirty images per second. Because of the way the player reads frames, any of these one-thirtieth of a second images can be held as long as desired, whether for one second or three hours.

The ability of the laser disc player to read single frames offers new opportunities for the way the disc can be used for motion sequences. Frames may be released one by one at a speed of less than the thirty frames per second, resulting in high quality *slow motion* play. Most players have a "joystick" control by means of which the degree of slow motion play can be varied. At any point during slow motion play, a user may stop a disc on a particular frame.

Slow motion can be a powerful tool in instruction, enabling a viewer, for example, to study in detail the complex motions of surgical procedures, analyze bodily movements in athletes, or carefully examine the steps of a physics experiment.

Disc players are also capable of reading frames in *scan* or *fast forward*. Played thus, at from three to thirty times "normal" speed depending on the capabilities of the player, it becomes possible for a viewer to search past material already seen, or to "browse" through a disc's contents much as one would leaf through the pages of a book. Slow motion and scan/fast forward work in both reverse and forward directions.

The main limitation to still frame, slow, and fast play on a videodisc is that the accompanying audio signal is interrupted when the player is in one of these modes. Although digital audio compression techniques enable players to produce sound over stills, this solution, which has been used primarily in experimental settings, has so far been implemented through the use of a device external to the player.

Laser discs have two audio channels, which can be used together to produce high quality, stereo signals, in some cases with CX encoding. Developed and patented by the Columbia Broadcasting System (CBS), CX is a means of reducing noise and improving dynamic range in an audio signal. The two audio channels may also be used for dual language programs or programs that incorporate two separate levels of instruction geared to varying levels of user experience or sophistication.

Like audio records, laser discs that provide access to still frames play at a constant rotational speed and so are known as *constant angular velocity*, or CAV, discs (see Figure 1). Their fifty-four thousand frames or tracks per disc are equivalent to thirty minutes of linear play; like a record, the disc must be turned over for an additional thirty minutes of play. The rotational speed of a CAV disc is a constant eighteen hundred revolutions per minute — one of the reasons that laser disc players have lids that must be firmly closed before the disc can begin to spin.

Consumer demand for movies at prices competitive with those for videotape put pressure on manufacturers of laser discs to devise a method for putting more than thirty minutes of standard play material on a side. The result was the *constant linear velocity*, or CLV, format. Unlike the CAV disc, which stores the same amount of information on each track, the CLV format, taking advantage of the fact that tracks near the edge of the disc are longer than those near the center, stores more information on the longer tracks. Whereas a CAV disc contains one video frame per track, CLV disc tracks can contain from one disc frame on inside tracks to three frames on outside tracks.

The rotational speed of the CLV disc varies from six hundred to eighteen hundred revolutions per minute to achieve a continuous frame release of thirty frames per second. While these "extended play" discs contain sixty minutes of linear play per side, they lack the still frame, random access, and other control capabilities of the CAV disc. Laser disc players have sensors that determine whether a disc that has been loaded is CAV or CLV format and will play the disc in the appropriate mode.

Development of the videodisc

The earliest experiments with videodisc were made in 1926, when James Logie Baird was cooperating with the British Broadcasting Company (BBC) to run a series of experimental television broadcasts. The Baird system used a Nipkow disc to scan both the subject at the transmitter and the picture for the receiver. Patented in 1884 by Paul Nipkow, the Nipkow disc translated images into electrical impulses and electrical impulses back into images by passing light through apertures in a rotating disc. Conversion of the light transmissions to electrical impulses was accomplished by means of a photocell.

One of the problems with the early Baird *Televisors*, as they were called, was that the scanning disc at the transmitter and the disc at the receiver had to be running at the same speed, and in synchronization, in order for the system to work. Because of the requirement for speed and synchronization, a Televisor might not have time to get warmed up before one of the experimental half-hour broadcasts was over, a problem Baird resolved by inscribing television signals on a phonograph record. The resulting *Phonovision record* was played on the device by the viewer to get it warmed up and ready to receive a live transmission.

A system using images recorded on a high-resolution photographic plate was patented in 1965, but apparently never built. This system would have used the beam of a flying spot scanner to read photographic images on a disc.

Westinghouse produced a system called *Phonovid* in 1968, which used a standard, long-playing phonograph record to record and play back television signals at the rate of one field (a field is one-half of a frame) per six seconds of rotation. A storage tube made it possible for the images to be released in real time.

Additional devices patented during the 1960s by 3M Company and and others paved the way for the development of modern optical videodisc

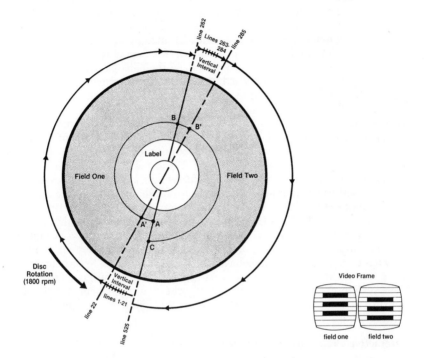

Figure 1: Format of a CAV disc

A single track of a videodisc consists of one 360° segment of a spiral. Each track contains the information for one video frame. *As seen on a television monitor, one video frame consists of five hundred and twenty-five horizontal lines, which are formed by a scanning device in the television set. The monitor very quickly scans alternate lines — all of the odd-numbered lines on one pass, all of the even-numbered lines on another. The human eye perceives this rapid scanning as a solid image. One set of alternate lines is called a* video field. *Field one of a video frame is the first set of scanning lines, which are numbered 1 through 262, field two, the alternate lines, numbered 263 through 525. The first twenty-one lines of each field contain not picture information, but synchronizing pulses, test signals, and such optical information as closed captioning for the hearing impaired. Taken together, these lines are called the* vertical blanking interval. *When a television's vertical hold adjustment is set incorrectly, the vertical interval appears as a black bar rolling through the picture. On the surface of a laser videodisc, the vertical intervals for each field appear as slices cutting through the tracks on the disc (A-A';B-B'). All five hundred and twenty-five lines of information, including picture lines and vertical interval lines are available on one disc track. Because the track is laid down on a spiral (the track that runs from A to C, for example), the laser must jump back from C to A in order to continue to play one track.*

systems. Refinement of the technology and evolution of practical applications for it have only come in the past five years, however.

The emergence of a new technology is usually characterized by a period of intense competition among technically incompatible products, the most successful of which become standards for the industry. Two videodisc formats have been developed, used, and then abandoned. Thomson-CSF developed a format that was laser-read, but was transmissive rather than reflective. The Thompson disc was transparent, floppy, and could not be handled directly. Although the disc, which had the single frame access and control aspects of the CAV reflective disc, contained only thirty minutes of linear play per side, it was capable of reading both sides simultaneously thereby doubling the pool of material accessible at one time.

Much awaited was the arrival of the *video high density*, or VHD, videodisc, a modified capacitance system that would share the low price of the capacitance player, but have the single frame and control capabilities of the laser system. In the VHD system, the stylus is suspended above the disc surface and kept over the appropriate track electronically. Because the motion of the stylus is not restricted by a groove, in its search and play features the system can behave like a laser disc player. Specifications were set for the format and producers began to prepare programs for the new system. Then, in December, 1982, the major partners in a joint venture to develop VHD suspended plans to introduce the format in the United States.

Interactive characteristics of videodisc

Even in a restricted linear play system, videodisc has much to offer. Videodisc replication is much less expensive than the equivalent process for videotape and, even in the capacitance format, discs tend to be more durable than tape. But the real excitement and promise for videodisc lies in the random access capabilities of the CAV laser system, or in any other system that can duplicate its characteristics. Such systems enable a viewer to determine the order and duration of viewing the succession of single frame images or motion segments. They are, like contemporary computers, interactive, meaning that they are in some way responsive to the requirements of the individual user.

Just as laser videodiscs vary in design, so, too, do interactive laser videodisc players. Variations in the interactive characteristics of videodisc players and systems are reflected in an organizational scheme developed by the Nebraska Videodisc Design/Production Group, which has described four potential levels of interactivity.

Level Zero systems are those dedicated exclusively to linear play. RCA capacitance, and CLV laser, disc players are included in this category.

Level One encompasses systems in which the basic controls of the videodisc player can be manipulated by the viewer. Typically included in this category are consumer model laser disc players such as the Pioneer VP-1000, LD1100, and PR8210 (described as a low-cost industrial player), the Magnavox 8000, 8005, and 8010, and the Discovision PR7810.

Such players are capable of performing the following functions: frame search; freeze frame; slow and fast play in forward and reverse; frame step "(stepping" from one frame to the next) in forward and reverse. In addition, they can respond to *picture stops*, codes recorded on the disc that instruct the player to stop automatically on certain frames when operating in standard, forward play mode.

Other codes that can be recorded on the disc, called *chapter interval codes*, or, more commonly, *chapter stops*, permit a viewer to request segments, the first frame of which will be found automatically when the chapter search command is used. Chapter and picture stops can be combined to cause a player to search out and stop on a single frame.

Examples of chapterized discs designed for Level One systems are the many "video records," such as Michael Nesmith's *Elephant Parts*. Chapters are listed on disc jackets just as songs are identified on the jackets of phonograph records. To play a given selection, a viewer specifies a chapter search, which is the functional equivalent of using a cue arm on a record player.

Using the simple devices of chapter and picture stops, innovative designers have developed sophisticated, interactive programs. Globalvision's videodisc about Boston, for example, presents a viewer with a menu of options on a still frame found automatically with a picture stop. Chapter segments end with a picture stop on a duplicate of the menu frame, thereby inviting further selections.

Some chapters on the Globalvision disc use motion segments to profile Boston neighborhoods; others consist of combinations of motion segments and still frames. A section on Boston hotels, for example, presents a motion segment describing a hotel, followed by a picture stop that presents a sub-menu. At this point, a viewer is invited to step through a series of still frames that provide an overview of hotel characteristics, including views of rooms in different price ranges. The same sub-menu, at the head of the motion segment, enables a viewer to bypass the motion segment in order to move directly to the still frames. Finally, by specifying the appropriate audio channel, viewers can select French or English narration.

Bruce Green's *Kidisc* demonstrates that interactivity is as much a function of program design as it is of player sophistication. The *Kidisc*, which is a selection of games and activities for children, relies on viewer control of a consumer disc player to achieve interactivity. A segment that teaches dance steps uses both audio channels, one to store music, the other, instructions (e.g., "step, one, two..."). A child can practice with the instructions, then shut off the audio channel that contains them and try dancing without the prompts. Another segment offers instruction in paper airplane folding techniques that the viewer can watch in slow motion, or by stepping through the frames one at a time. Slow motion can be used to make the rapid footage of an airplane ride, on another segment, appear "normal." A "guess the flag" game utilizes frame-stepping to achieve alternation of questions and answers.

In a target game, in which the rings of a bullseye turn red in dizzying succession, a quick trigger-finger is required to hit the "stop" (freeze frame) button just as the bullseye turns red; (a viewer could use slow motion to advantage in this game). An interactive adult video game, called *Murder, Anyone?* invites viewers to employ Level One interactive capabilities to solve a "whodunnit," complete with alternate endings.

Development of Level Two systems, which extend the capabilities of the basic interactive player, was based on the premise that a videodisc player could execute user instructions automatically, as well as manually, if a small amount of computer memory were incorporated in the player. Level Two systems comprise industrial grade players, such as the Pioneer 7820-1, -2, and -3, and the Sony LDP-1000. Such players are equipped with a built-in microprocessor, together with an EPROM (Eraseable, Programmable, Read-Only Memory), which holds the program that controls the player, and 1024 bytes of RAM (Random Access Memory), which provides a small amount of computer memory for storing programs that cause the player to execute a series of instructions automatically.

Keypads (see photos) that frequently accompany Level Two systems serve a dual function; they can be used to enter programs manually into a player's memory (a temporary "load" since the memory is eraseable), or as remote control devices to execute manual player functions, or to issue commands while the disc is under automatic program control, or both.

Level Two industrial players do not respond to picture stop and chapter stop codes; stops and search/play functions must be written as computer program steps if they are to occur automatically. If a disc with picture and chapter stop codes is loaded into a Level Two player, the player will simply ignore the codes.

Level Two systems, in addition to being able to receive programs manually keyed in via a keypad, can also take programmed instructions recorded as audio signals on channel 2 of a videodisc. When a disc, so programmed, is played, the program will be loaded, or "dumped," from the audio channel into the player's computer memory. Although more than one of these digital dumps may be played on a disc's audio channel 2, the limited size and eraseable nature of the player's computer memory results in each new dump obliterating the preceding one.

A major incompatibility exists between the Pioneer and Sony industrial players. Pioneer uses an F-8 microprocessor, a product of the Fairchild Semiconductor Division of Fairchild Corporation, whereas Sony employs a Z-80 microprocessor developed by Zilog, Incorporated. Each of these microprocessors has been programmed with a player control language unique to the manufacturer producing it. A given player is designed to interpret only its own manufacturer's control language. Consequently, users of Level Two discs with encoded program dumps must be prepared to either restrict their viewing selections, or to have available one of each type of player. 3M Company is the only one of the three mastering and replicating houses for laser videodiscs (Pioneer and Sony are the other

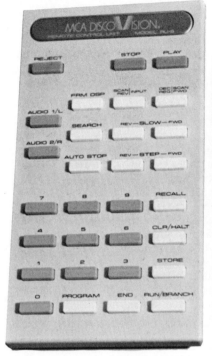

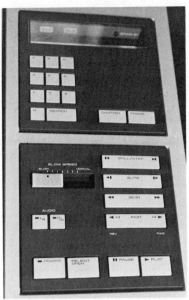

The labelling on most of the keys of the handheld keypad (left) for an MCA/ DiscoVision "Level Two" player clearly describes the nature of their functions, which include operations under automatic program control. A less extensive set of functions can be invoked by the keys on the control panel of the Pioneer VP1000 "Level One" player (right).

two) that has attempted to refine techniques for mastering discs that will accept both Pioneer and Sony programs.

Level Two systems, with limited computer control made possible by industrial player memories, approach a level of sophistication suitable for educational and training applications. Computer programs can be written to control automatically every function of such players, and the ability to execute successive program steps by pressing single keys on a keypad greatly simplifies their use.

Possibilities for interactive use are greatly increased in a system that can follow simple branching strategies. In the case of a multiple-choice question, for example, a user's answer will determine which segment a player will search out. A correct answer will bring some manner of positive reinforcement, an incorrect answer, remediation appropriate to the nature of the error. A decremental register in the program can control how many attempts a student can make to answer a question correctly.

Where appropriate, manual and computer control can be combined. If, for example, it is important to allow a student a limited time to view an image before answering a question, program control might be exercised to determine the length of time a frame is held. For study and review segments, in which it is more appropriate to permit a viewer to determine how long a frame is to be held, manual control may be employed to step through the frames. Program control could be restored by executing a command via the keypad.

Ford Motor Company and General Motors Corporation are using industrial videodisc players in dealer showrooms and for staff training. Ford introduced the Sony player to dealer showrooms with a videodisc containing an interactive golf game designed to familiarize dealers with the player through practice. The game provides viewers with a diagrammatic and photographic perspective of where a golf ball is in relation to a hole. Based on the viewer's club selection and force of swing, made by keying numbers on a keypad, the disc player searches out the segments on the disc appropriate to the results of the swing. Dealers subsequently received discs about Ford automobiles to use as point-of-sale tools with customers.

One of the more sophisticated Level Two videodiscs, *The Puzzle of the Tacoma Narrows Bridge Collapse,* was designed to aid students with varying levels of academic preparation learn some basic concepts in physics. A series of experiments provides clues that help students determine why the Tacoma Narrows suspension bridge mysteriously collapsed just four months after its completion in 1940. Using a keypad, students can explore a matrix of possible combinations of variables, and deal with mathematical calculations geared to the level of skill specified at the outset of the exercise. Because the visible frame display increments by one every one-thirtieth of a second, it serves as an absolute measure of time in certain parts of the experiment involving the frequency of a vibrating rope. Students can control the speed of the player in order to be able to see the rope clearly.

If Level Two systems constitute the marriage of video and computers, Level Three systems represent the fruits of that union. Any industrial or consumer player that can be connected to an external computer can be the basis of a Level Three system. Because Level Three systems have the full memory and computational resources of the computer available to them, they are not restricted by their own 1024 bytes of eraseable memory, and an extended level of program control becomes possible.

Additionally, a computer can enhance the function of a videodisc player through external storage of text, computer-generated graphics overlaid on videodisc images, and a host of add-on devices, or *peripherals,* that enable systems to be tailored to specific applications. A sampler of peripherals might include light pens, touch-sensitive screens, color graphics generators, random access audio devices (to provide an external source for sound over still frames), and special structures — ranging from a *Resusci-Annie* mannequin used in a videodisc-based cardiopulmonary resuscitation training program to a tank gunnery rig — designed to act as simulators and to provide input to the computer from yet another source.

The most familiar analogy for a Level Three videodisc system is perhaps that of a component stereo system. A stereo system may be simple or complex, relatively inexpensive or very expensive indeed, depending on the needs and budget of the individual putting it together. Level Three videodisc systems range from low-cost consumer disc players linked to inexpensive microcomputers all the way up to industrial players tied to mainframe computers.

Some Level Three systems employ two monitors, one for videodisc output, the other for instructions or for additional text or graphics generated by a computer. In other systems, an overlay interface makes it possible to do both on a single monitor by superimposing computer-generated information directly over a picture played back from a videodisc. Yet another type of single monitor system employs an interface that switches sources from the videodisc to the computer and back again depending on what a viewer needs to see for a given sequence.

Pioneering work with videodisc as an ultra high-density peripheral to a responsive computer has been done by the Architecture Machine Group at the Massachusetts Institute of Technology (MIT). Over a three-year period, beginning in 1977, MIT created the *Movie-Map,* an exercise in mapping that permits a viewer to "drive" through the streets of Aspen, Colorado. Controls on a touch screen enable the viewer to select the speed at which the "car" will move, speeding up or slowing down, as desired, and to decide, at each intersection, whether to turn left, right, or go straight ahead.

A viewer may drive around randomly, or plot a course in advance and sit back and watch the scenery go by. Buildings can be viewed as still images, seen in winter or in summer, and as they are "now" (at the time the films for the videodisc were made) or "then" (at some earlier period in their history). It is even possible to go inside the police station and be greeted by the Apsen sheriff. The notion of the exercise is to provide a preview of a new place that is sufficient in detail to enable a viewer to later visit with the familiarity of a native.

An MIT disc project on bicycle repair uses an image of a bicycle as a menu. Touching a part of the bicycle on the screen causes the disc player to bring up an information sequence on its repair. It is possible to call up close-ups of repair steps for a better view and to go to a glossary to learn about various tools.

An MIT project on the servicing and repair of automobile automatic transmissions extends the principles of the bicycle repair disc to create a personalized electronic book. One quadrant of the screen contains a picture from a disc still frame, the other three, high-resolution, computer-generated text. The text information is stored in digital form, by means of an experimental process, on the disc itself, and then processed by an external computer.

Overlays on picture quadrants make it possible for a viewer, by touching a particular symbol, to turn an illustration into a movie. Touching a different symbol blows the movie up to full frame. Other symbols invoke still frame, backward and forward play, and speed variations. Potential vocabulary problems on the text portion of the screen are displayed in red, rather than black, letters. When one of the red words is touched, the illustration quadrant is replaced by its definition. Vocabulary words in the definition are green, and may be touched for further amplification. A special graphics pen makes it possible for a viewer to annotate the text and images, and the "notes" can be stored or erased, as desired.

MIT's innovative work with videodisc has been funded largely by the Department of Defense for research and development purposes. Military and industrial users have thus far maintained the leading edge in the development and use of Level Three systems and programs. Flight simulators, maintenance training devices, battle game simulators, and even a national computer/videodisc network for Army recruiting centers are highly sophisticated replacements for less efficient and considerably more expensive methods of accomplishing the same tasks.

One Army videodisc casts the viewer in the role of a Second Lieutenant who must deal with a previously exemplary soldier who has suddenly become a discipline problem. The viewer must choose what the Second Lieutenant should do or say at each stage of the conversation. A similar type of interactive conversation has been adopted by industry in a set of videodiscs designed to train insurance salesmen.

In education, medicine as taken the lead in Level Three applications, with interactive retrieval systems for huge still-image databases. In law, an interactive disc requires a student to act as defense attorney in a criminal trial by entering objections. New science experiments are being developed using computer-controlled simulations on videodisc.

The ability to interface Level Three systems to external computers makes it possible to have performance evaluation and scorekeeping occur simultaneously with the use of the system, a significant advantage in educational applications.

A Level Three application designed for use with a broad-based population was demonstrated at Harvard in 1983. Developed by David Hon for the American Heart Association, the system is designed to train individuals to perform cardiopulmonary resuscitation, or CPR. (See "A Videodisc-Based Course in Cardiopulmonary Resuscitation.")

An unusual consumer application, designed for Neiman-Marcus by Perceptronics, employs a videodisc to display simulated travel footage on a wide-screen television in order to make exercising on stationary bicycles more interesting. A computer controls the entire apparatus; during uphill travel, it increases the tension on the bicycle. Considering that one of the "rides" is on the course of a roller coaster, the system is capable of providing an exhilarating workout.

The excitement and promise of videodisc technology notwithstanding, a number of problems have conspired to impede its more widespread deployment. Among the most important of these is incompatibility among hardware systems, which becomes increasingly acute as the level of interactivity increases. A case may be made, as in the example of the cardiopulmonary resuscitation training system, that the anticipated results of a project are compelling enough to warrant the purchase or creation of a dedicated hardware base, and certainly, for military and industrial applications, this has been the case.

In educational and consumer settings, however, it is desirable to have a standard player system. Unfortunately, players do not work identically, nor do interfaces, nor do computers. Some videodisc programs have been designed to work interchangeably on Level One and both Sony and Pioneer Level Two players. An example is a disc on *Producing Interactive Videodiscs* created by 3M Company. But most videodisc producers have made a marketing gamble by designing their programs for one player type and hoping that their choice anticipates trends in hardware purchases. For Level Three, the lack of complete interchangeability of computer software greatly increases the cost and risk of distributing videodisc programs designed to be driven by more than one type of computer.

Videodisc provides extremely high fidelity in the replication of video and audio signals. This high fidelity places new demands on producers. Producing very high quality materials for disc is at least two to three times more expensive than producing material of comparable quality for traditional linear media such as film or television.

Producers must also learn to think creatively in a medium that is radically different from linear media. As they abandon script treatments in favor of flow charts, and become project managers to teams of instructional designers and computer programmers, they must also struggle to create a new vocabulary for the art inherent in their profession.

Few early efforts to use the interactive capabilities of videodisc have been graceful or successful, and a shortage of well-produced materials has inhibited the widespread use of videodisc technology. Stringent technical standards and special equipment requirements imposed on producers by videodisc mastering and replicating houses have discouraged modest productions for in-house use. Videotape is still the favorite of educational institutions for such applications.

Although videodiscs provide very high-quality television images, they are currently limited by the five hundred and twenty-five horizontal lines of resolution provided by television monitors. For some applications, this level of resolution may not be sufficient. Depending on their age, quality, and frequency of maintenance, monitors are notoriously variable in color reproduction, making applications that depend on find discriminations based on color inadvisable.

Finally, the videodisc is still primarily a read-only medium. Although Matsushita has developed a "write-once" videodisc system that can accept a recorded signal, one time only, that cannot subsequently be erased or recorded over, the discs produced by the system hold less than thirty linear minutes per side, and it is not clear where applications for the device will emerge.

The current limitations of videodisc technology notwithstanding, the prevailing view is that the medium's promise outweighs its problems. Hardware manufacturers continue to refine old products and develop new ones, and the number of producers of videodisc software entering the market is increasingly steadily. If the enthusiasm generated by the videodisc in its still early stages of development is any indication, we will see a greatly increased use of videodisc in industrial, consumer, and educational settings in years to come.

A Videodisc-Based Course in Cardiopulmonary Resuscitation

A student places his hands flat on a mannequin's chest and executes five compressions. Two of the compressions cause low tones to issue from a computer. The student looks up at a television monitor. A middle-aged doctor wearing a light-blue lab coat says in a firm but friendly tone, "Now try again until you can get five good compressions in a row." As the student performs the compressions, a microcomputer screen adjacent to the television monitor plots the depth and placement of each compression, emitting high-pitched beeps to signal good compressions, low-pitched beeps to signal less than successful ones.

The student is learning cardiopulmonary resuscitation, or CPR, techniques interactively through an application of videodisc, microcomputer, and sensor technologies. Instructional motion picture footage and sequences involving the "doctor," together with still frames of glossary, illustrations, and textual materials, are stored on videodisc. A random access audio tape recorder provides sound over the still frames. The specially designed mannequin is wired with sensors that report to the microcomputer data regarding the student's performance. The microcomputer provides the overall intelligence for the system, presenting the student with menus of activities as well as with auditory and graphic feedback on performance.

The microcomputer also incorporates a real time clock, an essential component in the evaluation of CPR skills. Time is a crucial factor in the administration of cardiopulmonary resuscitation. It must be started before brain damage occurs, and compressions and ventilations must follow a specific rhythm and frequency to insure that circulation of oxidized blood is at an adequate level.

The real time clock also makes possible the "doctor's" seemingly personalized interactivity. For example, if the doctor asks the student to try five compressions and the student does nothing, the disc player will wait fifteen seconds, then search out and present a segment in which the doctor asks, "Have you tried that yet?" If the student answers "yes," he may be offered remediation. If he answers "no" (he hasn't done it yet), he is asked, "Would you like to try now?"

In creating the videodisc-based CPR training program for the American Heart Association, David Hon combined innovation and practicality to an extraordinary degree. User interaction appears elegantly simple, belying the system's tremendous underlying complexity.

The student's basic tools are a light pen and a mannequin. Interaction with the microcomputer is by means of the former; a student makes menu selections, or chooses quiz or exam answers, by touching the light pen to the screen. The position of the pen on the screen determines the nature of the output the videodisc player will display on the television monitor. A CPR student beginning training on the system is presented first with an exercise in the use of the light pen.

The mannequin is the vehicle by which students develop the physical skills associated with the administration of CPR. Sensors in the mannequin record the location, strength, and rhythm of compressions, as well as the force and frequency of ventilations. On the basis of the data cabled to it from the mannequin's sensors, the microcomputer evaluates performance and displays the evaluation graphically, in real time, enabling students to make adjustments to their technique.

A series of menus enables students to explore various facets of cardiopulmonary resuscitation at a speed, and in an order, of their choosing. CPR certification involves both knowledge and skill requirements. The videodisc training system addresses both, exposing the student to relevant medical information and providing a means for developing appropriate physical skills, but it makes no rigid assumptions about the best order of doing so. A student using the system to review CPR for recertification may bypass familiar instructional sequences and focus on aspects that have been forgotten. A medical student seeking a more in-depth understanding of cardiopulmonary resuscitation may access additional frames of glossary or textual information.

David Hon was inspired in the development of the CPR project by the works of cyberneticist Gordon Pask, and he relates some of his closed/open systems to theories of Stafford Beers. While CPR is essentially a

 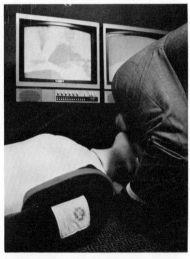

Developer of the videodisc-based cardiopulmonary resuscitation training system David Hon, in the left photo, momentarily responds to the photographer rather than the "doctor" on the videodisc monitor or the graphic evaluation of his compressions on the computer monitor. In the two-person exercise in the photo at right, he administers ventilations while the "monitor student" does compressions. The videodisc system provides for either student to make the decision to switch roles.

This photo shows more clearly the "doctor" who frequently occupies the videodisc monitor and the graphic feedback on the student's compressions provided by "Compy" on her monitor.

A student who is re-ordering a scrambled list of CPR steps presented as a quiz by "Compy," the computer with the female voice, has her correct selection displayed above the dotted line.

closed system, a training program in which fundamental objectives need to be met, Hon's goal was to render the system large enough, and design it strategically enough, to appear to a user to be an open system. A student is always free to leave a segment, or to leave the system entirely, and there are no time constraints on any instructional segment. Students may repeat segments as often as they wish.

One of the factors that contributes to the success of the videodisc-based CPR training system is the tremendous sensitivity built into it — sensitivity to the perceptions and needs of the CPR student, who has to cope with the somewhat frightening nature of what is to be learned, as well as acquire the requisite skills.

With respect to the two-screen system, Hon made a virtue out of necessity by giving each screen a persona. The "doctor" on the videodisc screen is a warm, constant, and reassuring presence. Instead of sitting magisterially behind his desk, he leans comfortably against the front of it, and much of the footage is shot as close-ups to make the presence of the character more strongly felt by the student.

A female voice (stored on the random access audio device) represents the computer. When the doctor has finished an explanation, he turns his head in the direction of the computer screen and asks "Compy," as the computer with the female voice is called, to take over the next bit of instruction. When Compy wants the doctor to take over, she refers students back to him. This technique, borrowed from television newscasting, has the effect of creating an intimate, personal atmosphere — not what one would expect from an automated information delivery system.

Similarly, when a student learns two-person CPR, an actor on the screen takes the role that a second student would play in a live CPR class. For the student learning two-person CPR, the shot on the monitor represents what he would actually see as he performs the assigned task. The student determines the time to switch roles and the computer instructs the videodisc player appropriately; or the student may respond to the "other" student's command to switch.

Tests conducted by the American Heart Association have shown the videosdisc-based training program to be at least as effective as traditional training methods (students trained and evaluated on the videodisc-based system were able to pass a CPR test administered by traditional CPR instructors), and less time-consuming, requiring significantly less than the nine-hour instructional time frame associated with live instruction.

Mr. Hon, Director of Advanced Technology for the American Heart Association, is currently at work on a new project designed to teach Advanced Cardiac Life Support (ACLS). ACLS techniques, used by hospital teams when cardiac arrest occurs, require split-second judgements by team members. The ACLS series will consist of eight disc sides, one of which will be CPR training. Whereas current ACLS instruction requires two and one-half days and eight physician instructors, the American Heart Association videodisc model is aiming at ten hours (segmented) and one physician instructor.

One of the highlights of the ACLS course will be a new method for teaching recognition of cardiac dysrhythmias. Traditionally, medical students have learned about dysrhythmia by studying electrocardiogram (ECG) printouts. Hon, however, wanted to impart a more organic understanding of dysrhythmia. Taking music as an analogy, he reflected that someone who plays an instrument has a much more intuitive grasp of how to read music than someone who does not. Similarly, he reasoned, a student who can take a large set of variables and create a pattern of dysrhythmia has a much more secure sense of what dysrhythmia is than a student who merely identifies a dysrhythmic pattern from a set of choices.

Hon wanted his set of possible ECG lines to appear on a videodisc; but the light pen works only on the computer screen. Hon experimented with the light pen, hooking it up to the output jack of the videodisc player, and with some engineering assistance to create synchronous outputs and displays, came up with the following system. A student touches the light pen to the video monitor to indicate choice of a line. The computer then replicates the line on its screen, adding lines until an entire ECG graph is constructed. The computer then evaluates how successfully the student has "drawn" a dysrhythmia.

One practical exam for the ACLS series will require each student to act as the leader of a four-person ALCS team dealing with a cardiac arrest. The other three team members will appear on the video screen to obey instructions, or, when appropriate, to question or challenge decisions. The real time clock will be the final measure of whether the "patient" lives or dies. Earlier discs will have instructed students in clinical detail and treatment options, but the exercise of those skills under severe time pressure will be the ultimate test of what students have learned.

8

Some Matters at the Heart of Computer Graphics: Why They Are So and Some of the Implications of Their Being So

George H. Stalker and John Simon, 1984

The proliferation of the heart that underlies this text — on boulders, overpasses, walls, and water towers — is testament to its simplicity. A human brain needs no formal art training to direct a hand to draw, carve, or paint it. Yet one of its electronic counterparts requires quite a considerable amount of instruction to drive a graphics output device to display the same figure. The aim of the authors, in the article that follows, is to impart an appreciation for why this is so, together with a sense of what underlies a computer's rendering of the various elements of so simple a drawing.

M uch of what is said and done in computer graphics is obvious; rather less is so lyrical and unexpected as almost to appear false. The result, when people try to explain the subject, is that at first everything they say seems self-evident. This suggests two broad categories of computer graphics-related knowledge:

- non-surprises — things you could probably deduce correctly if left alone in a quiet place;
- surprises — things you would probably deduce incorrectly if left alone in a quiet place.

There is a third:

- hardware facts — useful information about what equipment you can and can't buy.

In this article we'll visit several topics in computer graphics, implicitly distinguishing "surprises," "non-surprises," and "hardware-facts" whenever possible. We'll look first at the nature of computer graphics, at what, in very elementary terms, a graphics system is, and at some of the ways — ranging from the well-established to the relatively novel — in which computer graphics systems are being used to display information.

Subsequently, we'll apply our elementary understanding of the mechanics of computer graphics to some practical problems currently of interest to people designing computer graphics and find out how surprisingly hard it is to do some seemingly simple things.

Some fundamentals

There are two basic techniques by which people construct visual images, with or without computers: dots (e.g., in halftones) and strokes (e.g., in pen-and-ink drawings). Likewise, although there are many possible output media, the chief ones are: video-screen and *paper*. This gives us the following 2×2 matrix.

	Paper	Screen
Dots	I	II
Strokes	III	IV

Now let's consider the nature of an image area as pertains to computer graphics. A sheet of common graph paper, or better, two sheets with different grid spacings, will provide the background to a helpful analogy. Underlying all production of graphics images by computer is some sort of coordinate system. The one consistent aspect of such systems is that they are all Cartesian, that is, they employ x-y coordinate pairs (i.e., row and column positions) to identify locations.

Imagine creating an image on the more coarsely-gridded of our two sheets of graph paper by making dots at particular intersections of horizontal and vertical lines according to a list of x-y coordinates. Now imagine creating essentially the same image in the same physical space on the more finely-gridded sheet. Because we have more points available on this sheet, our list of coordinates will be longer and the resulting dots will be closer together resulting in an image of higher resolution.

Similarly, the number of points that can be individually specified, or *addressed*, by a computer graphics device that constructs images by means of dots determines the resolution of the images it produces.

This grid concept also applies, but less restrictively, to graphics devices that draw by means of strokes, the difference being that such systems reference coordinates only for start, end, and/or guide points among and between which they draw continuous lines.

Figure 1 provides examples of devices from each of the cells in the matrix, together with explanations of how each would go about drawing on the imaginary gridded surface we've just described. Devices are numbered for the cell they would occupy.

Modern graphics hardware devices such as those described in Figure 1 are designed to be controlled by *instructions* rather than simple electrical impulses. The requisite instructions must be transmitted to them the way data is sent to a printer. Instruction codes are naturally made as short as possible, but their meanings can be complex. Here, with English language translations, are some examples, both simple and complex, of graphics device instructions for an International Business Machines Corporation (IBM) PC personal computer.

To any color device — COLOR 4 "Use the color red until I tell you to change."
To a raster device — PSET (234,47) "Turn on pixel at location (234,47) using the color of the moment."
To a pen plotter — LINE (3,5)-(10,15) "Move the pen in a straight line from location (3,5) to location (10,15)."
or — CIRCLE (X,Y),N "Make the pen move in a smooth circle of radius N and center (X,Y)."

Different vendors' devices have very different capabilities and expect different instruction codes to carry out the same operations.

This all might seem rather straightforward, if a little complex — every device expects instructions based on the type of device that it is and on the vendor that manufactured it. Sometimes, however, a manufacturer provides a particular type of device with an understanding of instructions that are native to another type of device. For example, by building considerable computing power directly into a raster display device, we can enable it to receive vector-drawing instructions like a pen plotter and, in obedience to them, turn on an appropriate set of pixels. In effect, what this enables us to do is to substitute a single, simple instruction — of a type that would ordinarily direct a pen plotter to draw a line between a specified pair of coordinates — for a lengthy succession of raster type instructions of the form "turn on pixel (n,n)."

We can also extend an already-existing programming language so that it will be able to generate graphic output. We do this by augmenting the language to recognize certain special-purpose graphics "commands," which, when encountered, cause it to send appropriate instructions to some graphics device. (The "commands" may be part of the programming language or they may be directions, or *calls*, to specially-provided subroutines; it makes little difference to the user.)

Obviously, languages and programs must know which graphics devices they are instructing — otherwise the orders they send will be wrong. The idea that a piece of software must be "compatible" with a particular device has usually no deeper significance than this.

Graphic communication flows much more readily from a computer to us than it does from us to a computer. Graphics output devices, because they have been designed to do so, display graphic data in forms and shapes that we can recognize readily.

The devices that drive these devices, though, are digital, that is, they "think" in terms of discrete electrical states that correspond to binary

Figure 1: Graphics output devices

In general, graphics output devices form images by means of either dots or strokes drawn either a line at a time or at random. The output medium can be either a display tube or a piece of paper. The various combinations constitute a two-by-two matrix. The familiar dot-matrix printer *(cell I) creates characters and images by firing, according to instructions provided by a connected computer, pins in a writing head or stylus that moves horizontally across a piece of paper as it is advanced a line at a time. The pins form dots on the surface of the paper and the accumulation of dots forms an image. Most* interactive graphics systems, *that is, systems that allow users to change images while they are being displayed, employ a cathode ray tube. The following generic description of a cathode ray tube applies to both* raster scanning *devices (described in cell II) and* vector scanning *devices (described in cell IV). A phosphor coating on the interior surface of a cathode ray tube can be made to glow by bombarding it with a finely-focused stream of electrons generated by the* cathode, *a small, metal cylinder at the rear of the tube (see inset). These excess electrons combine with the phosphor's own electrons, driving it to a higher energy level. In order to return to its normal energy level, the phosphor gives off the excess energy in the form of light. The light decays rapidly and so this action must be repeated, or the display* refreshed, *many times per second. (Refresh rates of thirty and sixty times per second are typical; a faster*

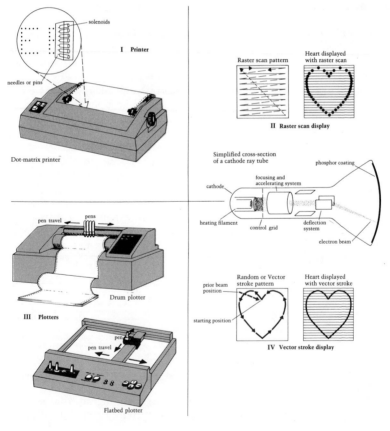

refresh rate provides a higher-quality image.) A raster display *device (cell II) is essentially a video version of a dot-matrix printer. If we think of the phosphor surface on the interior of a cathode ray tube as having a grid superimposed over it, a raster scan device will be aware only of the phosphor at the intersections of horizontal and vertical grid lines. These pinpoints of phosphor constitute the picture elements, or* pixels, *from which such a device creates its displays. The phosphor is swept, one grid line at a time, by the electron beam, which can be either* blanked *(that is, turned off), or* unblanked *(turned on), according to instructions that designate which pixels are to be lit and which left dark. The screens of almost all arcade games function in this manner.* Pen plotters *(cell III), unlike their electrostatic cousins, which* work *more like dot-matrix printers, form images by drawing continuous lines at random on a piece of paper, introducing another distinction among computer graphics devices — line, or raster, scan versus random, or vector, scan. A dot-matrix printer, as noted earlier, is a line scan device; image creation is accomplished by the coordinated operation of a paper advance mechanism and a writing head that sets down, a line at a time, the constituent dots that form an image. Random scan devices, such as pen plotters, can operate in a couple of ways. A* flatbed *plotter draws at random on a sheet of paper held flat on its bed by moving a pen mount latitudinally across a carriage, which is, itself, moving longitudinally over the bed. The pen(s) in the mount are raised and lowered by the actions of solenoids while mount and carriage are travelling. A* drum plotter *draws by moving its pen(s) transversely across the surface of a sheet of paper held securely to a drum that moves both clockwise and counterclockwise beneath it. As with the flatbed plotter, the raising and lowering of a drum plotter's pen(s) is accomplished by the actions of solenoids. Because they are continuous, the resolution of lines formed by pen plotters is greater than that for lines composed of dots. Although, like a raster scan device, a* vector stroke *device draws by lighting the phosphor surface on the interior of a cathode ray tube, the latter is not restricted to lighting only pre-designated points on the phosphor, but is capable of sweeping its electron beam in random strokes much as one might wield a fountain pen. The beam generated by a vector stroke device can be manipulated so as to function as a sort of pen, making line drawings on the screen. A vector stroke device requires coordinates only to identify starting, ending, and/or guide points.*

instructions, (which are characteristically represented as seemingly interminable strings of 1s and 0s). Because it is impractical for us to communicate with computers on their own terms, more direct and expedient ways of interacting with them with them have been devised.

Presently, interaction with computer graphics systems follows two general tacks: 1) we can use *special input devices* that allow us to show a system what we want; and, 2) we can use *symbolic languages* that specify, at an appropriate level of abstraction, what we want. We'll consider each of these approaches in turn.

Special input devices are, essentially, instruments that simplify the task of pointing or positioning in an interactive graphics system. A selection of these are shown in Figure 2.

Special input devices are particularly useful where large sets of arbitrarily-placed, non-computed points in a drawing must be communicated, once, to a graphics program. In some combinations — for example, a paper tracing used to guide a stylus over the surface of a digitizing tablet — they can be very fast.

Figure 2: Graphics input devices

Although it might seem, at first, that an instrument that allows us to pick elements directly from the surface of a graphic display would be the most efficient and easiest to use, in fact, devices whose movement over a separate, and often imaginary, but identical grid controls the movement of a light marker, or cursor, on the display are quite as effective and rather more popular. Trackballs *and* joysticks *(I and II), for example, which have long been used by radar operators and air traffic controllers, are also effective and easy-to-use input devices for interactive graphics systems. When one moves the arm of a joystick or rotates a trackball, one is essentially ranging over or rolling through an imaginary grid whose x-y coordinates correspond to positions on the display surface. Movement of the device is tracked on the screen by the cursor. Although the effecting mechanism is different, the operation of such devices is similar in concept to that of a child's toy in which the movement of a metallized object over a thin surface is controlled by a hand-held magnet moved about underneath it. In both instances, one moves one thing to move another. We can take the imaginary grid out of the input device and lay it on any flat surface. In essence, this is what is done with the now-familiar* mouse *(III). As a mouse is moved over a flat surface, wheels or rollers positioned at right angles in its base rotate. This movement is translated into the rotation of two potentiometers from which analog voltage measurements can be obtained, converted to digital measurements, and communicated to the display controller to effect a corresponding movement of the cursor on the display screen. The mouse, trackball, and joystick are usually provided with one or more buttons that enable one, having positioned the cursor, to tell the graphics system to "do something" at that location. As realized in a* digitizing tablet *(IV), the "separate but identical grid" has a physical presence. A digitizing tablet, or data tablet, comprises a flat surface, provided with a means (such as an embedded grid of wires) for identifying x-y coordinates, and a hand-held stylus capable of sending a signal to the display controller. Some means for signalling contact between the stylus and tablet, such as a pressure-sensitive switch in the point of the stylus, together with a means of identifying the x-y coordinates at the point at which contact is made, afford a user control over the cursor on an associated display screen. Digitizing tablets provide much finer control over cursor movement than any of the earlier-described devices. Broadly, two techniques are avail-*

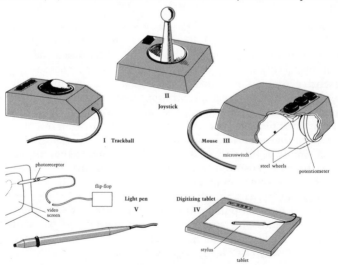

able for interacting directly with a graphics display surface. A touch panel *(not shown), a transparent screen fitted over the display surface, uses one of several technologies, including combinations of light sensors and sonar-style ranging, to identify to a controlling computer the location at which a user's finger impinges upon the panel's surface. The other technique involves the use of a* light pen *(V), or more appropriately, a light-sensitive pen. Such light pens as actually emit light do so only for purposes of highlighting the point on the screen at which the pen tip is directed. The effecting light is that being generated by the target pixels to which a photoreceptor in the pen is exposed by releasing a button or shutter. The light emitted by the pixel registers on the photoreceptor, causing a signal to be sent to the computer. The x-y coordinates of the pixel "picked" by the pen are recognized by the computer because it knows exactly which pixel was being illuminated at the time the signal was generated. The graphics application program can then be instructed to "do something" at that location.*

Symbolic languages work much as ordinary programming languages do. They can be easy to use if the objects we create are amenable to terse mathematical description. Likewise, they can be valuable (even if not easy to use) in situations where the objects we create are in some way *archetypes* — objects that will appear in many guises and must, therefore, be given to the system in a somewhat abstract form.

An example of the value of symbolic representation for archetypal forms can be found in a typefont-designing language called METAFONT. In typography, having created a particular set of letters and characters, or *typefont*, we want to be able to manifest it in different sizes, at various angles, in "light," in "bold," and in compressed and expanded form.

METAFONT enables us to do these things by allowing us to define an archetypal character set, which we can then render in any of a variety of forms by making only essential changes in our design definition. Accordingly, it accepts parameters for vertical and horizontal size, for slant, pen-width, pen-angle, and for certain other things that don't correspond to traditional type categories.

Displaying abstract information

Like many other computer applications, computer graphics has been refined to the point where — in some forms and in combinations with other applications — it can be used quite easily by the relatively uninitiated. Indeed, some applications have become so prolific as to suggest that among the deeper and more abiding issues in computer graphics are likely to be those of *what* to display.

A case in point is business graphics. Business graphics has a standard repertoire of simple graphic forms — chiefly line-graphs, several sorts of bar graphs, pie charts, and scatterplots — that is adequate for most business purposes and whose members are used consistently. Simple though the forms, their construction, before the age of computer graphics, was tedious and time-consuming. Accumulated data had to be analyzed, an appropriate graphic form identified, transformation of the data into that form effected, and the final graphic executed. Seldom could all of this be done by a single individual.

Today, a business user can accumulate data on a diskette, analyze it six-ways-for-Sunday, transform it into any number of graphic forms, including the one settled on, and generate and print the graphic without the aid or an artist or illustrator, and all in less time than it would have taken to perform a single analysis of the data with a calculator or on a general-purpose timesharing computer.

In fact, *automating* the production of these simple forms is a major issue (and a major obsession among vendors). With so many utilitarian graphics systems available to business users, getting an appropriate one into place is merely a matter of picking and choosing on the basis of need and cost. Having selected a system, the interesting problem becomes how to implement it so that it automatically provides helpful displays, or, rather, refrains from providing five hundred correct but unhelpful ones.

This is not just a matter of trying to display the right information, and do it clearly. It is a matter of reconsidering the whole subject of notation in light of new graphics capabilities. Consider the concept of the *generalized gauge*. Things we have always thought of as "gauges" — dial and indicator lights that provide continuous quantitative information about processes — can now be totally subsumed in screen monitor displays. Trivially, we can do this just by presenting a picture of a dial or an indicator.

We can, though, do much more than this. Continuously computed quantities that we are now displaying digitally can be displayed graphically. Projected future values, historicity, and rates of change can be displayed. Logic of various kinds can be used. Simple genres of static displays — the bar graphs, scattergrams, and pie charts that are used so often — can be implemented as continuous displays. Competing candidates for human attention, that is, competing potential subjects for display, can be selected for realization according to complex measures of salience.

Daily human experience has already provided viewers certain kinds of visual expertise. This *already developed perceptual virtuosity* can be used to advantage in coding information for graphic display. Some of us are, for example, "good at faces." Thus, we can profitably code certain information as faces in some systematic way. Figure 3 shows an application of this approach to a display of test data for integrated circuits.

Each face in Figure 3 represents a single manufactured unit for which twenty measured variables have been encoded as facial characteristics. Specific variable measurements appear as variations in the facial features. In addition, the plots are color-coded to differentiate good, marginal, and defective units. Attributes of particular units are far more identifiable in the plots than they would be in a more traditional tabular arrangement of numerical test data.

Often, the first thing we think of when we want to display some piece of complex information is more dimensions. As a result, we are always trying to find visual conventions to represent abstract information in more dimensions than are available with our output device; it usually has two. Where three dimensions of numerical scientific data are to be

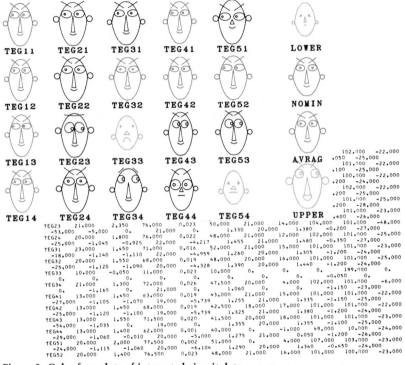

Figure 3: Color face plots of integrated circuit data

Defective and/or marginal integrated circuits can be picked out readily from this plot on the basis of color and the relative values of various measurable variables determined from the arrangement and shapes of particular facial features. Making any sort of preliminary assessment from a more traditional tabular arrangement of the same test data (shown overlaid) would be rather more difficult.

displayed, a number of methods have been proposed. Figure 4 shows two of these. Prior to the advent of computer graphics, displays such as 4b were practically impossible to create.

It is interesting to note that, even as computer graphics systems are simplifying the creation and manipulation of far more complex figures than even those reproduced in Figure 4, designers of graphics systems are still preoccupied with such seemingly trivial concerns as how to draw straight lines and curves and how to "erase" hidden lines in three-dimensional figures. In the next three sections, we'll look successively at problems that are currently facing system designers and at some of the ways they are being resolved.

Diagonal straight lines and aliases
Drawing a straight line would seem to be one of the simplest possible tasks, almost embarassingly easy for a computer graphics system; and, in a way, it is simple.

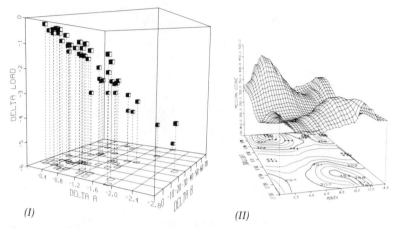

(I) *(II)*

Figure 4: Techniques for displaying numerical data in three dimensions
Several depth cues — including perspective gridding, projection, and connectors — have been added to (I) enabling a user to determine x-y coordinates of specific points from the plot. Illustrations such as (II) — which shows the behaviour of stratospheric ozone over contour-mapped landforms — were practically impossible to create before the advent of computer graphics.

Recall our earlier discussion of a graphics display surface composed entirely of points or dots arranged in a grid of rows and columns. As noted in that discussion, the dots that make up this grid in a video system are called pixels. An electron beam scans the grid line-by-line, lighting individual pixels as directed by instructions stored in the computer's memory.

One obvious way to draw a diagonal line on such a display, given endpoints, is to interpolate on each row or column in between, making a "line," as in Figure 5a. This works, after a fashion; but, with the exception of a line drawn at an angle of forty-five degrees, the result is jagged, like rectilinear comic-strip lightning. Such jaggedness in most diagonal lines drawn by dot- or pixel-oriented graphics systems is the most easy-to-see symptom of an interesting general phenomenon called *aliasing.*

Aliasing is a problem of frequency, like the problem of *sampling* for digital recording of music. In the latter instance, we are concerned with breaking down a continuous function into discrete values and then reconstructing the continuous function from them; that is, we sample the value of continuously-varying sound waves at specified intervals, record the sample values, and then try to regenerate from them the original continuously-varying waves.

Objects such as straight (or curved) lines having no appreciable thickness can also be thought of as "high frequency objects." A simple thought experiment shows this to be true: if we try to draw a diagonal line on a piece of graph paper at other than forty-five degrees between other than

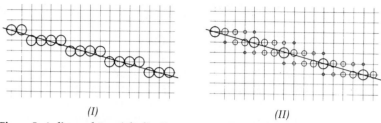

(I)   *(II)*

Figure 5: A diagonal "straight line"

(I) As drawn on a raster device

If we let line intersections in the background grid represent pixel (light point) locations on a raster display, it can be seen that an "ideal" diagonal line drawn between the designated endpoints will pass between many of these intersections as it would on an ordinary piece of graph paper. Wherever it does so, the best that can be done is to light the nearest pixel with the result shown.

(II) As drawn on a raster device with variable pixel intensity

If we draw a diagonal "straight line" on a raster device as in (I), but vary the intensity of the interpolated pixels such that those most central to an "ideal" line are brighter, those furthest away, dimmer, we can achieve a much straighter-appearing "straight line."

non-adjacent end points, the line will, at one or more points in its horizontal or vertical travel, pass between rather than through grid coordinates. If we are "drawing" such a by turning on pinpoints of light located only at grid coordinates, it can be seen that, however close the grid spacing, which is to say, whatever the limits of resolution for a particular digital device, there will be aliasing (jags) at some level if we don't thicken the line.

The resolution of the display device screen cannot represent high-frequency aspects of certain objects created in central-processor computations. Moreover, instead of degrading the image into fuzziness (as we might wish it would), it falls through to certain particular lower frequencies; that is, it lights the pixels nearest to the desired locations — thence the jags. Unfortunately (in this respect) the human eye has much better resolving capability for certain kinds of objects, such as thin lines, than a graphics display device (viewed at a reasonable distance) can realize; so the eye sees the jags, and the line does not appear straight.

The issue, then, is: how do we reduce aliasing problems produced at the weakest link in our chain — the point where pixel locations for the graphics display device are computed?

Generally what is done is to forget about how the eye works and concentrate on removing high frequency components from the image, as or before pixel locations are assigned. In effect this means making lines thicker and fuzzier. This works fairly well, since our perception (both cognitively and, it is believed, in the eye itself) correctly abstracts a smooth line from a slightly fuzzy streak.

Computational techniques for doing "anti-aliasing" in the central processor have been studied a great deal. Generating the right sorts of fuzzy streaks, especially when it is not merely straight lines we are handling, but curves and edges in general, can be hard from a computational point of view. It is easiest if whatever is being represented has a simple mathematical description.

Some manufacturers make their display devices do rough-and-ready anti-aliasing as part of the task of executing higher-level graphics instructions (instructions such as "draw a line from (a,b) to (c,d) "). This works fairly well for straight lines. The complicated, general-purpose anti-aliasing algorithms that would be required for curves, however, are now a little too slow to implement within an output device as it is working.

A pleasant sort of accommodation is possible if pixel *intensity* can be individually articulated in the output device. When this is the case, it is possible to cushion jags by making pixels brighter to the degree that they are central to an "ideal" line or curve. Figure 5b shows this schematically using circle size as a metaphor for brightness.

"Digital" french curves

A graphic artist will typically visualize a desired curve in its entirety, without reference to specific points along its arc. Using the traditional "Santa's sleigh" template, or "french curve," the artist can draw the conceptualized curve by patching together pieces of smooth curve drawn along various edges of the template.

A computer can also generate pieces of smooth curve without much trouble, and programs have been written that, insofar as possible, connect the pieces in a coherent manner. Because a computer cannot hold a mental image of the "idealized" curve, but must work, instead, from specified guide points along its arc, the goodness of a result generally depends on how adequately the guide points are deployed.

Other methods of generating curves systematically take distant control points into account. One such approach works as follows. Given an ordered collection of points in some space (usually, but not necessarily, two- or three-dimensional), it is possible to construct a mathematical function peculiar to it that will, if fed graduated values over a specified range, generate a continuous stream of points (a curve) in the neighborhood of the original collection. Unfortunately, most of the control points are not on the resulting curve. What we get is something like curve (I) in Figure 6, in which the line swings *around* the control points, touching only the first and last.

At first, this approach might seem to be almost useless. In building the mathematical function, however, we are able to specify how many control points we want to use and a "degree" n to the effect that no one point on the resulting curve depends on more than n ($=3,4,5$,etc.) nearby control points, and herein lies a virtue.

Notice that the number of control points for both curves in Figure 6 is the same, six. For curve (I), however, a degree of "5" has been specified. This means that five of the six control points are tugging at each of the individual points in the stream that is being laid down by the mathematical function. Thus, between the starting and ending points, no point

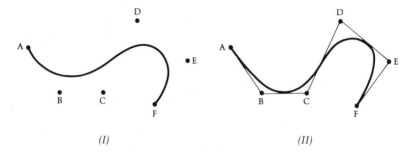

(I)   *(II)*

Figure 6: Two curves drawn with identical control points

One way to direct a computer graphics system to draw a curve is to supply control, or guide, points and starting and ending points. The difference between curves (I) and (II) — for which identical sets of control points have been supplied and identical starting (A) and ending (F) points designated — is attributable to our ability to vary, in the mathematical functions that generate the curves, the number of control points that will influence any single point on the drawn curve. For curve (I), five of the six control points have been allowed to simultaneously exert an influence over each point that will make up the drawn curve with the result that none of the points on that curve come close to any of the control points. We report the number of control points that are simultaneously active in the formation of the curve as the "degree"; thus, curve (I) has a "degree of 5." If we think of the active control points as tiny magnets, then specifying a lesser number will result in the drawn curve being pulled simultaneously in fewer directions at any given point; consequently, it can come closer to those points that are pulling it. We can see the effect of reducing the number of simultaneously active control points in curve (II), for which a "degree of 3" has been specified. As explained in the text, it is a characteristic of degree 3 curves drawn with this particular mathematical function that a straight line drawn between any two control points will intersect, or be tangent to, the curve drawn in that region.

on the curve can get close to any control point because four other control points are each pulling it toward them.

Now look at curve (II) in the same figure, for which a degree of "3" has been specified. Because only three control points are exerting an influence over individual points in the stream being laid down for this curve, certain of them come much closer to the control points.

The mathematical functions spoken of here are called *Bezier* functions, and the resulting curves, *B-splines*. The B-spline of degree 3, or *cubic B-spline*, (curve (II) in Figure 6), allows us to implement an interesting construction method. Notice that if we construct polygons from the control points for this curve, (that is, connect the dots), the resulting sides are tangent to, or intersect, the B-spline curve generated from the points. This is more than a curiosity. It allows us to *start* with tangent lines and their constituent points and then construct control points *from* them. As with techniques for eliminating aliasing, declaring lines to be "tangent to" a curve that doesn't exist yet may not be a particularly straightforward approach, but it is one that works for many applications.

Let us look at a practical graphics system whose basic curve-producing method is that of cubic B-splines, the METAFONT typefont-design program written by Donald Knuth.

A METAFONT user defines a particular character by designating points on it and then specifying the order in which an abstract "pen" passes through them in drawing the character. Optionally, the user indicates the exact *direction* in which this "pen" is moving as it passes each point. The information on direction is to help METAFONT construct tangent lines. (See Figure 7.)

We have said that METAFONT augments simple B-spline generation in special ways. For example, there is a parameter called "velocity," controlled by METAFONT, that manifests itself as resistance against making sharp turns.

But more general-purpose ramification of the B-spline concept is possible. Such is the concept of the *Beta-spline*, a B-spline with two parameters for "tuning" — *bias* and *tension*. From the point of view of someone using it, the bias parameter introduces lopsidedness — the same set of points connected in opposite directions will yield different curves. The tension parameter makes the curve hug more closely to its control points with the result that, if tension is increased without limit, the spline curve may start to look very like its own control polygon. Figure 8 shows the effects of bias and tension.

Figure 7: A METAFONT "heart"

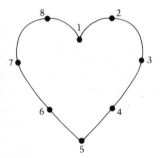

METAFONT might be made to generate the accompanying heart shape roughly as follows. First the user designates points using some convenient coordinate system. Having defined coordinate pairs (i.e., row and column positions) for each of the designated points, the METAFONT user can then draw the two sides of the heart by indicating the direction of the pen at each point. This is done by specifying number pairs that tell the pen how far to move, across and up, at each point. For example, because the points at 3 and 7 are farthest from a vertical center line their direction should be straight down. To achieve this direction, we would specify a distance of zero across, and a negative number up, which would result in the pen moving down. If the user doesn't provide any direction, as one might not for points 4 and 6, METAFONT does the best it can — it envisions, solely for purposes of constructing tangents at 4 and 6, a circle through 3-4-5, and one through 7-6-5.

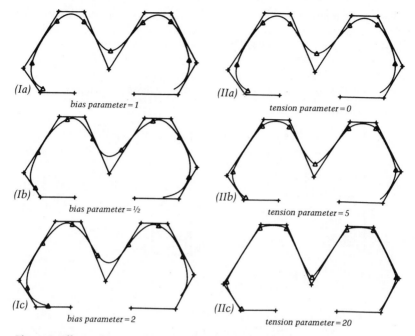

Figure 8: Effects of bias and tension on "Beta-spline" curves

Curves drawn within identical sets of control polygons (control points with connecting tangent lines) by the mathematical functions referenced in Figure 6 (so-called Beta-spline curves) can be "tuned" by varying either or both of two parameters. The effect of varying the bias parameter (shown in Ia-Ic) is to cause a curve to become lopsided in one direction or the other. Taking as a starting point a curve generated with a bias parameter equal to one (Ia), we can see a shift in the control points (small triangles) as a result of first halving (Ib), and then doubling (Ic), the value. Relative to the original curve, the resulting curves are lopsided, (Ib) to the right and (Ic) to the left. The effect of varying the tension parameter is shown in (IIa-IIc). Setting the tension parameter equal to "0" yields curve (IIa). If we increase the value of the tension parameter, say to "5," we get a curve like (IIb). Supplying the tension parameter with a very high value, such as "20" in the instance of (IIc), causes the resulting curve to follow the tangent lines of the control polygon almost completely.

Three-dimensional graphics

There is much about three-dimensional graphics that is mildly surprising. Many things that "ought" to be easy are hard and vice versa. For example, it is surprisingly *easy* for a computer to manipulate three-dimensional line drawings. Concretely:

- relocation and rotation of objects (Figure 9(I) and 9(III)) is easy;

Figure 9: Examples of computer manipulation of 3-dimensional drawings
*It is relatively easy for a computer to manipulate a 3-dimensional line drawing.
Generally, simple matrix computations are all that are required to relocate (I),*

An object constructed of lines can be *relocated* in the screen coordinate system by translating endpoints of the lines by a constant factor, in the instance of the house below, by (-3,-3).

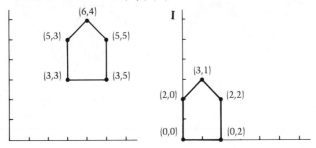

We can specify, in addition to width and height along an x- and y-axis, a third dimension, that is, the depth of an object along an axis perpendicular to the x-y axes which we'll call the z-axis.

IV

projection plane

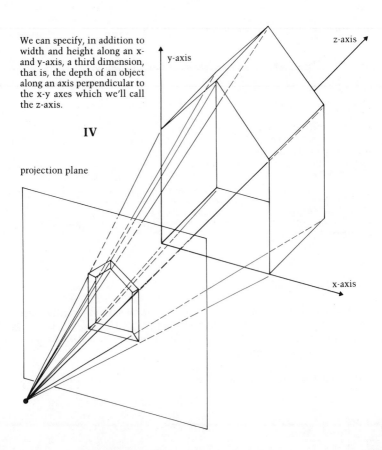

scale *(II), or* rotate *an object (III),* project *a transparent 3-dimensional object onto a 2-dimensional display (IV), or* simulate perspective *by implying distance with convergence and vanishing points (V).*

Multiplying the endpoints by a constant factor allows us to *scale* an object proportionally; let's multiply the endpoints of our relocated house by (½,½).

The mathematics of *rotation* are a bit more complex, involving sine and cosine functions, but essentially what we do is rotate an object through a particular angle.

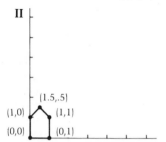

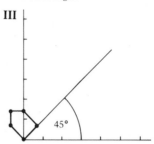

To represent this added dimension for our house, coordinates of points on the lines which compose it must assume the form (x,y,z). A computer can handle this representation of three dimensions internally, but usually is constrained to give it back to us on a display surface which has only two dimensions, i.e., coordinates of the form (x,y). We can convert point coordinates from three dimensions to two by dividing by the depth of each point. However, because any line has an infinite number of points, to apply this mathematical conversion exhaustively would be impractical. So we use the computer's ability to draw lines between specified endpoints and only convert the endpoints of the various tangent lines which make up the house. In effect what we do is project the endpoints of the lines which comprise a three-dimensional image to a particular viewpoint. In any plane that cuts the z-axis along this projection the points of the projecting lines will have two-dimensional coordinates. The computer can draw tangent lines among these various points with the result shown.

The image thus produced, although it provides perspective, is ambiguous; it could as easily be perceived to be an oddly-shaped picture frame as a three-dimensional house.

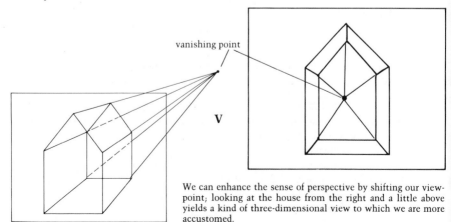

We can enhance the sense of perspective by shifting our viewpoint; looking at the house from the right and a little above yields a kind of three-dimensional view to which we are more accustomed.

- scaling objects, that is, shrinking or expanding them (Figure 9(II)), is easy;
- projecting transparent three-dimensional line drawings onto a two dimensional display (Figure 9(IV)) is easy;
- Simulating perspective, that is, implying distance with convergence and vanishing points (Figure 9(V)), is easy.

All of these things are done with simple matrix computations.

On the other hand — to give one example — it is surprisingly *hard* for a computer to copy the behavior of light as it would interact with a three-dimensional object. Let us consider some of the problems associated with this task.

Reflection and *refraction* are troublesome. Actual light may be bent (as in glass), broken (as at a reflective surface), blocked (as by an opaque object), filtered, colored — the list goes on. Realism, even comprehensibility, can quickly be lost if a computer presents us with three-dimensional images in which the apparent behavior of light does not conform to our expectations.

The most straightforward method for making a realistic image of some illuminated three-dimensional realm is called *ray-tracing* (see photo I). The idea is to trace light rays and find out which ones end up a the viewpoint. However, because an infinite number of light rays, most of which never reach the viewpoint, emanate from each point light source, the approach that is taken is to trace light backward from the viewpoint through each pixel on the screen to its imaginary source, or more often, sources. This is done by mathematically computing a path for every "ray." The result of the computations is a tree structure for each.

Care is taken to give separate treatment to specular reflection (from shiny surfaces) and nonspecular (from chalky surfaces); the most careful systems even attend to color variations within specular reflections, a phenomenon characteristic of metallic surfaces.

If ray tracing is carried through to its logical conclusion, *each* original and *all* secondary rays are followed until they encounter a perfectly matte (chalky) surface, or reach a light source, or until they leave the space being modelled. So, at least if thoroughness is any guarantee, the method ought to work.

Ray-tracing does work; but at worst it is terribly slow. We can see why; using the method is like filling a space with a three-dimensional handmade tapestry. Producing a single image by this method can take hours, or days, of computer time. For this reason, a major preoccupation in the field of computer graphics has been finding ray-tracing shortcuts. A number of strategies have been explored.

One strategy is to exploit the fact that, at times, objects in a three dimensional image are familiar "mathematical" objects, so we can compute, in advance of the ray-tracing, what the overall behavior of rays encountering them will be.

Another strategy is to simplify the computation itself, accepting a partial loss of realism. An example of this might be the following: we might elect to stop following the progress of rays and secondary rays after *n* collisions, reflective or refractive, with objects in the image.

Because of the enormous amount of calculation associated with it, ray-tracing is an excellent candidate for parallel processing; multiple processors independently tracing separate rays might significantly speed up the process.

A more radical approach is to abandon the ray-tracing technique altogether and treat all surfaces simply as quilts of opaque, dull-surfaced polygons. If we do this, computing a moderately believable brightness value for a particular flat pane of the quilt is easy — it depends only on the distance of light sources(s) and the attitude of the particular pane with respect to such source(s). Of course, no shred of "photographic" realism remains, but this is often an acceptable loss since we can generally interpret the result just as we do paintings and drawings that represent systems of illuminated physical objects but do not employ local "photographic" realism anywhere within the system (see photo II).

Hidden lines and surfaces can be a problem in representing three-dimensional objects. The practical question is "how can the program decide which lines, surfaces, and points would be hidden if our images were real and opaque?"

The fastest methods for eliminating hidden lines and surfaces generally depend on a computer program having some prior knowledge about the object(s) being represented.

The nature of this knowledge is different in different situations. For example, when objects to be represented correspond to simple geometrical objects, (or when they can be closely approximated by composite objects, each of whose components has this property), the relevant "prior knowledge" may simply be knowledge of geometry.

On the other hand, if the program is doing animation, "prior knowledge" may simply mean "memory of the previous frame," since that frame, by our very definition of what animation purports to do, must resemble the current frame in many useful ways.

Depth in three dimensions can be hard to represent in an unambiguous, quickly perceptible, way. So long as we have to view three-dimensional images in two-dimensional projections that are flat and uniformly sharp, we must leave unused a great deal of our everyday skill in spatial perception. There are several things we can do in an attempt to bring this skill into play.

We can use stereoscopy. The results of doing this are just as one would expect — successful, but either rigid or expensive. The usual, relatively inexpensive approach — stereo pairs for viewing with fixed images — works; but it doesn't really let us change our plane of attention as we could if we were seeing a truly three-dimensional display.

We can make ordinary two-dimensional projections and then impart an illusion of depth by giving them a particular plane of sharp focus. The effect is like that of a still photograph made with a lens of large diameter in which a subject that is in focus is surrounded by a foreground and

Figure 10: Examples of techniques for simulating the behaviour of light

It is surprisingly hard for a computer to simulate the behaviour of light as it would interact with 3-dimensional objects. A straightforward, but time-consuming and expensive, method called ray-tracing, *actually attempts to trace the path of every ray that ultimately reaches the viewpoint of the viewer. An image produced using a ray-tracing technique is shown at (I). Other methods achieve economy and time-savings by foregoing "photographic" realism in favor of creating an "interpretational" representation of light much as an artist might in a painting or drawing. An image produced by such a method is shown at (II). Still another method introduces an artificial "haze" that produces a contrast gradient such as we are used to from interpreting distances out of doors. This method yields somewhat surreal images, as that shown at (III).*

(I)

(II)

(III)

background that are hazy or out of focus. Generating such an image is actually quite difficult as it entails simulating the operation of a real lens.

We can introduce artificial "haze." This produces a contrast gradient we are used to from interpreting distances out-of-doors, and it has the interesting side effect that it makes all objects appear large and majestic, even chessmen and paper clips. The result is a trivial but pleasant surrealism (see photo III).

An impossible-sounding approach is to build viewing devices that look at eye-movement. Experimental devices of this type have been built that actually monitor viewers' eyes to determine how deeply they are trying to look, and then display a computed two-dimensional representation of subject material from just that depth, providing an effect like that of a high-magnification optical microscope, wherein objects before and behind the plane of focus are invisible and functionally transparent.

We have been ascending a staircase — to higher and higher levels of accommodation with machines that will display the world graphically for us. At the foot of the stairs we encountered the tools — the input and output devices — through which we accommodate the machines to our senses. Further up, we descried mechanisms for accommodating the rigid, point-by-point construction techniques employed by graphics devices to our need for straight lines and arcs. With the latter examples, of how we accommodate the two-dimensional image characteristics of graphic displays to our three-dimensional perceptual acuity, we are approaching what is, for the moment, the top of the stairs. Our ascent amounts to tricking the software that we write into tricking the hardware that we build into showing us something that, while imperfect, is intelligible and frequently helpful. This self deceit affords us novel and complex insights not only into the world we inhabit, but also into refinement of the machinery that provides them and that enables us to extend our stairway yet a few steps more.

9

Artificial Intelligence: a Long and Winding Road

John Simon, 1986

Many hundreds of years elapsed between the debut of talking oracles and dancing mannequins and development of the prototypes of the analog and digital computers; some two hundred years of experimentation with calculating machines preceded conception of the general-purpose computer, another one hundred years elapsed before the concept was resurrected, and yet a few more years preceded its realization; meanwhile, formalization of an algebra of thought lagged some two hundred years behind the origin of the notion and nearly another century passed before such an algebra was applied to the switching of electrical circuits such as are found in computers; and all of this is whence artificial intelligence derives.

"Be just what you iss, not what you iss not; 'cause what you iss, iss da happiest lot." This advice Mr. Wizard, a character in a circa 1960s Saturday morning cartoon program called the King Leonardo Show, proffered repeatedly to fellow character, Mr. Turtle, each time he returned the latter from another disastrous adventure in the role of someone else. The field of artificial intelligence, given the debate and occasional rancor that has intermittently characterized it over its brief twentieth century history, might be stood in good stead by heeding such advice; that is, the happiest lot, as far as artificial intelligence is concerned, might very well be to be just what it is, and to decline any pretence of being what it is not — yet.

The qualification is warranted. Like computing, the field of artificial intelligence, in the modern sense of the term, is young; it is only now entering the hands, and heads, of a third generation of students, and many of the first generation still linger. Computing itself has been both sustenance and sedative for artificial intelligence; computing machinery and techniques are the "stuff" in which "artificial intelligence" would be realized, yet computer manufacturers were, for a time, among the most adamant decriers of the notion that machines might "think." Though born together, computing and artificial intelligence are at widely disparate stages of development; the latter is only now trundling a pushcart full of "expert systems" into a marketplace teeming with retail and mail order purveyors of computing's extraordinarily scaled up capabilities and dramatically scaled down packaging.

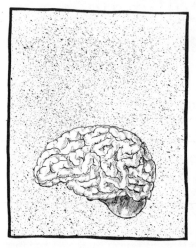

This is not to imply that things should be other than they are. Indeed, as it has turned out, realization of much that research in artificial intelligence has sought to accomplish has been contingent on the evolution of more appropriate and more powerful machinery. Nor is it suggested that artificial intelligence should have heeded Mr. Wizard's advice sooner. The reasoned debate and argumentation alluded to above will very likely, in retrospect, be deemed to have contributed to the enrichment of our understanding of human thought as much as, and possibly more than, actual machine-centered research carried out in the same time frame.

Though artificial intelligence, as a field or discipline, is relatively young, the notion of, and debate over, mechanization of human thought is many centuries old. Several contemporary authors with diverging views on artificial intelligence explore to varying degrees its antecedent myth and reality, among them, Stanley L. Jaki and Hubert L. Dreyfus, who write with a wariness of the terminology and its implications, and Frank Rose and Pamela McCorduck, whose prose strokes it with sensitivity, if not affection.

By some accounts, the first to entertain the notion of something akin to artificial intelligence lived several centuries B.C. McCorduck (1979, 4-5) recounts briefly, from Greek mythology, the story of crippled Hephaestus — son of Hera, god of fire, and divine smith — who variously fashions a bronze gentleman to patrol the beaches of Crete, a set of wheeled tripods capable of propelling themselves to and from Olympian feasts, and, to help him walk and assist him in his forge, a host of attendants for whom she turns to Richard Lattimore for a description:

> These are golden, and in appearance like living young women. There is intelligence in their hearts, and there is speech in them, and strength, and from the immortal gods they have learned how to do things. (Lattimore 1963, 386)

Even before we pose the question of whence intelligence derives, of what is the agent that imbues intelligence to a non-biological entity, we have at least one answer.

The mythology of the *The Iliad* is nearly three thousand years old. The line of reasoning that gave rise to the notion of logic is some four hundred years younger, Socrates being the first to entertain a vision of reasoning reduced to some kind of calculation to which all arguments might be submitted for resolution. Plato endeavoured to generalize that vision by suggesting that "all knowledge must be stateable in explicit definitions which anyone could apply" (1979, 67).

Jaki posits as the firmer footing attained a millenium and a half later by the mechanistic philosophy that began its precipitous climb from Plato's line of reasoning the realization that "for physics to make progress and sense, it must exclude from its range anything non-quantitative" (1969, 20). "As Galileo discovered that one could find a pure formalism for describing physical motion by ignoring secondary qualities and teleological considerations," Dreyfus explains, "so, one might suppose, a Galileo of human behavior might succeed in reducing all semantic considerations (appeal to meanings) to the techniques of syntactic (formal) manipulation" (1979, 68-69).

The real machinery of artificial intelligence to the fifteenth century, as distinguished from the mythical creations of Hephaestus, consisted largely in statues imbued variously with such attributes as movement and speech. These, McCorduck notes, were all as one to the people of the time, who detected "little difference between a human figure that nodded, bowed, marched, or struck a gong at a precise and predictable moment, and a human figure that answered knotty questions and foretold the future" (1979, 10-11).

What ensued, described by McCorduck as "a population explosion of automata" (ibid., 13), yielded within a century the prototypes of the analog and digital computers. "In 1621," Jaki explains,

> William Oughtred placed side by side two logarithmic scales, and by sliding one along the other . . . could perform multiplications and divisions. As there are . . . infinite numbers of points between any two positions on such scales, the slide rule, as the device came to be called later, can . . . be considered . . . a continuous function analog computer. . . . Its primitive digital counterpart, the adding machine . . . fully justified the proud remark of its inventor [Blaise Pascal]: "A calculating machine achieves results that come nearer to thought than anything done by an animal. But it does nothing to enable us to say that it has will, as we say animals have." (1969, 22-23)

It was in this milieu, of talking statues and rudimentary computers, that René Descartes formulated his mechanistic world view, which sought to "devitalize" biological organisms by describing them in terms of complex machines. But in treating the human organism, although Descartes carried the mechanical analogy all the way to the brain, likening it to an hypothetical hydraulic machine, there he stopped, admitting a dichotomy between bodily organs, including the brain, and "mind."

None of Descartes tentativeness was to be found in Thomas Hobbes, whom Jaki allows "fell captive to a flat theory of ratiocination in which all operations of the mind were traced back to addition and subtraction" (1969, 23-24); Hobbes, he observes, "greeted Pascal's arithmetic machine as the evidence of his views on human mind and thought. He described the brass and iron pieces of the machine as being invested with the functions of the brain and instructed to perform some of the most difficult operations of mind" (ibid., 24). By reducing human reason to a mechanical process and by ascribing to mechanical contrivances an artificial life, Hobbes sought to refute the notion of *dualism* inherent in Descartes' line of reasoning.

Hobbes having made explicit the syntactic conception of thought as calculation, all that remained was "to work out the univocal parcels or 'bits' with which this purely syntactic calculator could operate" (Dreyfus 1979, 69). This Gottfried Wilhelm Leibniz proposed to do.

McCorduck attributes Leibniz's fervent pursuit of an integral and differential calculus that would reduce "reasoning to an algebra of thought, a *calculus ratiocinator*," to his yearning "for a common language among scientists, so they could not only disseminate ideas, but also discuss them clearly and rationally" (1979, 33). Dreyfus suggests that Leibniz

> thought he had found a universal and exact system of notation, an algebra, a symbolic language, a "universal characteristic" by means of which "we can assign to every object its determined characteristic number." In this way all concepts could be analyzed into a small number of original and undefined ideas; all knowledge could be expressed and brought together in one deductive system. On the basis of these numbers and the rules for their combination all problems could be solved and all controversies ended. (1979, 69)

What Leibniz in fact found was the binary system of numbers; it remained for others to work out the algebra.

To the machinery of artificial intelligence Leibniz contributed a calculating machine, a refinement of Pascal's arithmetic machine, which could perform multiplication by rapidly repeating additions. Yet, though working from both directions that some present day researchers see converging in the realization of intelligent automata — devising a logical notation whereby human thought might be represented in a machine and creating a machine that might carry out logical operations of sufficient complexity to be classed as thought — Leibniz did not himself subscribe to such notions as were being put forth by Hobbes. "He took pains," Jaki records,

> to point out that a feeling or thinking being is not a "mechanical thing, like a clock or a mill." It was nonsensical to suppose, he [Leibniz] added, that "we might conceive sizes, figures and motions, the mechanical conjunction of which might produce something thinking and even feeling in a mass in which there was nothing of the sort, which thinking and feeling should cease also in the same way by the derangement of this mechanism." (Jaki 1969, 25-26)

Consider, in light of Leibniz's remarks, this observation by a twentieth century researcher in artificial intelligence.

Certainly you don't believe that neurons experience pain. Certainly you don't believe that the carbon, hydrogen, and oxygen that make them up experience pain. Yet science has told us the *incredible* and counterintuitive fact that if you take the ordinary molecules that are sitting around in this room and put them in the right configuration, they will feel pain.

Now that's *crazy* If anyone told you that, you'd have to laugh at them. But it's true. And there's a name for that in philosophy. It's the problem of emerging properties. How is it that something that you don't think of as having those properties can all of a sudden emerge with those properties? There's a mystery here, and it's a mystery that also applies to computers. (Rose 1984, 167)

Withal, Leibniz maintained the dichotomy between mind and body. He regarded these as "separate, but exactly matched, giving meaning to each other in a system of corresponding monads, clocks wound up to keep time together for eternity" (McCorduck 1979, 33).

Formulation of an algebra of thought was to come out of the work of a number of early nineteenth century English mathematicians, among them Sir William Hamilton, Augustus De Morgan, and George Boole. The latter is credited with laying the foundations of modern symbolic logic in a book published in 1854 entitled *An Investigation of Thought on Which Are Founded the Mathematical Theories of Logic and Probabilities.*

Though both are concerned with the general principles of reasoning, traditional logic employs words, whereas symbolic logic, to avoid the ambiguity inherent in natural language, uses ideographs. "Boole's system," McCorduck explains, "had 'elective symbols,' meaning arbitrary designations for classes of existing things, and 'laws of thought,' the rules of operation on these elective systems ... which ... significantly, would hold in an algebra of the numbers 0 and 1" (ibid.).

The earlier comparison of Oughtred's slide rule with Pascal's arithmetic machine identified the former as an analog, the latter a digital, device, the respective distinctions being the making of measurements of constantly varying quantities along a continuous scale versus the manipulation of discrete quantities. Because a logical algebra rooted in the binary system would, by definition, be implemented on the latter class of machine, an assessment of the progress being made by inventors of calculating machinery might be instructive.

Pascal's arithmetic machine, notes *The Annals of the Computation Laboratory of Harvard University, Volume I,* "was designed not to further scientific research but rather for use in his father's mercantile business. It was an accounting machine and as such was the forerunner of the modern accounting machine and cash register" (Harvard University 1946, 2).

A transitional phase ensued. "From the seventeenth century on," the *Annals* records, it was even more evident that precise and rapid methods of computation were required. The computation of tables of logarithms demanded by Napier's discovery of tables of sines and cosines, of tables of tides needed by faster and more extensive navigation and of the astronomical tables envisioned by Kepler, accentuated this need. Among many others, Gauss, Cayley, Tchebychev, Maxwell and Kelvin all attempted to devise or improve computational aids. . . . Despite this widespread interest . . . development of modern calculating machinery proceeded slowly until the growth of commercial enterprise and the increasing complexity of accounting made mechanical computation an economic necessity. Thus the ideas of the physicists and mathematicians, who foresaw the possibilities and gave the fundamentals, were turned to excellent purposes, but differing greatly from those for which they were originally intended. (Ibid., 4)

The prototype of the modern digital computer, a machine conceived, but never built, by Charles Babbage in the early eighteen-hundreds, was successor to a somewhat less ambitious calculating machine Babbage called a "difference engine." According to *The Annals*, the latter engine "was to 'perform the whole operation-(the computation and printing of a table of functions)-without any mental attention when once the given numbers have been put into the machine" (ibid.). Although twenty years of labor would produce, beyond a first working model, only what Rose describes as "a pile of sprockets and cogwheels" (1984, 30), which are today preserved in the collections of the Science Museum in South Kensington, Babbage abandoned the project not out of frustration but rather in order to undertake the creation of a far more ambitious general-purpose calculating machine.

Of Babbage's "analytical engine," *The Annals* observes:

Though the terms of the problem proposed were enough to stagger the contemporary imagination, he [Babbage] attempted to design a machine capable of carrying out not just a single arithmetical operation, but whole series of such operations without the intervention of an operator. The numbers in the first part of the machine, called the "store," were to be operated upon by the second part of the machine, called the "mill." A succession of selected operations were to be executed mechanically at the command of a "sequence mechanism". . . . For this latter, he intended to use a variation of the . . . cards. . . . used by the Jacquard weavers to control . . . looms to produce and reproduce . . . patterns designed by . . . artists. . . . Babbage required two decks; one of variable cards and one of operational cards. The first set was designed to select the . . . numbers to be operated upon from the store; the second . . . to select the operation to be performed by the mill. The . . . operation cards therefore represented the solution of a mathematical situation independent of the values of the parameters and variables involved. Thus the analytical engine was to have been completely general as regards algebraic operations. (1946, 5)

Interpretations of what Babbage thought of his designs vary. Jaki suggests that, although Babbage's appreciation for his computing device extended beyond its extraordinary capabilities to an anticipation that such devices would one day direct the course of science, it fell short of crediting the contrivance with the ability to think (1969, 47).

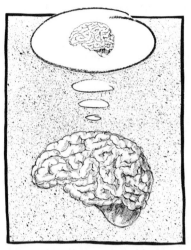

Although explications proffered by Babbage's friend and supporter, the Lady Ada, Countess of Lovelace and daughter of Lord Byron, are cited by Jaki and others as corroboration of Babbage's belief that his analytical engine was not a "thinking machine" (ibid., 47), an interpretation disputed by McCorduck (1979, 28), it may be that the Countess' observations regarding Babbage's work are merely reflections of the latter's own perceptions, with little appreciable weight of their own. A review by Tracey Kidder (1985, 6) of a biography written by Dorothy Stein raises questions about the Countess' mathematical astuteness and suggests that she had considerable assistance from Babbage in the composition of a set of notes appended to a paper on the Analytical Engine by Luigi Menabrea which she translated from the French.

That the analytical engine suffered the same fate as the difference engine was due partly to the inability of machinists of Babbage's time to meet required tolerances. Nevertheless, the unfulfilled design incorporated "the three essential elements of any modern computer: a 'store' (memory), a 'mill' (central processor), and a means of initiating various 'patterns of action' (programs")' (Rose 1984, 30), and "the rods and gears of the feedback apparatus in Babbage's machine performed exactly the same function . . . considered by several cyberneticians of our time to be the very essence of intelligent operation" (Jaki 1969, 46).

The most profitable of the late nineteenth-century calculating machines was Herman Hollerith's automatic tabulating machine, an early data processor whose successful application in the 1890 census enabled Hollerith to set up his Tabulating Machine Company (Rose 1984, 31).

At the turn of the century, H. P. Babbage, with the advantage of electrical circuits and improved machine tools and materials of construction, completed a portion of his father's analytical engine. "A table of multiples of π which it computed to twenty-nine significant digits," *The Annals* records, "was published as a specimen of its work" (Harvard University 1946, 7).

A contemporary of the younger Babbage, and himself an inventor of calculating machines and other automatic devices, Leonardo Torres y Quevedo built two electromechanical chess automata capable of playing the endgame of king and rook against king. "He declined," according to McCorduck, "to claim that his automata were actually thinking, but in 1915 he wrote, 'The inventor claims that the limits within which thought is really necessary need to be better defined, and that the automaton can do many things that are popularly classed with thought' (1979, 48). Further,

> Torres drew a distinction between the simpler sort of automaton, which has invariable mechanical relationships (the self-propelled torpedo was his example . . .) and the more complicated, interesting kind, whose relationships between operating parts alter "suddenly when necessary circumstances arise." Such an automaton must have sense organs, that is, "thermometers, magnetic compasses, dynamometers, manometers," and limbs, as Torres called them, mechanisms capable of executing the instructions that would come from the sense organs. (Ibid., 48-49)

McCorduck records that Torres' awareness of the general unreliability of electromechanical components and his lack of confidence in the ability of mechanical engineering to surmount the difficulties the elder Babbage had earlier encountered led him to view as dim the prospects for transforming his bolder designs into working machines. Nevertheless, she observes, "servomechanisms, which is what we would call Torres's machines, appeared in great numbers in the early twentieth century, and were the immediate inspiration for the field of cybernetics" (ibid., 49).

According to Jaki, it was "Vannevar Bush who rediscovered in the early twenties the principles embodied in Kelvin's differential analyzer and developed it into the first modern computer" (1969, 49).

Jaki observes a growing susceptibility to the brain-computer analogy with the debut of the Bush Differential Analyzer; the Massachusetts Institute of Technology's (M.I.T.'s) *Literary Digest* for 17 December 1927, he notes, variously heralded the device as a "man-made brain" and "an electrical machine which thinks for itself." Bush, rather less dramatically, described his construction as "an adding machine carried to an extreme in its design" (ibid., 49-50).

In abandoning his difference engine in order to pursue construction of the more complex analytical engine, Babbage had made a conceptual leap from calculating device to general-purpose computer. But realization of his grander design wanted a higher technology; it was variations on the theme of his difference engine that populated the century following his abandonment of it. Then, in the early twentieth century, with technology on the ascendant, the concept of the general-purpose computer was resurrected in the work of Alan Turing, a mathematician graduated from Cambridge University, and Claude Shannon, an engineering student at M.I.T.

Turing's contribution was an abstract universal computing machine, which he introduced in a paper written to prove that certain classes of mathematical problems were not solvable by any fixed and definite process. Turing likely drew on his familiarity with Babbage's work in conceiving what has come to be known as the "Turing machine," but, though he did go so far as to describe its workings, he did not, as Babbage did, actually intend to build the machine. "Turing showed," Rose explains, "that such a device, operating according to explicit instructions expressed in binary code, would be a universal computer, capable of doing anything any other computer could do" (1984, 32), a anything any other computer could do" (1984, 32), a concept, Rose avers, that was startling to mathematicians, implying, as it did, that "properly constructed and programmed, any one computer could in principle do the work of all computers. . . . [which], in turn suggested that a computer could be built that could do *anything* for which an algorithm — a precise and unambiguous set of instructions — could be written" (1984, 32). Known as Church's thesis (after Alonzo Church, a logician Turing worked with at Princeton), this latter proposition constitutes, Rose observes, "one of the cornerstones of computer science. . . . [and] the theoretical basis for artificial intelligence" (ibid., 32-33).

Contemporaneous with Turing's paper, Claude Shannon's masters thesis used Boolean algebra to describe the behavior of relay and switching circuits. "It supplied," according to Rose, "the link that connected binary math, symbolic logic, and the behavior of electronic circuits" (ibid., 32). Like Babbage's concept of a general-purpose computer, Boole's algebra lay dormant for a long time; some sixty years elapsed between his demonstration of the connection between mathematics and logic and the revival and perfection of the notion by Bertrand Russell and Alfred North Whitehead in their book *Principia Mathematica*. "Shannon's genius," Rose observes, "was to see that . . . the propositional calculus of symbolic logic could be used to describe the two-state, on-or-off behavior of an electromechanical relay switch. . . . and with this realization came the genesis of what has since come to be known as information theory — the idea that information, like energy or matter, is a quantifiable entity that can be manipulated at will" (ibid., 32).

Norbert Wiener, who took his Ph.D. from Harvard University at age eighteen, had, prior to the outbreak of World War II, shared with physiologist Arturo Rosenblueth a growing interest in analogies between electronic and biological devices. The interruption that was the War years found him paired with Julian Bigelow on a project to improve antiaircraft artillery.

Together, Bigelow, Rosenbleuth, and Wiener set about making a science out of the art of engineering design. They sought to reconcile with this new science the apparent unity of problems in communication, control, and statistical mechanics with a lack of unity in research in these areas. "They decided," McCorduck observes, "to call the entire field of communication and control theory, whether in the machine or the animal . . . *cybernetics*, from the Greek word for steersman" (1979, 45).

Supplementing their own knowledge about servomechanisms — mechanisms whose operation relies on some kind of feedback — with Rosenbleuth's familiarity with problems of excessive feedback in the human body, Weiner and Bigelow "devised a model of the central nervous system that explained some of its most characteristic activities as circular processes, emerging from the nervous system into the muscles, and reentering the nervous system through the sense organs" (ibid.). Their model, which emphasized the transfer of information rather than energy, provided a new paradigm for understanding many different kinds of scientific phenomena. Henry Mishkoff explains that "by describing interrelated systems in terms of the exchange of information," cybernetics pointed out functional similarities between humans and machines, which greatly contributed to our understanding of both (1985, 31).

Within a few years of the signal contributions of Turing and Shannon, Britain, Germany, and the United States hosted efforts to construct large computers. World War II lent impetus to some of these projects. Turing himself was associated with the British effort that yielded Colossus, an electromagnetic machine, completed in 1943, that provided a means to decode messages scrambled by a German automatic-encryption device called "Enigma."

By 1943, Konrad Zuse, a young German engineer apparently little heeded by his government, was, McCorduck relates, wondering of a calculating machine he had assembled in the parlor of his parents' Berlin apartment "whether it could play a master in chess." By 1945, she records, "he had developed a programming language . . . which, he felt certain, could be used for solving not only mathematical problems but also many other symbolic problems, such as chess moves" (1979, 50).

In the United States, 1943 saw completion of the Automatic Sequence Controlled Calculator, or Mark I. Jointly developed by Harvard University and the successor to Hollerith's Tabulating Machine Company, International Business Machines Corporation (IBM), under the direction of Harvard professor and Naval Reserve Commander Howard H. Aiken. this punched-tape driven calculating machine computed solutions to differential and integral equations using banks of telephone relays.

Commissioned by the War Department to compute trajectories for artillery shells, the Electronic Numerical Integrator and Calculator, or Eniac — a machine that substituted vacuum tubes for the Mark I's relay switches — was constructed at the University of Pennsylvania's Moore School of Electrical Engineering under the direction of John Mauchly and J. Presper Eckert.

That little quantitative data on the operation of the human brain existed in the mid-1940s was forthrightly acknowledged by a pair of the more thoughtful writers to suggest similarities between the brain and the computer. In 1943, Warren McCulloch, a neurophysiologist, with mathematician Walter Pitts, authored a paper that posited similarities between the operation of a network of neurons in a human brain and the operation of a computer. Mishkoff notes that although the precise correspondences suggested by McCulloch were not borne out by subsequent enlightenment about the operation of the brain, "his persuasive descriptions of the similarity between minds and machines contributed a great deal to the development of a field called *information science* and eventually to artificial intelligence" (1985, 29).

In the absence of qualifying data from brain research, refinements to the computer proved highly suggestive to imaginative writers who were quick to generalize novel characteristics in computer operation to operations in the human brain. One such refinement was the *stored program* computer, a machine, Rose explains, that "carried its instructions inside instead of having to be laboriously reprogrammed for each different task" (1984, 34). First realized in the Edvac computer, and its British counterpart, Edsac, the stored program concept made it practical to use a computer in the preparation of its own programs and led to the development of compilers, operating systems, and other programming aids.

A resurgence of popular literature's indulgence in hyperbolic analogy accompanied the unveiling of these newer machines; their massive size prompted references to "giant brains," while the descriptions of other writers ran a gamut from allusions to antiquity, such as credited the machines with "oracular" powers, to more conservative, contemporary estimations that held them to be, for example, "educated machines."

John von Neumann was associated with the group that built the Eniac and, subsequently, the Edvac, and contributed significantly to, if he didn't wholly originate, the concept of the stored program. In 1945, in the specifications he was commissioned to write for a larger, faster machine for the University of Pennsylvania's Moore School, von Neumann made many explicit comparisons between the parts of the proposed computer and the human nervous system. But, like Leibniz's deep involvements with calculating machines and an algebra of thought, von Neumann's penchant for making analogies between the computer and the human nervous system did not translate into a conviction that they were in any way fundamentally similar entities. Jaki (1969, 79-80) cites several qualifications regarding brain-computer correspondences offered by von Neumann, among them:

- the number of actions that can be performed (he suspected that the human brain outstrips its artificial counterpart by at least four orders of magnitude);
- their respective components (he observed that, whereas the brain utilizes a setup of numerous but slowly working components, a computer employs fewer but faster ones);
- the means of connecting their components (evidence suggested to him that the brain works mostly with parallel networks while computers are almost universally wired serially, which modes he regarded as not unrestrictedly interchangeable);
- their respective levels of precision (von Neumann noted that in the human nervous system a rather low level of precision, which he estimated not to exceed the level of two or three decimals, is associated with a very high level of reliability, which characteristic is not at all in evidence in computing machinery).

In his last public discussion on the subject, von Neumann suggested that "the nervous system appears to using a radically different system of notation from the ones we are familiar with in ordinary arithmetic and mathematics. . . . Logic and mathematics in the central nervous system when viewed as languages must structurally be essentially different from those languages to which our common experience refers" (ibid.). Von Neumann's views were corroborated by W. M. Elsasser, whose detailed study of the respective ways in which the two systems store information found in the brain an "'amazing lack of evidence for the existence of devices that would store information mechanistically after the manner of the storage components of electronic computers.' . . . [and] . . . lack of evidence in the brain for associated devices on which the distribution and sorting of information might depend" (ibid., 80).

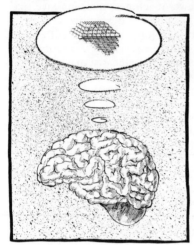

To afford issues such as these wider attention and further discussion, von Neumann, together with Aiken, who had just seen Harvard's Mark I to completion, Wiener, whose war work had helped spawn the field of cybernetics, and Pitts and McCulloch, whose early paper positing similarities in the operation of the brain and the computer had engendered the field of information science, formed, in December of 1944, the Teleological Society, its expressed purpose, to discuss "communication engineering, the engineering of control devices, the mathematics of time series in statistics, and the communication and control aspects of the nervous system" (McCorduck 1979, 66). Five years later, McCulloch addressed the first meeting of a similar organization, the Ratio Club, that had coalesced in Great Britain. Among the founders of the British organization were Donald MacKay, a physicist, and John Bates, a neurosurgeon, and among it members, Alan Turing.

Though they hadn't yet arrived at the term, the notion of artificial intelligence was being refined by members of these groups. McCorduck cites several relevant papers and creations by members of the Ratio Club. Grey Walter, the brain physiologist at whose laboratory the club was conceived,

> made significant discoveries about the electrical activity of the brain, and . . . to study some of these further . . . built the turtle, a dome-shaped electromechanical device that rolled its way around obstacles, and retired to its hutch when its batteries needed recharging. Walter intended it to show that complex behavior — what an observer might see as purpose, independence, and spontaneity — was in fact the result of rich interconnections of a relatively small number of original elements. (Ibid., 81)

Another member of the Ratio Club, a psychiatrist named W. Ross Ashby, had long been certain that much human mental behavior could be accounted for mechanistically. Ashby viewed organism and environment, taken together, as an absolute system whose parts interact with one another. Pondering the case for machines, he built one that McCorduck describes as "a self-organizing system, a system that responds to stimuli, changing its behavior, and in some sense its shape, in order to achieve stability" (ibid., 83). She describes this *homeostat* as a cluster of four units, each equipped with a governing device and capable of emitting a direct current output to the others and of receiving their output in turn. Relative to the settings of the governing devices, definite patterns of behavior would be exhibited by the homeostat as it sought to stabilize itself.

Ashby also contributed a pertinent observation to the evolving field of artificial intelligence: he pointed out that while both might be said to be designing a mechanical brain, the aim of one who wants his creation to perform a specific task, preferably better than a human can do it and not necessarily by methods humans might use, is substantively different from the aim of one who, like himself, is concerned with copying the living brain with such fidelity that the mechanical model would, in the same way that the human brain can, fail in certain characteristic ways. "Here," McCorduck notes, "Ashby articulated the distinction that would subsequently define two major branches of artificial intelligence: one aimed at producing intelligent behavior regardless of how it was accomplished, and the other one aimed at modeling intelligent processes found in nature, particularly human ones" (ibid.).

MacKay, during his years with the Ratio Club, "was wondering whether there was such a thing as the measurement of information, and in particular whether limits existed, in the ways that the Heisenberg Principle limits certain kinds of physical measurements" (ibid., 80).

McCorduck records that in 1949 MacKay privately circulated a document that discussed the possibility of combining analog and digital techniques in the design of an artefact that would be capable of responding to new information with adjustments in its behavior, that would, in effect, be capable of pursuing, independently of human intervention, a disciplined existence with at least an abstract sense of purpose and of developing purposes of its own that, while congruent with some overriding design principle, would not necessarily be predetermined by its designer.

In his own thinking about the notion of partial truth or probability, MacKay anticipated the present day concept of *fuzzy logic,* an extension of more formal logic to accommodate terms of a relative nature, such as tall, brief, and nearby. "In a 1951 paper," McCorduck notes, "MacKay proposed a statistical mechanism that would display many of the attributes of human cognition, including prejudices, preferences, originality of a kind, and learning" (ibid., 81). Taking up, toward the end of that paper, the question of how mind arises from matter, MacKay concluded that it isn't the descriptions of mind or matter that are exclusive but the logical backgrounds in terms of which they have meaning, like the dual descriptions of light as waves and as particles, each of which is valid in its own context.

Meanwhile, Turing, in an article published in 1950, proposed what has come to be regarded as the classic test of machine intelligence. Although the test he suggested to provide the answer to his opening question, "Can machines think?" has come to be called the "Turing test," Turing originally proposed it as the "imitation game." The game was to involve three people, a man, a woman, and an interrogator. The interrogator was to remain in a room apart from the man and woman and, by putting questions to them, try to determine which was the man and which the woman. Turing labeled the three A, B, and C, C being the interrogator and A and B the man and woman. Whichever of the two is A is supposed to try to cause the interrogator to make the incorrect identification; whichever is B is supposed to help the interrogator. Turing suggested the use of teleprinters to handle communication between the rooms to eliminate tone of voice and handwriting as clues. The game becomes a test for intelligence in machinery, Turing proposes, when a machine is substituted for A.

Of Turing's article, and particularly his test, Dreyfus remarks:

> The time was ripe to produce the appropriate symbolism and the detailed instructions by means of which the rules of reason could be incorporated in a computer program. Turing had grasped the possibility and provided the criterion for success, but his article ended with only the sketchiest suggestions about what to do next: "We may hope that machines will eventually compete with men in all purely intellectual fields. But which are the best ones to start with? . . . Many people think that a very abstract activity, like the playing of chess, would be best. It can also be maintained that it is best to provide the machine with . . . sense organs . . . and then teach it to understand and speak English. This process could follow the normal teaching of a child. Things would be pointed out and named, etc. Again I do not know what the right answer is, but I think both approaches should be tried." (1979, 73-74)

Both were. The same year that Turing's article appeared, an article was published by Shannon in which he discussed the options available to those who would program a computer to play chess. Shannon is credited, on the basis of this paper, with being the first to point out the impracticality of having a computer consider every possible combination of moves; he estimated that a computer that attempted to follow this approach, if it were capable of evaluating one million moves per second, would take 10^{95} years to make its first move.

Five years later, in a survey of the problems associated with programming a computer to play chess, Newell accompanied some suggestions for solving them with a proviso that the suggested mechanisms were so complicated as to make it impossible to predict whether they would work. Notwithstanding his cautionary hedge, a group at Los Alamos succeeded in programming a computer to play a poor but legal game on a reduced board the following year.

Although the Los Alamos group's program hadn't been written yet, chess-playing programs had been proposed when Arthur Samuel, in 1947, decided to build a checkers-playing machine. Samuel chose checkers specifically because it seemed a more tractable pursuit than chess, and the project was, for him, peripheral to his principal aim; the checkers-playing machine was intended to play in, and win, a checkers tournament gaining thereby notoriety and, hopefully, raising money for the construction of a computer on the scale of the Mark I or Eniac for the University of Illinois. Not only was the program, (not to mention the very small computer it was to run on), not completed in time for the tournament he had hoped it would play in, but Samuel was to work on the program, off and on, for some twenty years more, part of which time he would be employed by IBM, the company that had earlier cooperated in the creation of Harvard's Mark I.

Many of IBM's early data processing computers cut their teeth on Samuel's checkers program, which, because it was complicated and long-running, proved an excellent test vehicle.

Though too late for his Illinois venture, notoriety did begin to accrue to Samuel's program, somewhat to the chagrin of conservative IBM, which didn't mind using it to test computers, but worried lest it nurture public fears about thinking machines and computers taking over the world. Samuel's program was becoming increasingly sophisticated; ultimately, it could, to some extent, learn, supplementing the look-ahead approach to making moves with recollection of consequences of moves made in identical situations in previous games.

Samuel's approach to imparting learning ability to his program could very well describe the approach employed today by those working in the branch of artificial intelligence concerned with the development of expert systems.

> He did not believe that human learning processes ought necessarily to be imitated, because he believed that the differences between the human brain and the computer were simply too great. "I think you study the way people solve problems to get an insight into what the real problem is, not to get an insight into the method the brain uses to solve the problem. And then you sit down and you say, 'Okay, given the technology available, the speeds, and what the computer will do, how best can we solve the problem?'" (McCorduck 1979, 152)

Anthony Oettinger, then at the University Mathematical Laboratory, Cambridge, Great Britain, tried a variation on the latter approach suggested by Turing, that is, teaching a computer as one might a child. One of his programs, which he dubbed his "shopping programme," divided the University's Edsac computer into two parts; one part of the machine became the shopping environment, the other part the shopper. Oettinger summarized the program thus:

> The shopping programme may be imagined to define a small child sent on a shopping tour. If this child were asked by its mother to buy different articles in various shops, it would not know at first where to find these articles, and would hunt for them by going from shop to shop in a random fashion until it came to the desired one. Having found an article once, it would remember in what shop, and would go directly to this shop the next time the same article were requested. In addition, as its curiosity would prompt it to note the whereabouts of articles for which it had not had a specific request, it would often be able to go directly to the right shop. (Oettinger 1952, 1247)

Oettinger also developed a response-learning program that was capable of adjusting its responses, on the basis of feedback provided by an experimenter, to stimuli of varying intensity detected by a sensory device. The experimenter could, by rewarding, punishing, or simply ignoring particular responses made by the machine, cause it to tend toward certain responses over others. In contrasting the two programs, Oettinger suggests that the shopping program is "capable of performing functions which, in living organisms, are considered to be the result of intelligent behavior," whereas the response-learning program "is operating at a level roughly corresponding to that of conditioned reflexes" (ibid., 1251).

Oettinger admitted some severe limitations to the shopping program. These included limitations in the size of the matrix by which he defined the shops and their stocks, and the explicitness of the method by which the matrix and the memory were scanned. That Oettinger, in his shopping program, was thinking of emulating human thought processes rather than realizing intelligent operation by any means is clear when he suggests, by way of improving his program, "the introduction of memory decay or forgetfulness, [which] would give the learning process a greater degree of verisimilitude, that is a greater resemblance to the mental operations to which we are accustomed" (ibid., 1250).

Oettinger also recognized early, in his own programs, a characteristic that was to become endemic to artificial intelligence programming — that of limited domains. Commenting on the desirability of generalizing his shopping program, Oettinger observes that "while the shopping machine appears to learn, it certainly cannot be taught any subject the experimenter chooses" (ibid.). Describing a scanning method that would generalize the shopping program, Oettinger remarks that it would yield a machine that "is more powerful than the simpler machine only in thesense that its limitations are shifted to a higher level of abstraction."

Written before artificial intelligence programming was called by that name, Oettinger's paper not only anticipated a difficulty of generalizing limited-domain programs that continues to be experienced to the present time, but also provided some insightful observations on using digital computers as models.

> It is important to distinguish carefully between machines intended to be models of the physical structure of animal nervous systems and machines designed to perform specific functions of animal nervous systems. The fact that the . . . machines . . . can play restricted versions of the imitation game implies a correspondence between their functions and some functions of the human nervous system. But as there are usually many means of synthesizing a given pattern of functions it is dangerous to reason from functional to structural correspondence. A special machine could be built, for example, to do only the job of the shopping . . . machine. The physical structure and the internal mode of operation of this machine would need to bear no relation to the Edsac and, in turn, to the human brain, other than that of superficial correspondence of certain functions of input and output. (ibid., 1261)

Neither of the approaches outlined by Turing — abstract activities like game-playing or the teaching-learning paradigm that regards the computer as an infant to be acquainted with the world — offered anything like a general theory of intelligent behavior. "What was needed," Dreyfus remarks,

> were rules for converting any sort of intelligent activity into a set of instructions. At this point, Herbert Simon and Allen Newell, analyzing the way a student proceeded to solve logic problems, noted that their subjects tended to use rules or shortcuts which were not universally correct, but which often helped. . . . [and] decided to try to simulate this practical intelligence. The term "heuristic program" was used to distinguish the resulting programs from programs which are guaranteed to work, so-called algorithmic programs which follow an exhaustive method to arrive at a solution, but which rapidly become unwieldy when dealing with practical problems. (ibid.)

The term *heuristic* the two borrowed from George Polya, a mathematician whom Newell had studied under at Stanford University, and whose attempts to demystify problem solving techniques used by mathematicians had earlier been gathered together in a book called *How to Solve It.*

While at Rand Corporation in the early 1950s, Newell had applied card-programmed calculators to the simulation of radar screens, an activity, when he became acquainted with it, that "fascinated Simon, and opened his eyes to the possibilities of a computer as an information processor" (McCorduck 1979, 129).

When Newell and Simon came together again two years later, in 1954, they were in turn influenced by a third individual, Oliver Selfridge, who had come to Rand to describe his work with G.P. Dinneen on pattern recognition. Selfridge and Dinneen had developed a program that attempted to recognize visual patterns — a few alphabet letters and some simple geometric figures — by computing characteristics of the figure and comparing the returned values with norms. But more significantly, the program possessed the ability to generate new characteristics and to eliminate characteristics that it tried unsuccessfully, in effect, to learn from its experience. "It didn't learn very well," McCorduck notes,

> indeed, it tended to fix itself on one characteristic and improve that one to the exclusion of others. But that wasn't the point. . . . the thing that had so taken Newell, was that a complex process was underway that was the result of many simpler subprocesses. . . . [which] had been organized in a highly conditional and interactive way, and the system showed that, working in concert, a set of simple subprocesses that were easy to understand could lead to genuinely intelligent behavior. This conclusion seems altogether obvious and common sensical in retrospect, but at the time it wasn't at all obvious and it was counter to common-sense notions of intelligent behavior. This assumption — that sets of simple subprocesses could produce a system which behaved in a complex way — was to inform research in artificial intelligence through many, many more tasks of greater and greater difficulty. (Ibid., 134)

The effect of this on Newell, McCorduck explains, was to turn him from theorizing about how human organizations accomplish tasks to trying to build systems that exhibit intelligent behavior. His first step in this direction, she reports, was to write a paper "using chess as a vehicle to understand what Selfridge and Dinneen were doing" (ibid., 135). To carry his intention from paper to program, Newell left Rand for the Carnegie Institute of Technology (later Carnegie-Mellon University) to seek Simon's collaboration. The work Newell proposed to do

> was altogether congruent with Simon's growing convictions that the computer could be made to simulate human thought processes in ways that would yield insights which previous models — mathematical, statistical, behavioral — had not. The result would be the information-processing model, child of the new scientific paradigm of information theory. (Ibid.)

The two subsequently determined to create not only a chess machine, but also a program to prove mathematical theorems from *Principia Mathematica*. Work on the latter program, which Newell and Simon would call the Logic Theorist, eventually preempted work on the chess machine, and also came to include J. C. Shaw, a senior programmer at Rand, whose expertise was tapped remotely via long-distance telephone. In the closing days of 1955, these three were able to lay claim to a working Logic Theorist whose solutions to mathematical problems and puzzles seemed intelligent and creative, and to some significant contributions to the art of programming.

Memory, which is still a precious commodity in computers, was no less so in those early days, and computers then, as now, typically allocated it at the beginning of a program's run, irrevocably dedicating segments of storage to specific functions. So great was their Logic Theorist's appetite for memory that the Newell, Shaw, and Simon team were forced to come up with an alternate approach, which consisted in labelling each segment of memory and providing the computer with the means to keep track of the usable space available at any given time. It was from this "vacancy list" that their *list processing* technique took its name.

The notion of list processing carried into the organization of data, as well. "It happens," McCorduck explains, "that data arranged in lists, and lists of lists, lend themselves most readily to the simulation of human thinking processes. . . . [which] fact is unsurprising, for . . . one important source of the ideas for list-processing languages was what psychologists knew about associative memory in human beings" (ibid., 143).

Approximately twenty-five hundred years interceded between Socrates vision of reasoning reduced to a form of calculation and the vision of a group of individuals who sought to focus through the medium of the digital computer what had amounted to little more than a mirage for Socrates. This later vision took the form of the Dartmouth Summer Research Project on Artificial Intelligence, a two-month event made possible in part by a grant from the Rockefeller Foundation and attended by a core of some ten mathematicians, psychologists, neurologists, and elec-

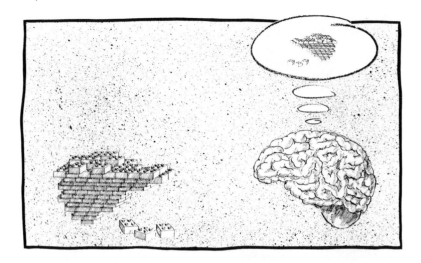

trical engineers from industry and academia. Four of the ten collaborated on a grant proposal calling for

> a . . . study of artificial intelligence [to] be carried out during the summer of 1956 at Dartmouth College in Hanover, New Hampshire. . . . to proceed on the basis of the conjecture that every aspect of learning or any other feature of intelligence can in principle be so precisely described that a machine can be made to simulate it. (Ibid., 93)

John McCarthy, an assistant professor of mathematics at Dartmouth and the conference's prime mover, drew the other three collaborators from associations past and present. Marvin Minsky, a junior fellow in mathematics and neurology at Harvard University, had been a graduate student with McCarthy at Princeton University and the two had subsequently worked at the Bell Telephone Laboratories with Claude Shannon. Nathaniel Rochester, Manager of Information Research for IBM, was known to McCarthy in connection with the gift of a computer that his company was making to M.I.T.; these two discovered they shared a mutual interest in intelligent machines, particularly in such machines as might be made to exhibit original behavior in problem solving.

Of the other conference participants, some have already been associated with ideas or lines of work — Samuel, Selfridge, Simon, and Newell. Also present were Alex Bernstein, from IBM, who, in developing a chess-playing program that employed sophisticated heuristic techniques for identifying best moves, was exploring various methods of eliminating possibilities, a concept that has become central to artificial intelligence research, and Ray Solomonoff, who was working on models of inductive inference and arguing the case for presenting simple problems to computers in order that the method by which the machines arrived at their solutions, and not the solutions themselves, might be more carefully scrutinized.

Reviewers seem to agree that the Dartmouth Conference is more note-worthy for the individuals it brought together than for anything that transpired during the course of it. McCorduck remarks that it represented a confluence of several different intellectual streams of the twentieth century which had, themselves, flowed from other streams (ibid., 95), and Mishkoff adds that in this confluence a new branch of computer science arose, the term *artificial intelligence* becoming firmly and irrevocably associated with it (1985, 32). "There were no spectacular scientific devel-opments at the conference," he observes, "no startling insights. . . . but the new field did come away with a name and with an "elite". . . . [and] even today, the leadership of the American artificial intelligence com-munity is composed largely of the conference participants, their students, and their students' students" (ibid.). The schools with which these lumi-naries became associated — Carnegie-Mellon, M.I.T., and Stanford Uni-versity — became early bastions of artificial intelligence research.

At Carnegie-Mellon, where they had produced the Logic Theorist, Newell and Simon pressed on with development of a successor program called the General Problem Solver, or GPS. In his tutorial work, *Artificial Intelligence*, Patrick H. Winston summarizes GPS thus:

> For some problems, it is natural to think in terms of current situation and desired situation. We speak of the collection of facts that specify the problem and where we are on it as the *current state*. Similarly, where we want to be is the *goal state*. Here are some examples:
>
> • In a travel problem, the current state and the goal state are defined by physical locations.
> • In a robot-assembly problem, the current state and the goal state are defined by the raw materials and the thing to be assembled.
> • In a geometry problem the current state is all that is known, both general and specific. The goal state is all that is know, as before, but also including the fact to be shown.
>
> Consider an approach to these problems in which *procedures* are selected according to their ability to reduce the observed *difference* between the *current state* and the *goal state*. This approach is known as *means-ends analysis*. GPS is a metaphor denoting a particular control strategy built on top of the means-ends analysis idea. (1984, 146-147)

In GPS, Newell and Simon did not, McCorduck avers, invent a new universe, but rather conceived a means for understanding some major aspects of an existing universe, that of human symbolic behavior. They associated their program with human problem solving, which they iden-tified as "a subspecies of thinking, concerned explicitly with the perfor-mance of tasks" (1979, 213). McCorduck notes successful trials of GPS with logic problems and puzzle solutions, and incorporation of its prin-ciple techniques in a host of successor programs.

GPS was not alone in providing insights. At other institutions, other targets were being hit with varying degrees of success. John McCarthy, who had left Dartmouth to help establish an artificial intelligence laboratory at M.I.T., was aiming at generalized problem solving with a twist; he proposed a program that would be able not only to solve a variety of problems, but also to take advice in order to improve it performance. McCorduck records that this Advice Taker program never became anything more than a proposal "because," according to McCarthy, "in order to do it, you have to be able to express formally that information that is normally expressed in ordinary language" (ibid., 218). McCarthy considered this to be the key unsolved problem in artificial intelligence and made several unsuccessful attempts to invent a formal language that would be able to express the events of everyday life. Lack of success in this endeavour — his or otherwise — McCarthy attributed to too few competent people having devoted themselves to it.

In addition to aligning another target for artificial intelligence researchers, McCarthy's specifications for the Advice Taker engendered the development of two tools — the LISP programming language and the concept of timesharing — that have become fundamental not only to work in the field, but also to computing in general.

The language and subsequent versions thereof that derived from the list processing technique developed by Newell and Simon in the creation of the Logic Theorist were called Information Processing Languages, or IPLs. The programming language McCarthy developed to accommodate the specifications of his Advice Taker program he called LISP. Minsky, in *The AI Business*, suggests that, at twenty-five years of age, LISP is still in its prime. "One of the things that we want in intelligent systems," he observes,

> is the ability to solve systems of complicated constraints automatically, but I am not sure that is the kind of thing you want to put into a language. The reason why LISP has retained its popularity in Artificial Intelligence is that it is not a language so much as it is a language that you write your own language in. When an artificial-intelligence person wants to make a program to reason by analogy, he starts with LISP because in a week or two he can write in LISP the elements of another language that he really wants to use. In PASCAL you just do not go around writing another language that you would rather have than PASCAL because PASCAL's syntax is too rigid and the way it allocates memory is too inflexible. LISP is really the machine language of high-level languages. (Winston and Prendergast 1984, 253)

Mishkoff describes some of the characteristics and functional attributes of LISP. One of the former is the list-orientation of the earlier IPLs. LISP lists comprise sequences of *elements*, each of which can be either an *atom* (a single object) or another list. A list can also be a sequence of lists. A term that is part of its own definition, as *list* is, is said to be *recursive*. What recursion allows in the present context is a program to arrive at a solution to a problem by working back through a series of antecedent problems, each of which depends for its solution on the solution of the preceding one. This technique, which is not supported by many programming languages, is regarded as an important component of intelligent problem-solving.

Data, which Mishkoff describes as *declarative* knowledge, that is, knowledge about the properties of an object, and instructions, which he defines as *procedural* knowledge, or knowledge about what actions to perform, take the same form in LISP (1985, 156). This consistency makes integration easy and enables LISP programs, which are themselves essentially lists, to be treated as data by other LISP programs, or even by themselves. Derivatives of this capability include LISP programs that can modify and add to their own instructions, and even write complete LISP programs, all of which is of great utility to a program that is attempting to learn a new task. LISP programs can also easily keep track of the order and frequency of the instructions they execute, an attribute that contemporary "expert systems" use to advantage in accounting for their actions to their programmers or users.

Although it was to become the single most widely-used language for developing artificial intelligence programs, "it happens," McCorduck explains, "that LISP didn't catch on for some time. McCarthy," she says,

attributes its late blooming to the fact that it could do things powerfully . . . but at the time of its invention, nobody really wanted to do them. The simple programs most people were aspiring to were actually easier to program in machine code, and not until aspirations rose did people realize that LISP existed and would provide a representation by which they could accomplish more complicated tasks. (1979, 216)

The extensive use it received when once it did catch on led to the creation of total programming *environments* around LISP. These environments comprise sets of programs — including editors (for writing and modifying programs), debuggers (for finding and correcting errors in programs), and windowing systems (for displaying multiple sections of programs simultaneously) — that work fluidly with particular versions of LISP to expedite program development.

McCarthy's design for LISP included the notion of "working with it interactively — giving it a command, then seeing what happened, then giving it another command" (ibid., 217). To accommodate this approach, he was compelled to invent a complementary kind of computing, earlier pondered but never implemented by Shaw, which McCarthy was to call "time-sharing," after a term used in communications to describe a technique for sending several signals over the same line.

McCarthy's implementation of timesharing, which he carried out at M.I.T. with the aid of a grant from the National Science Foundation, enabled several programmers to execute their programs interactively on a single computer. As with transmission systems, processing speeds of computers are so fast that, although the machines cycle serially among the programmers who are using them, the effect is of simultaneous processing. This was in sharp contrast to the then-prevailing mode of computing, termed *batch processing*, which called for programmers to read into a computer stacks of cards into which their program instructions had been coded in the form of punched holes, and then wait for the instructions to be processed and the results of the processing printed before making changes or additions and repeating the entire process. "It was," McCarthy remarked,

> one of those ideas that seemed inevitable in the sense that when I was first learning about computers, I was a little surprised that even if that wasn't the way it was already done, it surely must be what everybody had in mind to do eventually. It turned out it wasn't, and I promoted it as something for artificial intelligence." (Ibid.)

In the mid-1960s, McCarthy left M.I.T. for Stanford University, where he initiated a project in robotics research and continued his work on the formalization of common sense knowledge and reasoning.

Minsky was McCarthy's collaborator in the creation of the M.I.T. artificial intelligence laboratory and served for several years as its director. His early work in artificial intelligence, influenced by the brain-computer comparisons of McCulloch and Pitts, was concerned with trying to understand the operation of the brain in terms of neurons using the digital characteristics of the computer. "Prodded," according to McCorduck, "by his colleague, Ray Solomonoff, who complained that there must be a more direct way of working on ideas of intelligence, such as trying to define what the behavior was instead of the parts it comprised, Minsky moved away from the neural-net idea" (ibid, 84), but not before contributing something of a last word on one of the major efforts to utilize this approach — the Perceptron.

Central to the notion of a neural-net is the assumption that organic brain cells are largely undifferentiated and organize themselves into purposeful behavior as a consequence of experience and perception. The built-in redundancy in the brain — by which responsibility for functions carried out by a part that becomes damaged can sometimes be assumed by other another part — lends support to this notion, as does the seemingly random way in which connections are made between neurons, enabling impulses to detour when a route is damaged or otherwise blocked.

The Perceptron was an attempt to create an automaton that would be able to demonstrate equivalent capabilities, that is, that would be be able to organize itself, to do so in a random manner, and to learn and adapt in the process. Work on the Perceptron was led by Frank Rosenblatt at Cornell University. As originally conceived, the system comprised three levels: corresponding to the retina of the eye was a grid of photocells that reacted to light stimulus; below that, a group of associator units collected impulses transmitted from the photocells to which they were randomly wired; and at base, a set of response units acted upon the signals received from the associator units. Subsequently, to improve its performance, some of the randomness of the Perceptron's wiring was eliminated on the assumption that animals and humans enter the world with at least some neural connections already established.

Minsky's final word on Perceptrons took the form of a book on the subject which he coauthored with Seymour Papert, whom he met in 1961 at a conference in England while presenting some work on a Perceptron-like machine.

"One problem with a Perceptron," McCorduck notes,

> was that it could classify stimuli it received but it lacked an internal representation of that act. Therefore it couldn't refer in some symbolic way to the act of perception, but had to recapitulate the act itself exactly, which put it in the position of being no better off when repeating the act again. Symbolic representation, by which machines (and humans) deal with a host of phenomena without having to reiterate them in their totality, is central to intelligent behavior, to memory, and to consciousness. (Ibid., 89)

In turning his attention from brain structure to brain process, Minsky was drawing a bead on what has perhaps been the most persistent and intractable problem in artificial intelligence — knowledge representation. "We don't have to think about how to store what we know about love, say, or the behavior that's expected of us in restaurants," Rose observes, "we either store it or we don't." But for computers, he explains, "it's different: every fact . . . must be written out in code, and it must be organized in such a way that the computer can integrate it with every other fact it has" (1984, 55). It was to this end that Minsky introduced the notion of storing knowledge in *frames*. Within a given frame, a host of details is associated with a particular object or concept. A frame for a rose, for example, might contain details about color, number, fragrance, etc. When we think "rose" we typically assume default values for many of these details unless our immediate experience leads us to substitute different ones. For example, we might, at the mention of the word, call up the color red, only to change this image when the speaker presents us with a yellow rose. Details can be added to or eliminated from frames at will.

Roger Schank came to the problem of knowledge representation by way of language understanding. Donald Michie, who had earlier worked at Bletchley Park where the project that yielded Colussus was carried out and subsequently moved to Edinburgh University where he became involved in artificial intelligence research, notes that

> in the 1950s and 1960s, millions of dollars were spent in the United States on research-and-development projects aimed at . . . ["machine translation"]. The techniques of machines breaking up texts grammatically and looking up meanings in a computer dictionary proved too shallow to crack the machine translation problem unaided. Fundamental progress had to wait for the development of an adequate theory of what is involved in "understanding" a passage of English-language text. (1974, 103)

Schank was one who attempted to construct such a theory, applying to the problem a computational-linguistic approach that assumed that ambiguity could be minimized if language could be represented at a sufficiently deep level. At such a deep level, he reasoned, different sentences with the same meaning would take the same form, while similar, or even identical, sentences with different meanings would register those differences. Because Schank assumed that primitive units of meaning

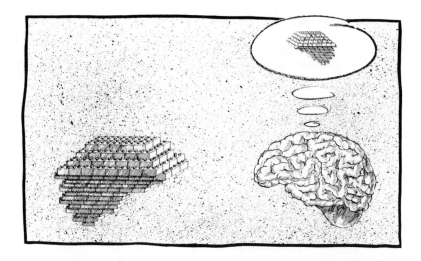

could be identified and were related to one another by dependencies, his view, which was similar to that of noted linguist Noam Chomsky, came to be described as the notion of "conceptual dependencies."

Later, with Robert Abelson at Yale University, Schank attempted to integrate these concepts into larger contexts. Out of this work came the notion of *scripts*. Like a frame, a script is a sort of atomic unit. It provides a set of default behaviors related to common situations. The script idea suggests that for almost any situation that we find ourselves in we have stored a pattern of behavior that is appropriate to it and that can be readily called up. As with frames, the elemental details of scripts can be augmented or reduced at will and possess default values that can be altered on the basis of present experience.

Subsequently, Schank undertook to effect in programs the ability to make inferences. His resulting story-understander programs have demonstrated the ability to digest and then answer questions about stories inferring information that isn't explicitly contained in them. Linking a number of these programs together, Schank created BORIS (for Better Organized Reasoning and Inference System), a composite entity with a limited understanding of, among other things, what motivates people.

One of Schank's students at Yale, Robert Wilensky, earned his doctorate trying to expand the skills-repertoire of story-understanding programs. "While most of his [Schank's] students," Rose explains,

> were working on his main story-understander program, SAM, Wilensky was put to work on a more speculative cousin known as PAM, for "Plan-Applier Mechanism." Where SAM was supposed to understand stories because it knew about scripts, PAM was envisioned as a program that could understand stories about situations for which no ready-made script exists. PAM would know about plans and goals. These, Schank theorized, are what enable people to function in situations they've never encountered before. (1984, 51)

Prior to Wilensky, Rose observes, work in planning had, like the theorem-solving programs of Newell and Simon, addressed only an aspect of planning, such as problem-solving, or was confined to "the area of 'robot planning' — programming robots to move blocks around" (ibid.). The business of "programming robots to move blocks around" entails providing the program employed by a robot's computer with detailed knowledge about an environment, as well as about plans and goals. Michie considers the level of difficulty of programming such knowledge to be equivalent to that associated with the language understanding task. A robot in the most elementary of environments is, he explains, not unlike a child in a playpen with a few commonplace objects; it is up to the machine's programmer to provide it with abilities equivalent to those the child employs "to come to terms with, and mentally organise, not only the visual and mechanical properties of material objects, but also the basic laws of nature, such as gravity, which determine their interaction" (1974, 103).

A robot, with its associated paraphernalia — cameras, moveable platforms, and manipulators — is incidental to this task; "we are concerned," Michie explains,

> with the use we can make of a robot in order to develop *theories* of "computer understanding" of the real world. The acid test of such theories is provided by the robot itself. If it can be got to *understand* what is involved in operations such as "find," "fetch," "build," "tidy," and so on; then, and only then, can we program it to do these things. (Ibid., 104)

In the early 1970s, at the Stanford Research Institute, formerly associated with Stanford University but now an independent research organization known as SRI International, a working model of a robot that "understood" a highly constrained environment sufficiently well to formulate and carry out simple plans within it was built. Nils Nilsson directed the project that resulted in the creation of Shakey, whose name derived, according to McCorduck, from the observation by one of the project staff that the mobile robot shook a great deal as it moved about (1979, 230).

Shakey was radio-controlled, stood about the height of a man, had no "hand," and could not climb. Michie proffers a report by Stephen Coles that describes a task-oriented situation in which Shakey was placed and recounts sketchily the strategy for enabling the robot to carry out the task.

> [Shakey] is in a room in which a box rests on a platform. The platform is too high for the robot's wheels to mount. Somewhere in the room is a ramp. The robot's task is to cause the box to be on the floor. . . . The capability to reason out the solution from first principles is programmed into the system. The key techniques are derived from mathematical logic. The trick is to dress up the formulation of a plan of action so that it looks exactly like the task of proving a theorem in some logical calculus. The kind of theorem the machine tries to prove is one which asserts that "a possible state of the world exists in which the box is on the floor." It is possible to arrange that,

as a side-effect of a successful proof, a chain of actions is produced for bringing about the desired state of the world. (1974, 108)

Coles' report also provides a "robot's-eye-view" of how Shakey goes about completing the task; it "sets out," he explains, "the stream of 'thoughts' . . . which go through the robot's 'brain' (. . . the program running in Stanford's SDS940 computer) in the form of the following informal English translation:"

> My first subtask is . . . to move the ramp over to the platform and align it properly. To do this, I must first see it. To do this, I must first go to the place where, if I looked in the right direction, I might see it. This sets up the subsubtask of computing the coordinates of a desirable vantage point in the room based on my approximate knowledge of where the ramp is. . . . Next I have the problem of getting to the vantage point. Can I go directly, or will I have to plan a journey around obstacles? Will I be required to travel through unknown territory to get there if I go by an optimal trajectory; and, if so, what weight should I give to avoiding this unknown territory? When I get there, I will have to turn myself, and tilt the television camera to an appropriate angle, then take a picture in. Will I see a ramp? The whole ramp? Nothing but the ramp? Do I need to make a correction for depth perception? (Ibid., 109-110)

"Shakey," according to McCorduck,

> taught its creators some surprising things. Perhaps one of the most important had to do with that elusive property of generality, for Shakey showed that you could not, for example, take a graph-searching algorithm from a chess program and hand-printed-character-recognizing algorithm from a vision program and, having attached them together, expect the robot to understand the world. . . . There are serious questions about the interaction between knowledge in different domains. . . . [and] with uncertainty in a complicated world. (1979, 232)

Terry Winograd, a doctoral candidate at M.I.T. in the early 1970s, created a "bodiless" robot in software that he cryptically called SHRDLU, the concatenation of the latter six of the twelve most frequently used letters in the English alphabet. "SHRDLU," Mishkoff explains, "works in an imaginary limited domain called the 'blocks world,' consisting of blocks of various sizes and shapes" (1985, 95).

"Early vision research in the late 1960s," McCorduck explains,

> had concentrated on the blocks world, the cubes and pyramids that robot arms moved around on command. To understand such a simple universe seemed . . . a summer's project. It wasn't. The problems were very hard . . . and depended not only on understanding image processing, but also on the predispositions of the observer, how far that system — human or robot — understood limits, and how it represented its knowledge internally. (1979, 258)

The question had been raised, McCorduck explains, of whether "intelligence — understanding both what one is told and what one can see for oneself — [might] turn . . . out to be the use of specific kinds of knowledge in a given context" (ibid., 259). Winograd's thesis, she notes, was one of a number of tests that sought to respond to it. Winograd suspected that programming methods, such as iteration, procedure, and recursion, had counterparts in human cognition, and he patterned SHRDLU's knowledge accordingly, arranging for the program's equivalents of reasoning, semantic analysis, and parsing to be carried out, as they are in humans, concurrently. "This simultaneous attack on several fronts," McCorduck notes, "saved SHRDLU from the embarrassing dead ends toward which semantic ambiguities had always led programs in the past, because at each stage of the understanding process, each bit of expertise made a contribution" (ibid.).

In deference to acknowledged limitations in the techniques available to him, Winograd, in order to provide his "robot" with sufficiently deep knowledge about its environment, severely circumscribed the world it would have to deal with. Further, by abstracting his blocks world, representing the totality of it — blocks, tabletop, arm, dialogue — on a video display, he sidestepped the mechanical engineering problems that would have attended a real world implementation.

SHRDLU, through the intermediary of a teletype, could be instructed to do things in its world, such as repositioning and stacking blocks; interrogated about what it had done and about the states of particular blocks; and, to some extent, even account for its reasoning. Gerald Sussman subsequently taught a program called HACKER, which he built in the image and likeness of SHRDLU, some new tricks. HACKER was provided with the ability to stop mid-course when it was stumped, analyze the subgoals that comprised its attempted solution, and try to detect and resolve conflicts among them — it could, in effect, debug the reasoning of which its predecessor was capable.

But SHRDLU did more than spawn more clever successors; it suggested something, McCorduck explains,

> that designers of other kinds of artificial intelligences, namely intelligent assistants, had simultaneously arrived at in their attempts to build programs that performed at the level of human experts in a given field. It was that humans operated successfully not by using powerful, underlying general rules, but rather by using a large amount of detailed knowledge, organized in special ways. This was the factor that distinguished the specialist from the amateur. (Ibid., 262)

McCorduck describes an "intelligent assistant" as a program whose extensive knowledge in a narrow but difficult task domain is used to relieve a human expert of some of the taxing but essential parts of a particular job. Perhaps the earliest of these was DENDRAL, a program capable of inferring molecular hypotheses from chemical data. Provided with a chemical formula of a compound and data from mass spectrometer analyses, the program proffers from the vast number possible the most likely arrangements of the atoms in each molecule (Michie and Johnston [1984] 1985, 49). The multidisciplinary effort that yielded DENDRAL, which began at Stanford in 1965, included Edward Feigenbaum, who had been a graduate student under Simon at Carnegie-Mellon, Joshua Lederberg, a professor of genetics and Nobel laureate, and Carl Djerassi, a physical chemist (McCorduck and Feigenbaum 1983, 61-62).

Research into DENDRAL-like systems continued at Stanford; in the early 1970s, under the aegis of the Heuristic Programming Project, work on what Newell would later call the "grandaddy" of all expert systems was begun by Bruce Buchanan of the Stanford Department of Computer Science and Edward Shortliffe of the Stanford Medical Center (Mishkoff 1985, 41). Their prototype "expert system," called MYCIN, brings to bear on the diagnosis of infectious diseases and recommendation of appropriate therapies the collective expertise of many physicians.

Newell's observation regarding the stature of MYCIN is well taken; open it up and one can detect the elemental fragrances whose adept blending is the essence of every successful, present day, expert system. The constituents of this essence include several facets of problem identification, conversational abilities, accountability, modularity of design, and reliability in operation.

MYCIN's problem definition is exemplary. It was conceived to operate in a vital domain, medicine, on real problems associated with diagnosis of infectious diseases, such as overuse, misuse, and side-effects of antibiotics, effects of antibiotics used in combination, and maldistribution of expertise. Additionally, its problem domain was constrained sufficiently to make it tractable to existing limitations in expert system design techniques.

Physician-program interaction is conversational; the former provides the latter with background information that it could not infer, such as data drawn from patient history and laboratory tests, and responds, typically with YES or NO replies, to questions generated by the program as it reasons toward possible diagnoses and therapies. "This style of interaction," explain Winston and Prendergast, "is similar to what goes on in hospitals. There are specialists on hospital staffs available for consultation whenever a less-specialized physician wants expert advice. MYCIN's authors designed the program to fit into the existing pattern of seeking and providing consultative help" (1984, 31).

Technically speaking, MYCIN's conversational skills derive from its *user interface*. "The communication performed by a user interface," Mishkoff explains, "is bidirectional. At the simplest level, you must be able to describe your problem to the expert system, and the system must be able to respond with its recommendation" (1985, 57). Because expert systems are frequently intended to be used by individuals who are generally unfamiliar with computers, English language exchanges are highly desirable; the techniques for implementing such interfaces, Mishkoff notes, derive from a related discipline called *natural language processing*.

"In practice," Mishkoff adds, "a user interface generally is expected to perform additional functions. You may want to ask the system to explain its 'reasoning,' for example, or the system may request additional information about the problem" (ibid).

What MYCIN "knows" is a set of "if-then" rules of a form such that "if certain conditions obtain, then there is suggestive evidence that — ."

A physician or medical assistant who wants the program to account for its reasoning

> can type RULE, and this will cause the machine to display the rule that it is currently evaluating. This gives the user an idea of what is happening. For a more detailed explanation, the user asks WHY and gets a summary of the logical process that is being worked through. . . . The explanations are composed from the English text that is held in the machine in conjunction with each rule; the rules that the machine actually operates are held internally in advice language. (Michie and Johnston 1985, 44-45)

Modularity of design is another key facet of expert systems. The user interface might be thought of as a door to the expert system proper, which, in turn might be thought of as a library with its associated support structure. In expert system parlance, these latter constitute the *knowledge base* and the *inference engine*, respectively.

Like the books on a library's shelves, the knowledge base is the collection of all the information available to the system. Mishkoff makes a useful distinction between the more venerable concept of computer *database* and the knowledge base of an expert system. Although storage and retrieval of information in a particular domain are implicit in both, the knowledge in a database, he explains, "is only declarative (factual) knowledge," whereas "a knowledge base contains both declarative knowledge (facts about objects, events, and situations) and procedural knowledge (information about courses of action") (1985, 54,56).

As the knowledge base is to a library's collection, so the inference engine is to its control structure, that is, all of the mechanisms by which the institution acquires, orders, integrates, and makes accessible, the constituent pieces of its collection.

Randall Davis, an early contributor to the MYCIN project and the developer of TEIRESIAS, a tool for knowledge acquisition, describes the

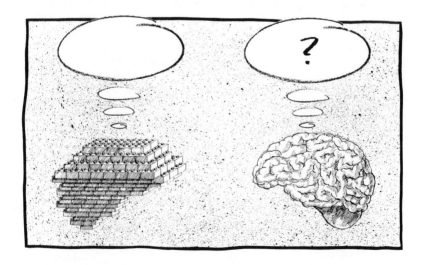

modular design of the former in *The AI Business*. MYCIN's architecture, he explains, set a pattern for expert systems. It comprises a knowledge base whose nearly five hundred rules represent most of what is known about infectious disease diagnosis and therapy, and an inference engine that attends to finding, extracting, and applying that knowledge (Winston and Prendergast 1984, 33).

MYCIN's inference engine, given the name of a suspect organism, locates and extracts from the knowledge base all of the rules that make conclusions about identity and works recursively through these until it exhausts them, at which point it asks the physician a question.

The if-then form of the rules in MYCIN's knowledge base renders individual rules simple and understandable even out of context, unlike traditional program code which usually makes very little sense when read a few lines at a time. Davis suggests that successful applications for MYCIN-like technology require a domain that can be so chopped into a few hundred or thousand rule-sized chunks, each of which constitutes a separate, distinct, and comprehensible piece of information (ibid., 34-35).

Modularity has yielded another benefit — generalizability of the inference engine. Davis explains that this separation of inference engine from knowledge base gives the former wider application; unplugging one knowledge base from a generalized inference engine and plugging in a different one yields a consultation system for another problem domain for the labor of creating the knowledge system alone (ibid., 34). By way of example,

> to help construct expert systems in other spheres, the disease rules were taken out of MYCIN, leaving a general-purpose system called Essential MYCIN, or EMYCIN. Using this, a quite separate expert system was constructed to diagnose lung disease. . . . PUFF. . . . takes data from a spirometer, a machine that measures air flow rates and volumes as the patient breathes in and out of a tube. . . . asks questions about the patient's history — how many cigarettes a day and so on — and then, using a knowledge base of about a hundred rules, produces a detailed description of the patient's apparent condition and a diagnosis of disease. (Michie and Johnston [1984] 1985, 47)

With regard to reliability, Michie and Johnston add that "the doctors who check . . . PUFF's reports sign 85 percent of them unchanged," and of MYCIN they report that a panel of experts assessing the anonymous prescriptions for ten difficult cases made by MYCIN and nine physicians assigned the highest score to the program (ibid., 46-47).

The efficacy of expert systems continues to be demonstrated by successor systems in a growing number of fields. Michie and Johnston recount several, among them, the sixteen hundred rule Prospector system, developed by SRI, International, which has elicited interest from mining corporations and from government agencies concerned with energy conservation and exploitation of natural resources.

What is perhaps the first commercially viable expert system to achieve routine use began as a joint development project between Digital Equipment Corporation (DEC) and Carnegie-Mellon University in 1978. Two years later, the system, designed to verify configurations of DEC VAX computers, matriculated to the firm's industrial environment. XCON, so dubbed for its expert configuration skills, brings to the task of reviewing the plethora of possible configurations of the firm's VAX computers approximately forty-five hundred rules and a database of more than nine thousand components. The system verifies configuration feasibility as well as completeness, checking components for adequacy and compatibility, evaluating memory size, and making determinations relative to the type and length of connecting cables. The system "knows" about the sizes and shapes of the cabinets the firm uses, even to the location of the slots that components fit into.

XCON addresses a very real problem for DEC, a hallmark of whose computer sales is diversity. In the first two years of production use, XCON analyzed more than twenty thousand unique orders at an average time of two minutes per order, as opposed to from twenty-five to forty minutes for expert technical editors, and at a level of accuracy of more than ninety-five percent as opposed to between sixty-five and seventy percent for the editors.

DEC's success with XCON has led to the development of two complementary expert systems, XSEL, a highly interactive system that, imbued with all of XCON's knowledge and more, will enable a DEC sales person to prepare quotes on a portable terminal at a customer site, and XSITE, a system capable of producing, for a given configuration, a floor plan depicting the arrangement and connections among system components, and of specifying environmental requirements, such as air conditioning and electrical power.

XCON is also known as R1, the latter appellation apparently deriving from the head of the project team that developed it, Carnegie-Mellon professor John McDermott, who reportedly uttered the the following variation on a classic phrase: "Three years ago I wanted to be a knowledge engineer, and today I are one" (Winston and Prendergast 1984, 41-46). "Knowledge engineer" has only recently entered the vernacular, but the notion implicit in the term was expressed in print as early as the late 1960s in Jaki's book; discussing the simulation of thinking operations for useful purposes, Jaki referred to "thought engineering" done by "information engineers," whose training, he noted, "is not geared to developing appreciation for basic scientific and philosophical questions" (1969, 248).

MacKay once referred to the computer as the "honest hodman par excellence" (ibid., 242). The phrase is equally apropos of the expert system. Like agricultural robots, these systems are engineered to labor tirelessly and reliably in fields large and small, and differently planted, but in every case bounded.

Expert systems and their component pieces, inference engines and natural language processors, are the current commercial products of artificial intelligence. Work going on at other universities and, increasingly, in corporations and small specialty firms, will yield others. Mishkoff cites a host of research efforts — variously involving industry, academe, and academic-industrial alliances — in such areas as automatic programming, self-contained vision systems, planning systems for robots, speech recognition and generation systems, and "intelligent" tools for developing expert system components (1985, 42-43).

It may be that the hype accompanying the commercialization of artificial intelligence will one day describe actual system characteristics and capabilities; the progeny of artificial intelligence research a decade hence might be as unimaginable today as expert systems were a few decades earlier.

Douglas Hofstadter, speculating on whether emotions will ever be explicitly programmed into a machine, suggests that the notion

> is ridiculous. Any direct simulation of emotions . . . cannot approach the complexity of human emotions, which arise indirectly from the organization of our minds. Programs or machines will acquire emotions in the same way: as by-products of their structure, of the way in which they are organized — not by direct programming. Thus, for example, nobody will write a "falling-in-love" subroutine. (1979, 677).

Except, perhaps, a pair of graduate students at the University of California at Berkeley. Peter Norvig and Joe Faletti are subjects in Rose's humanistic study of artificial intelligence research at Berkeley. They were, while he was writing about them, trying to marry a frame-based memory system to a story-understander program called PAM and a problem-solving program named PANDORA; the object? — the courtship of John and Mary.

The composite program, called PAMELA, was intended to be able to make distinctions about love and to entertain a flood of associations at certain suggestions. Frames possessed both characteristics and defining features, which the designers defined as things one might expect to find in a frame, and things that had to be there, respectively. For the Romantic Love frame, for example, a defining characteristic is that a man and a woman share an attitude called "love"; a characteristic might be that the man and the woman are both adults. The flood of associations the two wanted PAMELA to make were the kinds of connections that are made unconsciously by humans, as between marriage and wedding rings, honeymoons, and baby carriages (Rose 1984, 70-71, 79-80).

Faletti had earlier attempted to imbue PANDORA, the problem solving component of PAMELA, with a knowledge of the weather and its consequences. As the "raincoat program," PANDORA was provided with a desire to learn more about the world upon waking. It knew that one could learn about the world from newspapers, and that a newspaper was to be found on its front lawn. PANDORA the raincoat program also had an understanding of the states of being wet and dry, a preference for the latter, and the knowledge that rain resulted in getting wet and that a raincoat could help preserve the state of being dry. In its infancy, PANDORA learned to put its raincoat on — and on, and on. It fell into what is known in programming jargon as a loop. Though its programmers remedied this situation, succeeding in getting PANDORA to put its raincoat on but once and then retrieve the newspaper, their success was tempered by some confusion on the program's part regarding indoors and outdoors; having determined that it was raining, the program put its raincoat on and retrieved the newspaper but, alas, elected to read it out-of-doors (ibid., 59, 62-68, 177-180).

PAMELA, too, was to have limited success. Told that "John loves Mary," PAMELA appropriately invoked the Romantic Love frame which put it in the state of knowing that there was associated with John a mental object, which was an attitude of love for Mary. Where PAMELA bogged down was in the Ask frame, which was to be full of knowledge about asking questions and getting answers. Poor PAMELA interpreted one of Faletti's questions as the answer to it with results little less devastating than can occur when one human lover misconstrues another's question for an answer (ibid., 81-83).

The difficulties of trying to get programmed machines to act in the manner to which we are accustomed to perceiving one another act provide many such amusing anecdotes.

The bases of PAMELA and PANDORA are the understanding and observation of human mental processes as these are experienced by the programs' human progenitors. That some might prefer deeper access to such processes is suggested to Jaki by the observation of one author that "it is undesirable and illegal to put a human being in a completely non-operating state . . . and once this is done, the human being can never be returned to an operating state — he is dead . . ." (1969, 255). The missing text implied by the ellipses are Jaki's own observations: relative to the first part of the sentence, that "old fashioned humanists would have said 'to kill him,'" and of the concluding qualification, that "this explanatory remark is probably added for the benefit of those who are no longer familiar with 'anthropomorphic' notions such as death" (ibid.). Jaki's concern is for what could occur were we to give over too fully to the tendency that has persisted throughout the history of artificial intelligence — to impart, as Hobbes did, an artificial life to our automata, while at the same time reducing our own life to the most elementary of mechanical terms.

Michie and Johnston extend Jaki's concern to the artificial automata that might one day contain some representative characteristics of human organisms. Noting, under the heading "Killing an expert system," that "animals often have to be 'put down' for practical reasons, and so will robots," they posit that

> an interesting question arises concerning expert systems. One of these constructed with the cooperation of a particular human expert can capture his skills in such faithful detail that colleagues and friends interacting with the system may recognize his personal style of thought. Long after he is dead, they could respond to the foibles and fancies of the intellectual companion they knew. This would be for him a kind of immortality, more vivid and direct than authorship of books, or passive relics such as photographs and tape recordings, since it would include fragments of responsive behavior. How should we regard the wiping out of such a system irretrievably? It would surely be reprehensible, in the same way as was the burning of the great library of Alexandria. (Michie and Johnston [1984] 1985, 222)

Would it be? How is one to judge? Perhaps it is too early for such conjecture. Perhaps. But very probably it is not too early to reflect on what might seem by comparison more pedestrian issues related to the anticipated proliferation of artificial intelligence-based products, and perhaps our ability to deal with more radical possibilities will be abetted by this earlier questioning.

Margaret Boden, of the University of Sussex in Great Britain, suggests that a new kind of computer literacy is wanted. To the notion that education of users is not going to be necessary "because the whole point of AI is that with these natural language interfaces, and reasoning power, and interactive facilities, the user is not going to have to know about computers," Boden responds that,

> certainly, they are not going to have to know about the way the thing is built, and they are not going to have to know about the details of the programming languages. But there are certain things that they *are* going to have to know, and which I think are going to have to be taught. (Bernold and Albers 1985, 224)

One of the things Boden suggests needs to be made clear is the nature of the limitations that can apply to such programs, and it is important, she believes, that such knowledge be shared not only with those who actually use the programs, but also with those who might be affected by their use. Such limitations, she proposes, might best be flagged by those who write and market the programs.

The other thing that Boden contends should be kept in mind by all — programmers, non-programmers, users, and non-users, alike — is that it is always reasonable, in principle, to question a computer program. "You can do this," she explains,

> on three levels: You can question its data. That is to say you can ask: "Does it have all the necessary data, all the relevant data?" (because it may not).

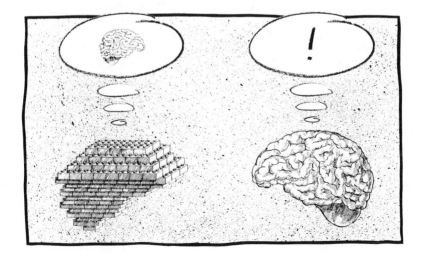

And you can ask: "Are all the data which it has actually true?" (which they may not be). In the same way you can ask about a human being: "Do they know all the facts, and are all their beliefs which they take to be relevant, in fact true beliefs?". . . . Similarly, you can always in principle question the rules of inference that the thing is using, just as you can in principle question the rules of inference that the human being is using. . . . And thirdly, in principle, it is always possible to question the values, or decision criteria, which are built into the program — just as you can with human beings. What you think is "best" may not be what the programmer assumed was "best." (Ibid.)

Finally, Boden points out that artificial intelligence programs are basically knowledge systems that comprise models of the world that are analogous to those humans carry around with them, and that we have an obligation to question these models as well. Boden contends that many people do not, that "they take the answers, the judgements, the advice given by computer programs to be, if not absolutely objective, at least somehow more objective than the decisions of mere human beings" (ibid., 225).

So we come full circle; if we heed Boden's advice, we are granting that artificial intelligence systems are just what they are, and treating them accordingly. Mr. Turtle never gave up, however. If only in reruns on UHF television stations, he even today pleads with Mr. Wizard to let him be something other than what he is. Artificial intelligence programs will undoubtedly become something other than what they are presently. Very probably they will become more than they are now. Will we recognize them for what they've become, for all that they become? Or will we impose upon our own minds the kinds of boundaries that the artificial intelligence programs of today admit, perforce.

While at Berkeley, Rose observed taped on the door of the office of the artificial intelligence group a cartoon clipped from the pages of the science fiction magazine *Beyond*. "The comic strip," he relates, "was called 'Boid' . . . [It read] 'Think yer smart, don't ya?' said a bird to a computer. 'Mebbie you can compute numbahs faster than us livin' creatures . . . But can you feel? Can you laff & cry, an' hate, an' love? Na, computer, fer all yer smarts, you'll never replace us.' Then the bird flew away — and the computer said, 'Oh, well, I can dream, can't I?'" (Rose 1984, 61).

If someone would doubt my results, I would say to him: "Let us calcu-
late, Sir," and thus by taking pen and ink we should settle the question.
— Leibniz

Calculating and Searching

T hose who hold that a computer is nothing more than a fancy calculating machine have a point — on one level at least. Whether on another level the exceedingly rapid and extraordinarily complex calculation that takes place in a computer's circuitry results in something akin to thought — conscious or otherwise — is a question that is entertained, with frequent reference to others who have entertained it, in the preceding article.

The lead quotation from Leibniz reflects a millenia-old desire to reduce human thinking processes to a kind of precise calculation such as forms the basis of every modern computer's processing abilities. But while the computer has presented the long sought after structure, the means for transferring to it any but the most superficial forms of human thought has not attended it. Below a certain, relatively high, level we are not aware of our thought processes, whereas all we know of a computer's processing is confined to the very basic level of computational manipulation of electrical states. The problem this presents is summarized, rather succinctly, by one of the students whose work in artificial intelligence is recounted by Frank Rose in *Into the Heart of the Mind* (Harper & Row, New York, 1985): "When you educate a human, you don't have to figure out what they're doing inside their head. You just have to tell them things, and somehow they do all the remembering automatically. But here [in the computer] we have to figure out how things should be stored and how connections get made."

Trying to reconcile the way we think with the way our machines must, by their very nature, think has been perhaps the greatest problem facing those who would create a thinking machine in the likeness of a thinking human. The general tack for getting the two closer together has been to persist in the age-old pursuit of a consistent and precise method for representing human thought. The artificial intelligence community refers to the problem as that of *knowledge representation*.

In *Understanding Artificial Intelligence* (Texas Instruments, Dallas, 1985), Henry Mishkoff, in a chapter titled "Symbolic Processing," offers some insight into the nature of present day techniques for representing knowledge in computers. These schemes, he points out, owe much to the ancient Greeks who codified the system of human reasoning and deduction called *logic.* Indeed, logic has found hearth and home in the computer, which, as we know it, is a much more logical system than any human who has ever lived. The principal problem with logic has been the intractability of much of human knowledge to representation in its rigid, formal structure.

What can be represented in logical notation are propositions, hence the system that, working from statements whose "truth values" (true or false) are known, can calculate the truth values of related statements is called *propositional calculus*. To illustrate his progressive definition of the logic employed in artificial intelligence, Mishkoff enlists the aid of the noted feline, Garfield. Propositional calculus, he explains, enables us, working from the following pair of statements whose truth value has been established as true:

- Garfield is a cat.
- If Garfield is a cat, then he is a mammal.

to infer for the following statement a truth value of true:

- Garfield is a mammal.

Predicate calculus introduces the ability to specify relationships and make generalizations. Again, Garfield demonstrates. Given known truth values of true for the following statements:

- Garfield is a cat.
- All cats are bigger than all mice.

we can, using predicate calculus, arrive at, and know to be true also, the conclusion that:

- Garfield is bigger than all mice.

The generalizations included in the foregoing statements are "all cats" and "all mice" and the relationship is "are bigger than."

Most often employed in artificial intelligence work is a variation of predicate calculus, called *first-order predicate calculus*, that extends the boundaries of logic to include functions and other analytical features. A *function*, Mishkoff explains, is a logical construction that returns a value. Thus we might have an "is-owned-by" function for Garfield that would enable an artificial intelligence program that incorporated it to respond to the question "Who owns Garfield?" with "Jon."

In order to further reduce the constraints on expression posed by logical notation, Lotfi Zadeh, a professor at the University of California at Berkeley, introduced the notion of *fuzzy logic*, a still less formal system that can accommodate such relative and approximate concepts as "tall," "expensive," and "normal."

Specifying highly complex interrelationships among knowledge elements yields a *semantic network*. A simple semantic network depicting the interrelationships of the facts we have regarding Garfield is shown in the accompanying illustration. The several knowledge elements constitute *nodes*, whose *links* define their functional interrelationships. The characteristic that enables us to make deductions from this network, such as "A cat is a mammal and is bigger than a mouse; Garfield is cat; therefore, Garfield is a mammal and is bigger than a mouse," is called *property inheritance.* Within the context of the semantic network, Mishkoff explains, a cat has the properties of being a mammal and being bigger than a mouse, and since Garfield is a cat, he inherits those properties.

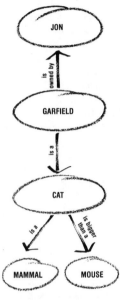

A form of logic was employed by what is generally considered to be the first artificial intelligence program, the Logic Theorist. But while expressing facts about, and relationships among, objects is amenable to logical representation, expressing knowledge about what to do with a collection of facts — the kind of working knowledge present-day expert systems must have in order to be able to recommend courses of action on the basis of analyses of the factual data available to them — is best accomplished by introducing a set of rules. These usually take the form of "if-then" expressions, in which the "if" (conditional) clause specifies a condition that must exist in order for the "then" (action) clause to be invoked. Such rules, (also known as *production rules*), are formal representations of the relevant heuristics, or "rules of thumb," by which we would ourselves evaluate and act upon the available facts. A personal heuristic of Jon's might be: *If Garfield is rubbing against my leg and meowing plaintively; then* I should take the necessary steps to feed him.

The structure of *rule-based* or *production* systems is advantageous for several reasons. Such systems can be modified relatively easily by incorporating new, or elmiminating existing, rules; their method of operation, which entails the successive "firing" of rules, makes building in accountability for their reasoning relatively straightforward; and, because knowledge in the form of such rules tends to be very readable, even persons unfamiliar with such systems can often use them.

Any artificial intelligence system required to reason its way to a conclusion must be able to search its store of accumulated knowledge rapidly and effectively. Little is known about how humans search their mental stores; much of the process seems to be informal and subsconcious. That humans know practically everything about how computer programs search their knowledge bases is attributable, quite unremarkably, to the fact that humans conceived the search strategies employed by computer programs.

Having conceded our possession of precious little knowledge about what goes on inside our heads, we must turn to what goes on outside of them for an analogy by which to explain some of the characteristics of searching as it is conducted by an artificial intelligence program.

Consider the prospect of travelling from Boston to Tokyo. To simplify the analogy, a westerly direction of travel is dictated. In the parlance of artificial intelligence, Boston is your *initial state* and Tokyo your *goal state.* All that lies between is your *search space.* An inverted tree structure, called a *search tree* is often used to depict a search space graphically.

Your search space could conceivably include every foot of highway and railroad track in this country and on the Japanese mainland, most of the vastness of the Pacific Ocean, and all of the airspace over that great body and two of the countries she separates. Considering the number of initial paths open to you, and the number of additional paths that open up at every fork in each of those paths, and at every fork in each of the paths that emanate from those forks, etc., will provide an understanding of what computer scientists are referring to when they discuss the problem of *combinatorial explosion.* Your initial state, the goal state, and every fork in between, are *nodes.* If you were to undertake your journey by first travelling to each node that is connected directly to the node that is your initial state, then travelling to each node that is directly connected to each of those nodes, then travelling to each node that is connected to each of the nodes connected to those nodes, you would, again in the terminology of artificial intelligence, be conducting a *breadth-first* search. Such a search would not be practical for you, and it would also not be practical for any program that is trying to reach a goal state that is separated from its initial state by many levels.

Alternatively, you could select one from the many paths directly connected to your goal state and, without looking back, select one of the available paths connected to each of the nodes that you encounter thereafter until you reach a *terminal node,* that is, a node with no further branches. The terminal node might be, but is not necessarily, the goal state and a trip to it in the manner just described is called a *depth-first* search. The disadvantage of a depth-first search becomes apparent when you consider that if the terminal node you reached was not the goal state, you have to start over from the beginning, and if the terminal node you reach at the end of that trip is not the goal state, you have to — etc.

Working, as you have been, from your initial state to the goal state is termed *forward-chaining.* It is also possible to start from the goal state and work backward toward your initial state, which approach, it follows, is called *backward chaining.* You would very likely in your situation, and many artificial intelligence programs do, use a combination of forward and backward chaining to identify a route. This constitutes a *bidirectional search.* You would alternate from one to the other, but an artificial intelligence program can initiate simultaneous searches from both initial and goal states and terminate the process when the two searches meet at a common node.

As performed, both of the searches described above — breadth-first and depth-first — were *blind* searches. Node-to-node progress was governed by nothing more than whether a given node corresponded to the goal state or not. This is termed the *generate-and-test* method. It would clearly be an impractical method for you and, when the search space is extremely vast, it is also an impractical method for an artificial intelligence program.

To the end of making searches more practical, ways of *pruning* a search tree have been devised. Just as you, in your Boston to Tokyo trek, would have recourse to maps and agents for air, bus, and rail lines, so an artificial intelligence program can be afforded various means to achieve a more direct transition from an initial state to a goal state. For example, the generate-and-test method can be enhanced through a technique called *hill-climbing*, whereby the program is provided with the ability to calculate the difference between the current node and the goal state and, by comparing the computed differences at successive nodes, determine whether it is moving toward or away from the goal state. Having determined that it is moving away from the goal state, the program can look for a more optimal path with a minimum of backtracking.

Another method of search space reduction uses a bidirectional search strategy in conjunction with heuristics and subgoals. A program might, for example, have a heuristic that would lead it quickly to its goal state, but not be able to apply that heuristic from the current node. If, however, the heuristic could be applied from a nearby node, the program might set aside its ultimate goal in order to establish a subgoal of getting to the nearby node.

You might suspect that it will be a long time before an artificial intelligence program will be able to find the optimal route from Boston to Tokyo, but recently the author had an opportunity to interact with a program that, provided with his Cambridge (Massachusetts) street address (initial state) and only a Cambridge telephone number for his destination (goal state), was able to relate street-by-street directions from the former to the latter.

Cognitive Science and Artificial Intelligence

Donald S. Bradshaw

"T he progress of science tends to be limited by the tools available to it." This statement may seem obvious and therefore unnecessary, but the problem runs deeper than the simple assumption that most scientists tend to formulate problems in such a way that they can be solved using tools and instruments available to them. This process can slow progress for long periods of time when problem-definition, thus circumscribed, becomes accepted wisdom in a scientific community, affecting how scientists perceive their work — forming their "models of perception."

The study of the human mind has suffered this disease more than most fields of inquiry. Probably the most ancient, and still pervasive, limitation of our view of the mind is that what we perceive as our mind is what we remember of our conscious thought. This has been true since the unrecorded beginnings of human introspection. It is still true. In the era from the time of the ancient Greek philosophers to the present, this model of perception has persuaded us that the mind is an engine of logical thought. Here is how that notion arises — and persists.

Introspection tends to concern itself with the mental process that is usually observed by this method — conscious thought which is remembered and re-perceived, a selection and modification process. It is undeniably evident that the conscious mind is capable of symbol-manipulation, computation, and ratiocination, the dominant conscious mental activities of the philosophers and scientists who were observing their own minds at work. It was — and still is — likely, perhaps inevitable, that these thinkers would believe that logic or reason is the primary function of the mind.

This view of the mind persists to the present day, reinforced by, and reinforcing, the traditional western view of man as a rational being — an essential conceptual underpinning of western social philosophy and democratic institutions. This cultural bias exerts a powerful, almost irresistible influence on our perception of the human mind.

The development of the digital computer has further reinforced this perception. The first computers were referred to as "mechanical brains," then "electronic brains." These early characterizations of the computer as functionally identical to the human mind arise from the deeply-rooted consensual notion of the mind as the seat of reason, a logic machine, more complex than, but essentially the same as, a man-made logic machine, the digital computer. And as the computer has become more powerful, it has been used increasingly for analysis and decision making. Such programs now fall into a class known as *artificial intelligence*, a term which to many means artificial *human* intelligence.

Thus the digital computer has become the latest model of perception of the human mind and is shaping much of the work done in the developing field known as *cognitive science.* Some who work in both fields — artificial intelligence and cognitive science — believe that these two disciplines will ultimately converge, and that, some day, a computer will faithfully replicate human mental activity.

Others disagree, arguing that logic, computation, and ratiocination are functions the human mind can learn to perform (albeit slowly and imperfectly), but that they do not constitute basic brain function. They maintain that whereas the circuitry of a serial digital computer makes it a logic machine and nothing else, the logical operations that the human mind sometimes performs *are but one among many mental operations,* all of which are produced by a *neural network, the organization of which bears no resemblance to computer circuitry.*

Toilers in the field of artificial intelligence will probably not be deterred by these obstacles. It is well that they should press on, for their work contributes much of value to the development of computer science, which continues to yield highly useful results:

- *More useful software* for the control and management of the processes of human enterprise, programs that can "learn" from shifting patterns and re-program to cope.
- *More powerful hardware:* cheap, virtually unlimited internal memory; multiple-channel simultaneous processing with cross-talk; sensory input devices to collect data directly from processes in real time; output devices directly connected to and controlling processes.
- *Integration of computers with processes* on a larger scale. As these systems become more complex and independent of human intervention, we may start thinking of them as "organisms."

Shall we then have *artificial intelligence?* Certainly. We have it now. Later systems will be so smart as to appear superhuman — and so they will be in some respects. And with their self-programming ability to adjust to changes in their environment, they will appear to emulate the human organism. Some will even, at times, run amok, prompting some of us to attribute to them human characteristics such as madness or evil intent.

But will they be models of the mind? They will certainly be *used* as models of the mind, but if this use is based on the notion that the mind is fundamentally and primarily a computational organ, they will teach us something about cognitive processes, but not much about the mind.

10

Robotics: Toward the Evolution of a New Working Class

John Simon, 1984

". . . a working machine must not play the piano, must not feel happy, must not do a whole lot of other things. Everything that does not contribute directly to the progress of work should be eliminated."
Karel Capek, R.U.R. (Rossum's Universal Robots), 1923

D ie-casting is a technique for producing relatively finished metal castings in a single operation. The die-casting process consists of injecting, under very high pressure, molten metal into a tightly clamped mold, or *die*, whence derive the name of the process and of the machine that carries it out. The die-casting machine is essentially a press between whose jaws, or platens, the separate parts of a die are mated under a pressure of from hundreds to thousands of tons. The high-pressure injection of molten metal, called a shot, drives air from the die through vent holes and fills all cavities of the mold. Some amount of molten metal is forced between the mated surfaces of the die creating overflows called gate runners, or flash. Typically, the removal of this unwanted material by trimming is all that is required to render a casting produced by this method a finished product.

A human operator who attends a die-casting machine must lubricate parts of the injection system that feeds molten metal into the die, lubricate certain of the die surfaces to prevent hardening metal from sticking to them, transport a charge of molten metal from the crucible that conveys it to the machine into the injection chamber, remove the casting from the cooled and separated die and pass it along along to the trimming stage, and, finally, clean the die of any remaining pieces of solidified metal before repeating the entire series of actions again, and again.

The die-casting process produces — in addition to metal castings — noise, heat, and fumes. It is also a repetitive process which, insofar as it involves moving machinery, hot metal, and high pressures, has the potential to be hazardous to limb, and even to life. A human operator who attends a die-casting machine adds to such operational variables as physical and chemical states of the molten metal, machine adjustment, and cycle timing, the variables of his own physical and mental states.

The die-casting process is exemplary of a type of work from which Rossum and son, characters in a 1923 play written by Karel Capek, sought to free mankind through the construction of humanoid creations they called "robots" (from the Czechoslovakian word "robota" meaning "drudgery, servitude, or forced labor"). "A man", says Rossum in *R.U.R.* (Rossum's Universal Robots), to distinguish his own species from his humanoid creations, "is something that feels happy, plays the piano, likes going for a walk, and, in fact, wants to do a whole lot of things that are really unnecessary." It followed for him that a machine replacement for a man should want to do none of these things.

In 1962, in the United States, a squat, insensible machine was bolted in place beside a die-casting machine, replacing the human who had previously attended it. Possessed of a single "arm," which it could extend and retract, raise and lower, and move to the left and right, the machine, called by its creators a Unimate, constituted the first installed industrial robot.

To call it humanoid would require a considerable stretch of the imagination, but in spirit the Unimate was the embodiment of a Rossum robot. It wanted to do none of the things Rossum had identified as human proclivities. Indeed, bolted to the floor in the midst of heat, noise, and noxious fumes, its relatively monstrous arm having only a limited repertoire of movements, the Unimate could hardly feel happy, play the piano, or go for a walk. What it could do, and all it could do, was move its sole appendage through a programmed series of motions related to the operation of a die-casting machine. This it could do over and over with great precision and without tiring.

The first of what has, as a class, come to be known as America's "steel-collar" workers, the Unimate had its origins in a 1956 patent application by George C. Devol labelled Programmed Article Transfer. It was produced by Unimation, Incorporated, a machine tool manufacturer located in Danbury, Connecticut.

Another company, A.M.F. of New Rochelle, New York, began research and development on its own "robot" product, a device called Versatran (from *versa*tile *trans*fer) about 1958 and commenced commercial activity in 1963. Prab Conveyors, of Kalamazoo, Michigan, followed Unimation and Versatran into the business and, for about a decade, these three companies and their handful of customers were about all there was of industrial robotics.

Laura Conigliaro (1983, 1-3,1-4) characterized the period as being one of "a series of uses, a few users, and a few vendors" and suggests that the beginnings of a "robot industry" did not occur until the middle to late

Unperturbed by heat and fumes, a Unimate robot quenches a casting. Unimation, Incorporated installed the first Unimate in a die-casting plant in 1962.

1970s, when the vendor base was expanded by the entry of such companies as Cincinnati-Milacron, Autoplace, DeVilbiss, and ASEA, Incorporated, and when the auto industry, which had earlier "discovered" and begun to use robots in a modest way, began a major retooling effort in which they played a prominent part.

Looking back, one might find prophetic the series of events that preceded the First National Symposium on Industrial Robots held in Chicago in April, 1970. When the sponsoring ITT Research Institute was ready to release the general announcement of the Symposium, its service department went on strike. When the prospective attendees might have been expected to respond to the announcement — which the chairman and his staff had prepared and distributed — the postal workers went on strike. When the persistent attendees, who had substituted TWX and wire communication for the United States mails, might have been expected to arrive in Chicago, there was a sit-in by the air traffic controllers. Finally, on the morning the symposium was to open its doors, nine inches of snow fell on the city.

On its way to becoming an industry in the United States, robotics, too, had obstacles to overcome, but labor and nature were not chief among them. Industrial management and an unfavorable economy were the major stumbling blocks to the development of a robotics industry in this country. Robotics typically requires a relatively substantial initial investment and its greatest promise lies in longer-term productivity gains. But even as a handful of hatchling robot manufacturers struggled to extricate themselves from their shells, a generally worsening economy was placing constraints on the availability of investment capital and escalating interest rates were causing U.S. industry to seek ever shorter payouts on investments.

An exported robotics technology found a rather more auspicious spawning ground in Japan. Kawasaki Heavy Industries became a licensee of Unimation while that firm was still manufacturing, and trying to sell, its robots one at a time in this country. Unlike its U.S. counterpart, which initially regarded robots with caution, and often, decided disinterest, Japanese industry responded to them with alacrity from the outset. By the 1970s, Japanese automobile assembly lines were heavily populated by Unimate look-alikes. Even allowing for the somewhat more liberal definition of a robot to which Japan subscribes, working Japanese robots probably outnumber working U.S. robots by two-to-one. This rapid growth has occurred in a markedly different industrial context.

Among the distinctions that have been made between United States and Japanese industry is one of management perspective. In the United States, in a prevailing climate of which specialization and mobility are the chief constituents, managers tend to transport their particular expertise from company to company and, in so doing, pursue short-term goals that can be realized during their brief tenures and avoid innovations that might pose a threat to their particular areas of specialization. With lifetime employment almost assured, mobility for Japanese management is usually within a single company among different positions which are often unrelated to one another. Such a context gives rise to managers who are "generalists" and to a climate more indulgent of an appreciation for the longer-term benefits of innovation.

The geographic proportions of the two countries has also played a role. Market penetration by robot manufacturers in this country has been hampered both by the distribution of United States industry across a vast continent and by regional differences over that area. Being concentrated in a geographically smaller, and more homogeneous area, Japanese industry presented a comparatively easier target for Japanese robot manufacturers.

Casebound copies of the *Proceedings* attest that, despite all obstacles, the First National Symposium on Robotics was held. So, the current proliferation of robots, increasingly varied and adaptable to an ever-broadening range of jobs, attests to the existence of a thriving robotics industry where once a single Unimate labored. As the market for robots has increased, so has their cost-effectiveness, with capital recovery through savings in wages alone being realized in as little as twelve to eighteen months in some cases.

Robotics is a progeny of two technologies, a century-old industrial engineering automation technology and a several decades-old computer science and artificial intelligence technology. The industrial robot was conceived as a variation on traditional automation and, in most, the "genes" of the former parent are dominant.

Traditional automation, often called *hard automation,* is usually introduced in the form of machinery rigorously engineered to produce a very specific product. The initial investment is usually high and, to the extent that it is possible to alter the machinery to accommodate changes in the product, such modifications are usually extremely expensive. Consequently, automation is best suited to the manufacture of products for which long and continuous runs are expected.

The precursor of the robot was the numerical control (NC) machine, the debut of which occurred in the 1950s. Originally developed to fabricate contoured aircraft parts, NC machines use a numerical control method to activate tools in response to predetermined commands stored on punch tapes, magnetic tapes, or in semiconductor memories. These commands variously direct the selection of tools, their proper positioning in three dimensions relative to work pieces, the feeding of work pieces, the flow of coolant, and so forth. The use of numerical control methods to automate the operation of machine tools that drill, grind, cut, punch, and mill raw materials into complex finished parts has spread throughout industry. Subsequent generations of control techniques have lent various prefixes to the original acronym: CNC (computer numerical control) refers to numerical control as executed by an adjunct minicomputer; DNC (direct numerical control) describes the simultaneous control of multiple NC or CNC machines by a host computer. By whatever acronym they are called, the techniques remain those of hard automation; a significant change to a product manufactured by a numerical control machine will probably involve a retooling, as well as a reprogramming, effort.

By contrast, redeployment of an industrial robot entails primarily changes to its programming. A robot is basically a manipulator. Whether it is engaged in moving objects from one location to another, as it might be in a warehousing task, or in the loading and/or unloading of machine tools, or in drilling, painting, or welding, the principal activity of a robot is the movement of its arm. Because this movement is controlled by stored programming it can be altered or adjusted merely by changing the program that is producing it or by introducing a new program to drive an entirely different set of movements. Thus, if the shape or orientation of a part being handled by a robot changes, the program that directs the movement of its arm can be changed to accommodate it. Similarly, a robot can be used on shorter runs of different parts by providing a program for each part to be handled and causing the appropriate program to be activated for each run. Seldom does a robot require any physical altera-

tion, other than a possible change of the tooling at the end of its arm —
an action roughly equivalent to the exchange of a wrench for a screwdriver
in a human hand — and robots have been programmed to make such
changes themselves.

"An arm on a post"

An industrial robot might be thought of as a human arm mounted on a
post. If one allows for a wide range of variability in the size, shape, and
flexibility of the "arm," one can see the analogy in practically any industrial robot from the first Unimate to contemporary welding robots that
"look" at their work through cameras and adjust their torches accordingly.

Robot arms are basically capable of two types of movement — linear
or straight-line movements, and rotational or swivelling movements. A
robot's "reach," called its *work envelope,* or sphere of influence, is the

Figure 1: Robot arm types and work envelopes

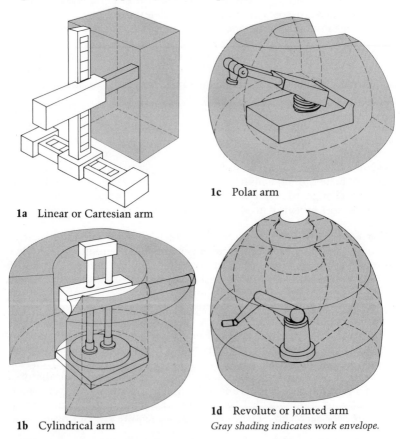

1a Linear or Cartesian arm

1c Polar arm

1b Cylindrical arm

1d Revolute or jointed arm
Gray shading indicates work envelope.

sum of all the points in space upon which, through every possible combination of movements available to it, the robot can bring its arm to bear. Various movements and combinations of movements employed by industrial robot arms are demonstrated by the four generic robots shown in Figure 1. Each robot's work envelope is represented by a shaded area, the shape of which varies with the configuration of the arm and the total area of which is determined by the lengths of arm and post.

In combination with their bases, each of these robot arms is capable of three articulations, that is, it can be moved along or about three distinct axes. These axes can be in different coordinate systems.

Consider the robot at 1a. It can adjust the position of its horizontal arm by moving its support laterally along its base, and by moving the arm itself vertically on its support. The robot is also capable of *extensional* movement, which is realized through the telescoping part of its arm. These three articulations, all of which are linear movements that can be plotted on Cartesian coordinates, are sufficient to position the robot's arm anywhere within the work envelope whose boundaries are established by the physical limits imposed on its side-to-side, up-and-down, and back and forth movements.

Although it possesses an arm and support identical to that of the robot at 1a, the robot at 1b, because it rests on a circular base capable of rotational movement, has a significantly different sphere of influence. The work envelope that results from the combination of one rotational and two linear articulations shares the attributes of a cylinder and a doughnut and has cylindrical coordinates.

The robot arm at 1c combines a single linear movement, an extensional movement of the arm, with two rotational movements, one of its circular base and a see-saw motion of its extensional arm through polar coordinates. This type of robot usually has a wedge-shaped work envelope.

Figure 1d shows a robot capable of three rotational movements. Each segment of this robot's arm can be swung through an arc — the lower portion swiveling on the base and the upper portion swiveling on the lower portion — while the base rotates the entire assembly. Such an arm is said to have revolute coordinates and its work envelope typically has a sort of quasi-spherical shape.

Three additional articulations are usually provided by a "wrist" assembly at the end of a robot's arm. Labelled for equivalent aircraft motions, these are called pitch, yaw, and roll (see Figure 2). They equate to tilting, bending, and twisting of the human wrist.

Not all robot arms are provided with six articulations. The number of articulations necessary to do a particular job can often by reduced by configuring a workplace with a robot in mind. If, for example, the beds of machine tools with which a robot is to interact are located parallel to one axis of a Cartesian robot or on a radius of base rotation for a cylindrical, polar, or revolute robot, one axis of articulation can be eliminated. This is a desirable end, since the mechanical complexity, difficulty of programming, and expense of a robot are usually directly related to the number of articulations it possesses.

Frequently, the nature of the work to be performed will dictate a particular type of arm configuration. The so-called "pick-and-place" function — that of lifting an object in one location and moving it to another — can usually be handled by a simple Cartesian robot. Considerable rigidity can be built into the supports of these robots, and into the columnar supports of cylindrical robots, enabling both to lift quite heavy loads. The ability of cylindrical robots to swivel back and forth very quickly and extend and retract their arms at fairly high speeds gives them an advantage over Cartesian robots in some applications, such as the loading and unloading of machine tools. Welding and spray-painting are most often handled by polar or revolute (jointed-arm) robots. If a robot is required to reach into a tub, as is the case in investment casting, only a revolute robot may do.

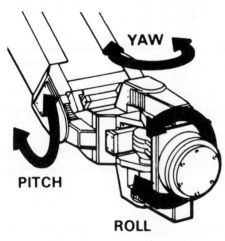

Figure 2: Robot wrist articulations

Without some kind of tooling at the ends of their arms, the robots in Figure 1 would be capable of little more than pummeling, punching, and dislodging. Most industrial applications of robots require more refined actions than these. Consequently, robot "wrists," like human wrists, usually terminate in a hand.

The very characteristics of the human hand that make it so adept at manipulating such a wide range of materials through feeling and touch render it too sensitive for use under some conditions. Because they lack such sensitivity, robot hands can grasp hot metal ingots, manipulate materials coated with corrosive substances, and handle objects with extremely sharp edges without employing tongs, gloves, or special precautions.

The robot equivalent of a human hand is called by the unglamorous but descriptive term *end effector*. It describes, quite simply, an implementation at the *end* of a robot arm designed to enable the machine to *effect* a desired operation. The operation might be grasping, lifting, or manipulating a workpiece. It might also involve effecting a change to a workpiece without physically touching it, as in welding or painting.

Some robot hands bear a rudimentary resemblance to the human hand. Some have two or more fingers, and some even attempt to model finger joints and to educe in them movements that correspond to the movements of human fingers. Generally, though, robot hands are much more utilitarian. In fact, for robots whose job entails wielding a tool, such as a welding torch or a paint-spraying gun, it is often possible to dispense with a hand altogether, fitting the tool instead directly to the robot's wrist.

The construction of such "hands" as do serve industrial robots is dictated not by any consideration of resemblance to the human hand but rather by the exigencies of the job to be performed. A sampling of end effectors, including tools attached directly to robot wrists, is shown in Figure 3. Pivoting pads at the tips enable some robot fingers to align to flat-sided surfaces for a more secure grip. Wide-opening fingers enable other robot hands to sweep imprecisely positioned objects into their grasp. Objects that will accept a thin finger underneath them can be picked up and repositioned with dispatch by a simple robot hand with one rigid and one moveable finger. A similar configuration, arranged for end-to-end grasping, can be employed for lifting articles such as cartons. Vacuum cups enable robots to handle materials like plate glass, and magnetic pickups can expedite the transfer of metallic objects.

In addition, many robots are capable of accepting interchangeable end effectors, extending their reprogrammability to a broader range of jobs. In some installations, robots have been programmed to change end effectors themselves, disconnecting from and depositing one hand on a specially designed rack, and retrieving another from it.

The design within

Primitive man considered air, water, and fire to be the elemental forces of nature. The corollaries of these elements, in pneumatic, hydraulic, and electrical systems, are the forces that drive robots. There are examples of industrial robots powered exclusively by each of these systems but, more often, they are employed in combination.

A robot requires a drive system for each articulation of its arm and wrist as well as for any actions and articulations of its end effector. Pneumatic and hydraulic systems create the power to move robot limbs by regulating the actions of compressed air and fluid, respectively, on pistons that slide back and forth inside of cylinders. Electrical systems turn motors to achieve the same end. The source of a robot's power does not have to be, and often isn't, contained within its "body." Most pneumatic, and many hydraulic, robots derive power from compressors or pumps external to them. Also, single power sources are sometimes used to drive multiple robots.

The power produced by a drive system can be delivered to a robot limb in a variety of ways. A human bicyclist pumps pedals positioned conveniently for his or her legs to produce power that is transferred to the vehicle's rear drive wheel by means of a chain. Similarly, the power-producing component of a robot's drive system need not necessarily be located at or in the part to be driven. Ballscrews, rods, electrical lines, compressed air and fluid lines, and bicycle-type chains can all be found transferring power through robot anatomies. Like robot drive systems, robot transmission systems are often used in combination. In one robot, for example, power to tilt the wrist is delivered by means of a linkage

Figure 3: A sampling of robot end effectors

The human hand is a remarkably versatile manipulator, the operation of which is still little understood. By merely changing its configuration we can pull a brush through our hair, hold a pen, turn a wrench, or open a car door. Robots, because their hands, or end effectors, are much simpler and less flexible than their human counterparts, rely on interchangeability to extend their manipulative abilities. A two-fingered robot hand can be afforded a more compliant grip on flat-sided objects by fitting the fingertips with pivoting pads (a). Objects that will accept a slender robot finger underneath them can be lifted by a relatively simple robot and with but two fingers, only of which need be moveable (b). Turning this arrangement sideways, and broadening the span of the fingers (c) yields a hand useful for lifting objects such as cartons. If a hand with fingers contoured for gripping a particular shape is allowed to open the fingers widely (d), it will be able to sweep imprecisely-positioned objects into its grasp. Fitted with vacuum cups, a robot hand can lift flat sheets of glass or plastic (e). When a robot is called upon to wield a tool, a hand is usually dispensed with in favor of fitting the tool directly to the wrist. Two of the tools most frequently used by robots are the welding torch (f) and the paint-sprayer (g).

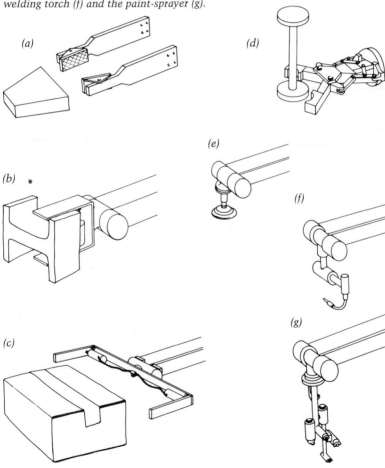

(a)

(d)

(e)

(b)

(f)

(c)

(g)

disc, while power to turn the same joint side-to-side is transmitted through an angled gear.

The conventional automobile provides an example of a machine powered by mixed drive systems. Through the operation of a switch, stored electrical power is amplified and directed to a mechanical starting unit that turns over an internal combustion engine by means of gearing. Power produced by the combustion taking place in the engine's cylinders is transferred, by means of belt drives, to both an alternator, which, in turn, powers a set of electrical subsystems, and to a water pump that powers the hydraulic system that cools the engine. By engaging a gearbox, one can direct the bulk of the power to a mechanical drive train capable of turning the vehicle's wheels. Stopping the motion of the moving wheels is accomplished by a mechanically-actuated fluid hydraulic system.

An automobile is not a robot, however, because control of its motion is always in the hands of a human operator. A robot is programmed initially by a human, but thereafter is capable of functioning automatically under the control of the program. A robot is essentially a composite of a set of moving parts — the support, arm, and wrist combination — collectively called the *manipulator*, and a *controller* by means of which movements of the manipulator can be recorded and caused to be replayed at will.

Electricity has from the beginning played a significant role in robot control. Even robots, mostly of the earlier types, which employed mechanical, pneumatic, or hydraulic controllers used electricity to signal the opening and closing of control valves.

A rough parallel can be traced between the evolution of computers and that of robot controllers. Just as the earliest computers comprised banks of relay switches that had to be manually set for the particular computation to be performed, so the movements of the earliest robots were controlled by setting a series of limit switches, which, when tripped, would shut off the drive system and stop the motion of the arm. Later computers, which employed vacuum tubes, could be programmed by changing the configuration of wire plugs on an electrical patchboard. The equivalent in robot controllers was the sequence controller, which comprised a matrix of diodes in which the positions of contact pins could be changed.

With such control systems, a programmer could specify little more than the most basic of movements and the order in which they were to occur. It was also necessary that a movement on one axis be completed before a movement on another could begin. "Reprogramming" such controllers was usually tedious, involving a complex resetting of switches, or rearrangement of wires, or both, and the movement of the machines they controlled, aptly called *limited-sequence robots*, was often sufficiently jerky to lend them the less flattering appellation, *bang-bang machines*.

Robots became amenable to more refined control through the combination of servo-mechanisms and magnetic storage devices. A servo-mechanism is capable of varying the position of a robot limb in proportion to

Figure 4: To teach a robot

Teaching a robot is like recording a symphony; both endeavours involve preserving a series of movements in such a way as to be able to replay them, on demand, just as they were originally performed. When one wants to hear a Brahms symphony, one plays a phonograph record or a tape recording of it. When one wants a robot to apply sealant along a seam on an automobile body panel, one causes a recording of the requisite motions, as the robot was originally led or driven through them, to be replayed. The robot arm may be led through the original movements manually, as in the illustration, or, like those in the photos, driven by means of a "teach-box," a hand-held device resembling a calculator, with labelled keys and, often, a small display window.

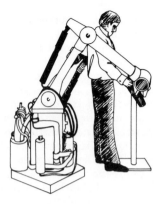

the value of an electrical control signal. With a control panel on which the rotation of a knob associated with each robot limb varies the signal, and hence the position, of the limb, and a switch triggers the operation of the magnetic recording device, a programmer can easily drive a robot through a series of movements and record the end points of each. Two points would be sufficient to guide a linear movement; a third, intermediate point would serve to guide a rotational movement. The complete set of end points, together with information necessary to control their execution in the proper sequence, constitutes a *program* that can replayed by the controller to cause the robot to repeat the series of movements precisely by moving its arm from recorded point to recorded point. These *point-to-point* robots are under direct program control only when the arm is at a recorded point, the paths between points being interpolated by the controller.

Although minicomputers were used as controllers for some very early robots, computer control did not really become economical until the proliferation of the microprocessor in the early 1970s. The computer provided the large store of memory required to specify complete trajectories for robot limbs, a requisite ability for a robot expected to follow a continuous, and perhaps complex, path at a prescribed speed, all the while maintaining a tool at the end of its arm at a specified attitude. This is precisely what is required of a robot engaged in seam welding.

A logical extension of the point-to-point robot, the *continuous-path* robot can be taught in real time. As it is led by its programmer through the required motions, the controller of a continuous-path robot is not only continuously recording the position of its hand but also the speed at which it is being led.

Toward the well-being of machines and men

Twenty years before the first industrial robot was installed, author Isaac Asimov proposed a set of three commandments to govern the behaviour of the fictional robots that populated a series of his stories. The essence of these was that: 1) robots were never to harm humans, nor to allow harm to come to humans through inaction, 2) like the robots in Capek's play, they were always to obey humans except as such obedience might violate the first law, and 3) they were to care for and protect themselves except as doing so might conflict with either of the foregoing laws.

Unlike Asimov's robots, contemporary industrial robots can do little to care for themselves and, although they act always in accordance with human will as it is programmed into them, they cannot act otherwise when the programmed action places a human life in jeopardy.

Robots have injured, and killed, humans. Many industrial robots are capable of lifting several hundred pounds and of swinging their arms at speeds of three feet per second. Movements set in motion by a particular program are carried out blindly and without variation. Robots have neither the tactile sensitivity and reflex action that would enable them to recoil their arms upon contact with a human nor the visual acuity to detect the presence of one.

Because robots of themselves cannot observe Asimov's laws, it is left to those who build and use them to do so. Contributions of robot manufacturers range from arm drives that will preserve rigidity in the event of power failure to prevent a robot from unexpectedly dropping its arm or releasing it gripper to robot "teach" controls that incorporate emergency stop switches and operate arms at reduced speed while they are being programmed.

Although industrial robots may be found painted in safety-striping and sporting rotating beacons on their moving arms, barricading is by far the means most frequently employed by industrial users for discouraging unintentional human-robot contact. Early attempts to restrict the swing of robot arms by erecting concrete posts were largely abandoned when it was realized that these introduced a further hazard in creating "trapping points" where a human might be caught between a robot arm and a post. Many robot work areas are enclosed by fences, sometimes supplemented with sensors that shut off power in the event of an intrusion.

Yet, with robots, as with many other potential hazards of the industrial workplace, the greatest risk is occasioned by the complacence that seems inevitably to derive from familiarity. Robots have the added disadvantage of being targets of the human propensity to anthropomorphize, with the attendant danger that is engendered by attributing to a machine far more "intelligence" than it actually has. Until robots do become significantly smarter, a concerted and continuous effort by humans to instill in humans a respect for the speed, strength, and potential unpredictability of robots is warranted.

If a robot is not to have positive human traits, neither should it be perceived to have negative ones. A robot should not, for example, appear to be stupid. It should not be seen grasping at air and moving an empty gripper from one location to another. Nor should it place its arm into a press during an inappropriate cycle. While it is unquestionably better to have a robot arm crushed between the jaws of a press than a human arm, it is clearly best if the jaws close only on the intended casting.

To preserve their robots from disorientation and disaster, industrial engineers have applied to them some of the very same devices they have employed in the preservation of human life and limb. Mechanical, electrical, and electronic controls and interlocks have long been used to forestall accidents among human machine operators. Because they are themselves machines and can be fitted directly with such devices, robots can be much more intimately married to the machinery they operate than can humans.

Mechanically-operated limit switches, microswitches, pressure and vacuum switches, and photoelectric and infrared devices are among the controls commonly used to insure that parts are delivered to an appropriate location and are properly oriented for robot pickup, that robot movements are correctly synchronized with the cycles of the machine(s) it is operating, and that robot gripper mechanisms are actuated before attempting to lift objects.

Hardiness is one of the foremost attributes of the industrial robot. It was in replacing humans in jobs deemed undesirably heavy, hot, or hazardous that it first found a niche. Despite their inherent ruggedness, robots are often further "hardened" against particularly harsh environmental conditions by being fitted with protective gear and/or ancillary systems. Robots exposed to extreme heat can be provided with radiation shields or fitted with air or water cooling systems. Robots can be shielded from sparks, liquid sprays, gases, and harmful particles by skirts and rubber booting around exposed joints. Jobs involving volatile materials usually employ robots that have no potential for creating a spark nor any drive system actuated by a flammable fluid. Also, because stray signals that would at worst cause a computational error or result in a burst of "garbage" output from a computer can cause unprogrammed and potentially hazardous movements in robots, it is desirable to shield them from electrical noise and interference.

The abilities of even relatively "unintelligent" robots — to attend multiple machines at a pace that would quickly exhaust a human operator and to handle objects too heavy and/or too dangerous to be grasped by human hands — more than offset the limitations imposed upon them by less-than-human sensibilities. Nevertheless, rudiments of certain of the human senses are being built into robots.

Two types of elementary "vision" are in use by contemporary industrial robots. Both rely on video images, the principal difference between them being the amount of image data processed.

A typical "seeing" robot is a system comprising a robotic manipulator, or arm, one or more camera "eyes," and a computer component capable of processing, and correlating robot movement with interpretations of, images recorded by the camera(s).

A camera records an image as a continuous gradation from white — through all the shades of gray between — to black. Offset printing, like digital computing, is a process that deals in discrete quantities. At any given point on a piece of paper, ink is either deposited or not deposited. To "trick" an offset press into printing shades of gray, a continuous-tone image is re-photographed through a screen with the result that an image composed entirely of minute dots — whose concentration varies proportionately with the shades of gray in the original — is formed. Similarly, by means of complex formulae, a computer can convert a continuous-tone image into mathematical values that correspond to the various shades of gray contained in the original. The more complex the formulae used, the more shades of gray can be represented.

Binary vision is the most elementary type of robot vision. A binary vision system establishes a threshold value for what is to be "seen" and then essentially throws away, or gives a value of zero to, any lesser values and keeps, or gives a value of one to, any values at or above the threshold. The resulting binary image has the characteristics of a purely black and white picture. Supplied with patterns or templates of the parts they are to look at, such systems can variously detect the presence or absence of a part and determine part location and orientation.

For parts spaced too closely together, or parts difficult to differentiate from their backgrounds because of their respective colors or inadequate illumination, it may be impossible to set a threshold value that will yield a representative black and white image. Gray-scale vision systems employ more complex formulae, or *algorithms*, that make much greater use of the density information contained in video images. Such systems can represent an image in as many as sixty-four shades of gray. With gray-scale vision, a robot can variously detect edges of images and analyze scenes in terms of "blobs" of gray.

Tactile sensitivity, too, is being built into robots. Retractable, pin-like probes in the end effector of a Cincinnati-Milacron robot used in an automatic drilling operation help it to gauge the insertion of a drill into a bushing and lock fitting. An experimental end effector fitted to a Unimation Puma robot in the United

An air jet attachment enables this robot to lift single pieces of cloth.

Kingdom enables it to lift single pieces from stacks of cloth. An air jet above and forward of a pair of slender flat fingers has the effect of lifting the topmost piece of material allowing the lower finger to slide under it. Infrared sensors in the fingers trigger their closing upon detecting the cloth between them. Italian researchers have tried to emulate some of the mechano- and thermoelectric sensing properties of human epidermis with electrically-conductive synthetic polymers. Conceivably, a robot with fingers constructed of such piezo- and pyroelectric polymers might be provided with a human-like sensitivity to mechanical stresses and thermal conductivity in the objects it touches.

While growing numbers of personal computers are being afforded the ability to recognize limited vocabularies and to respond verbally to their operators with speech too slow and too succinct ever to be mistaken for that of a human, the vast majority of robots remain mute. The kind of responsiveness exhibited by the golden *Star Wars* robot, C3PO, is a very long way off, if indeed it is deemed worthy of realization at all.

More representative of a type of robot we may see in the nearer term are those featured in the 1972 Universal film *Silent Running*. Programmed to tend the vegetation removed from a nuclear polluted earth under the great glass domes of the space freighter *Valley Forge*, these speechless robots waddle about the length and breadth of the ship occasionally making excursions onto its exterior in the performance of their duties. Largely under automatic program control, supplemented with vision and sensor data to guide their movements, the robots also respond to commands addressed respectively to Drone 1, Drone 2, or Drone 3 (later renamed Huey, Dewey, and Louey by the ship botanist). The awkwardness of their gait, the maneuverability of their manipulators, the modularity of their design, their modicum of "eye-hand" coordination, and the nature of their programming are all representative of characteristics and capabilities that can be found in extant working and experimental robots.

Eye-hand coordination and integration with other elements of automation, such as computer-aided-design (CAD) and computer-aided-manufacturing (CAM), have far greater implications for industrial robots than do speech and hearing. Very complex assembly tasks will probably remain out of the grippers of robots until a reasonably sophisticated level of robot eye-hand coordination can be attained. But for the problem of parts orientation, there are many tasks that could be in the hands of robots even now. Feeding computer-aided-design systems information about the arm and gripper characteristics of in-plant robots could help to put some of them there.

Where in-plant technologies are most effectively interfaced, the truly unattended factory is approached. Isolated examples of such factories exist in several countries. End-to-end automation is achieved by designing a manufacturing process, and the plant that will carry it out, together and by letting the particular functions and configurations of machines and parts fall out of this design.

Realistic robot from the Universal film, Silent Running.

In 1984, Fanuc, Limited, the Japanese parent of GMF Robotics Corporation of Troy Michigan, erected on eight thousand square meters at the base of Mount Fuji a two-story plant that manufactures several types of drive motors for robots. On the first floor, fifty-two robots variously unload materials delivered by unmanned carriers from an automatic warehouse, load and unload machine tools that finish the materials, and reload the unmanned carriers with machined parts, which are returned by them to the warehouse for temporary storage.

Under the control of a centralized computer system, and in accordance with a stored assembly schedule, machined parts are delivered, again by unmanned carrier, to the second floor where forty-nine robots on four different assembly lines assemble the motors and transfer the finished products to unmanned carriers for delivery to an automatic packaging machine. The packaged motors the machine disgorges back onto the unmanned carriers are then returned to the automatic warehouse where they are stored until shipped.

Although the one hundred and one robots share this facility with some sixty humans, the ten thousand motors produced there each month are assembled entirely by the robots under the control of the central computer.

Meanwhile, back at the ranch

If one could interface a speech synthesis device to a sheep's brain one could learn first-hand from a group of the creatures in Australia what it's like to be shorn by a robot. The Australian Wool Corporation has, since the early 1970s, funded a broad research program on robotic sheep-shearing. A prototype computer-controlled robot, equipped with sensors and cutter, has successfully sheared the backs, sides, bellies, and necks of sheep. A mechanism for automatically retrieving sheep from a race and presenting them to the robot has also been successfully demonstrated. To be practical, a fully automated shearing system will have to be sufficiently rugged to operate under remote, harsh, and dirty conditions and to withstand the rigors of repeated transportation and start-up and of sustained periods of inactivity. A system design that will satisfy these criteria, together with the resolution of a handful of remaining technical problems, could lead to the sheep ranch becoming the first "primary industry" to employ robots.

If a robotics system posited by Abraham Manimalethu of General Electric Company in Peru, Massachusetts is built, the orchard may follow the sheep ranch in providing agricultural employment for robots. The basis of the proposed "fruit-picking" robot would be a simple Cartesian robot with a slender arm capable of very fast, but highly-refined movement. A rubberized "skin," inlaid with pressure switches, would enable the arm to detect, and avoid breaking, tree branches. The robot would require a vision system sufficient to identify the location, orientation, and size of objects of a strikingly characteristic shape for its contoured grippers. Tactile sensors would prevent the grippers from crushing the picked fruit. The robot would travel on a tractor driven by a human operator and would be expected to be able to spot and pick individual pieces of fruit at least as fast as a human, that is, in approximately ten seconds.

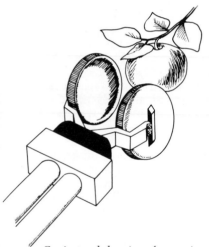

Before robots will be found down on the farm in any great numbers, experiments and speculation such as are cited above must be carried much further. By far the greatest employment of contemporary robots is in welding, with machine loading and unloading and foundry work vying for second place. Painting employs the next greatest body of robot workers while assembly and miscellaneous applications account for the least.

The potential economics of utilizing robots in assembly operations has aroused considerable interest, however, and while researchers continue to investigate techniques for imparting to robots the human-like eye-hand coordination that would render the task of assembly relatively

Conjectural drawing of an agricultural robot.

trivial, industrial users are applying their own ingenuity to the application of traditional robots to their immediate assembly tasks. Some fairly complex assembly operations have been automated using single-arm, visionless robots. A research group at Shugart Associates, for example, programmed a Unimation Puma robot with a highly adapted end effector to assemble, with the aid of specially-designed feeders and air-operated presses and controls, the eight components of a floppy disk.

For many years, robots were introduced to the workplace as simple replacements for the one or more humans who had performed the job at hand before them. The approach emphasized the ability of the robot arm to perform a routine function that had previously been performed by a human arm. A whole range of new possibilities opens up, however, when characteristics peculiar to the robot begin to be more fully exploited. With no diminution of the significance of the robot arm, the utilization of its ability to be interfaced to computers and other computer-controlled machinery has made possible the likes of the Fanuc factory described earlier. In other instances, the existence of robots has given rise to jobs that would be virtually impossible without them.

The robot arm of the National Aeronautics and Space Administration's Space Shuttle is well known. What is perhaps less well known are the roles played by other robots in the Shuttle program. The Materials and Processes Laboratory of the Marshall Space Flight Center has employed robots in several processes related to the fabrication and refurbishment of shuttle components. Of these, the spraying of an insulating thermal protective coating over the large external tank, which has a diameter of thirty feet, and the twelve foot diameter solid rocket boosters that are attached to it for lift-off, are jobs that exist because there are robots to do them. Manual spraying by humans is rendered nearly impossible by the need for protective clothing and the dimensions of the workpieces, neither of which considerations are relevant to the Trallfa and Cincinnati-Milacron robots NASA employs to do the spraying.

Two other Cincinnati-Milacron robots are employed by NASA. One manipulates a Tritan Corporation "Hydro-laser," a specialized device that delivers a narrow, high-pressure stream of water capable of cutting away the remaining thermal protective coating from recovered solid rocket boosters, a necessary step in preparing them for reuse. The other serves as a "welder's helper" to an elaborate automated tooling system that does primary welding on the large external tank. Parts that have to be reworked are offloaded to the robot for repair enabling the automated tooling to proceed with the welding of additional units.

Robots helping automated machines and other robots will become a more common occurrence as their numbers increase. One could project a time when the robot work force will be of such proportions that instances of robots replacing other robots will become common. In this idealized labor camp, displacement would be a problem of a different order, since unemployed robots, unlike unemployed humans, can simply be traded in, sold, scrapped, or, if the economics allow, removed to a corner and left to accumulate dust.

Walking and rolling

From a pair of early A.M.F. Versatrans that spent their working lives transferring one hundred and ninety-five pound lots of brick between a feed conveyor and kiln cars at a rate of over ten thousand per hour while they hung suspended from overhead beams, robots have shown themselves to be a relatively oblivious lot with respect to placement. Besides hanging upside-down and sitting bolted-upright, robots have worked sideways, their bases firmly anchored in walls.

Where it is impossible to arrange the workplace so that everything required by a robot is within its grasp, a variety of techniques can be employed. Stationary robots have been afforded access to areas outside their work envelopes by having them work in concert with nearby robots, by presenting their work via a "lazy-susan" arrangement, and by fitting them with additional arms with different work envelopes. Where none of these approaches is adequate or appropriate, it is possible to transform the stationary industrial robot into a mobile creature. Through the ingenuity of industrial engineers, inverted robots can be found traveling along overhead monorails while upright relatives ride two-rail trolleys from station to station.

In general, such industrial robots as do move about do so by rolling. Rolling is also the means of choice for mobilizing a class of non-working robots that have taken their qualifying adjective from the computer industry; in many so-called *home*, or *personal*, robots, mobility is provided in lieu of utility. Most personal robots are employed by aficionados or by the children of indulgent parents as experimental vehicles or expensive toys. Collision avoidance in personal robots is usually achieved by means of infrared or sonic range-finding systems that operate on the basis of body heat and echo detection, respectively. Camera-based vision systems would render the average personal robot prohibitively expensive without contributing significantly to its collision-avoidance capability, since most contemporary industrial-grade vision systems impose extensive limitations on the visual world of the robots that use them. Some personal robots forego the expense of object detection altogether, instead excusing themselves in synthesized "robot" voices every time they bump into something.

A typical "personal robot."

Much of the off-the-shelf utility of personal robots relies on relatively inexpensive speech recognition and synthesis chips. Some are capable of voicing a set of stock phrases, such as "I do not do windows." Others can recognize, and respond to, a specific set of spoken commands.

The usefulness of the arms, or manipulators, with which some personal robots are equipped is subject both to the sophistication of the limb itself and to the interest level of its owner. A security application advertised for one personal robot consists in its accosting an intruder detected by its infrared sensors with an upraised manipulator and an announcement that it is going to call the police.

The most versatile personal robot manipulators, like their industrial counterparts, are more often mounted on a stationary base than fitted to a mobile robot body. Such arms usually find homes with the more devoted robotics experimenters, be they children or engineers, and will likely find their way into elementary school classrooms much as personal computers have. The more sophisticated personal robots, whether of the mobile type or of the more traditional "arm on a post" variety, are provided with some means for programming their actions, often including the ability to be interfaced to a personal computer.

Personal robots can be pieced together much as personal computer systems — from an assortment of hardware and software components obtained from a variety of vendors. One version of a "sentry robot" was mentioned earlier. Commercially available software will enable another robot to record, at a prescribed set of locations, the times of any "intrusions" as detected by its sensors. The robot can later be made to play back the recorded times. Yet another "security robot" makes its rounds and concurrently recharges itself by detecting and plugging itself into any electrical outlets it encounters in its patrol area.

It's easy to draw a parallel between the limited value of many of these early personal robot abilities and the limited capabilities of the earliest personal computers. The cause of personal computers was advanced considerably by so-called "hackers," individuals possessed of a consuming preoccupation with low-level programming and microelectronics. Although we earlier referred to them as the "non-working" relatives of industrial robots, the potential of personal robots is evident even through the sheen of silliness that veils some of their current occupational repertoire.

As experimental subjects in the hands of robotics hackers, the current generation of personal robots may contribute significantly not only to the greater sophistication of subsequent generations of their own kind but to the enhancement of the industrial robot as well.

In elementary schools, personal robots will serve a dual role. As personal computers have made affordable an introduction to computer science at the elementary school level, so personal robots will provide a springboard from the primary grades to the formal "robotics science" disciplines that are emerging in the wake of the industrial robot just as computer science and its related disciplines followed widespread application of the business computer.

Additionally, with its potential for animated behaviour, the personal robot could succeed the personal computer as a teacher's aide, helping students with traditional subject matter, such as mathematics, reading, and spelling. A remotely-controlled robot named OPD2, which incorporates an integral tape deck and chest screen by means of which music can be played and movies shown, is credited by the Orlando, Florida police who own it with teaching elementary school children about safety in a way that is retained by them much better than when an officer does the training.

In considering mobility in robots, it is helpful to turn to the human infant for parallels. The relatively stationary newborn has at its disposal abilities just sufficient to draw to itself the necessary attention to insure its survival. The traditional industrial robot is similarly restricted, having a limited set of motions it is capable of executing from a fixed position in fulfillment of the particular task that constitutes its reason for being.

As infants learn to crawl, so robots have learned to roll. Notwithstanding the learning that takes place as a consequence of the activity, crawling in babies is superficially regarded as a playful exercise. So, underlying, and perhaps in part owing to, the entertainment value of the rolling robots that variously apologize for bumping into walls and raise the hackles of the quadrapedal pets whose tails they inadvertently traverse in their programmed travels, there is an educational value in providing the inspiration to "build a better robot."

Ultimately, the human infant walks. For robots, the skill of walking is orders of magnitude removed from that of rolling. For this reason, walking robots are primarily still a thing of laboratories. An experimental Japanese robot, named To-Rover, combines two levels of rolling action to achieve a sort of quasi-walking sufficient to enable it to climb stairs.

Odetics, Incorporated of Anaheim, California, demonstrated a prototype of a spider-legged creature, called ODEX I, that "walks" by moving its six legs, or articulators, three at a time in a tripod gait. ODEX I can attain a speed equivalent to what would, for a human, be a brisk walk while carrying a load equal to nearly two and one-half times its weight and can change direction in mid-stride. It has climbed into and backed out of the bed of a twenty-two hundred pound pickup truck and then hoisted the rear of, and dragged, the truck along at its normal walking pace.

Actually a hybrid, ODEX I is a robot insofar as many of its functions, such as stair-climbing and normal walking, are carried out entirely under program control. But as it is not completely autonomous, relying on a human operator using a control device with a few knobs and switches and a joystick for some interpolated instruction, such as finding the precise edge of the tailgate in the truck demonstration, it is a *teleoperated* machine. It is, nevertheless, a very remarkable machine, which can quickly change from a narrow profile that enables it to pass through a twenty-one inch doorway, to a squat profile with articulators fully extended for maximum stability. In what Odetics terms its "tucked" profile, ODEX I, which is capable of lifting more than five and one-half times its own weight while stationary, compresses itself to a mere four feet high by two and one-half feet wide.

Attempts to model the human gait in a bipedal robot are at the frontier of robotic walking experiments. Such machines as have been built are doddering things indeed. They are as infants taking their first steps, wholly consumed by the effort to maintain their balance while putting one foot in front of the other. As robots teeter on the brink of this major accomplishment, we will undoubtedly urge them on. In spite of their potential threats to employment, in spite of their association with things sinister through decades of fanciful films and literature, we are in their corner. In fact, we have been there for some time.

Joseph Engelberger, past president of Unimation, Incorporated, relates an anecdote about a robot installed in a Cleveland, Ohio sheet metal stamping plant. Though it struggled with the unwieldy automobile dashboards that were being manufactured, the robot could not make the production rate dictated by the foreman, and when the working pace was increased, its hand began to drip oil and drop parts. Robot and programmer persisted for fully two months, in the course of which circuit changes and a reconfiguration of the work area improved the robot's performance. All the while, the plant's human work force watched, rapt, and when the robot finally made the foreman's rate, it responded, to a man, with a standing round of applause. Perhaps it was gratitude, to a machine that bore witness to the wonder of human movement by virtue of struggling so mightily to emulate it. Or perhaps it is that human sympathy transcends the species. We can take heart in the latter.

In Japan, at the base of Mount Fuji, robots labor continuously and tirelessly in the manufacture of parts for robots yet unborn. With equal ardor, in divers laboratories and research facilities, their human progenitors strive to marry in their indefatigable frames a complex package of ever more refined movement and sensitivity. Though it may not be a specific target, the robot-manned factory of Capek's *R.U.R.*, which produced not parts but entire robots, looms closer. If the way to emulate human-like movement and sensitivity lies, as some suggest, not in the further exploitation of raw computing power, but in the incorporation of biological components in our machines, we will have realized yet another parallel with Capek's farsighted play. For though, alas, Rossum's robots eventually revolt, to the chagrin and, ultimately, elimination of the species that both created them and sorely misused them, two of their number, Primus and Helena, are altered by a formula devised by one of Rossum's biological scientists. The rest of Rossum's robots will eventually succumb to mechanical fatigue. Primus and Helena alone share a biological potential manifested first in their caring one for the other. Capek chose to draw the curtain on these two exiting, holding hands, to a reading from *Genesis*.

11

Much To Do About Books: the Late, Great Handshake of Libraries and Technology

John Simon, 1985

Forecasts of a stay-at-home population that conducts most of its work and social intercourse electronically have flowed liberally from the supposed imminence of telecommuting, electronic funds transfer, and shopping via interactive videotex. The state of major traffic arteries at rush hour, the lines at the drive-up windows of banks, and the parking lots of shopping malls and downtown areas bespeak the rate of progress toward such a society. Similarly, electronic publishing and dial-up bibliographic and full-text databases are but the first cobbles in the road toward putting a national, and perhaps someday global, library at the other end of our telephones.

One need look no further than the struggle to manage the growing body of human knowledge to substantiate the time-worn assertion that "necessity is the mother of invention". When the store of human learning became too great to be remembered, mankind began writing it down. When it became so voluminous as to overwhelm the scribes who were writing it down, the development of moveable type ushered in an era of hand-set printing. Four hundred years later, to keep apace of the demand for printing, the setting of type was turned over largely to machines. Today, following more than half a century of intimate association with chemical, optical, and electronic technologies that has not only significantly enhanced the mechanization of typesetting and printing, but also spawned competing alternative media, such as video, the annual yield of a highly automated publishing industry lies somewhere in the hundreds of thousands of different titles.

The titles are, of course, of books, which have, since the invention of writing, been the principal vehicle for recording and disseminating human knowledge. Even when they were produced exclusively by the meticulous, hand-copying of scribes, books proliferated beyond the ability of even all learned persons to keep one of each, a situation mankind addressed by accumulating them in public buildings and thereby making individual collections accessible to many. Thus did the "library" come to us.

Libraries of yore

Religious and political transactions probably constituted the first "bodies of knowledge" for which written records were systematically preserved. If we consider such archival collections to have been libraries, then the first library buildings were probably temples and the first librarians, priests.

At Nineveh, among the remains of the extensive library of Ashurbanipal, Assyrian monarch and patron of literature, were found, transcribed in cuneiform characters on clay tablets ranging in size from one to twelve inches square, ten thousand distinct documents, some extending over several tablets. Covering the floor of the room in which they were found to a depth of one foot, the tablets appeared to have been methodically arranged and catalogued and to have been available for general use by the king's subjects. Being essentially accumulations of official literature, libraries such as this sixth century B.C. example constituted national encyclodediae of religion and science.

The concept of a truly comprehensive library, one whose collection would transcend national boundaries, seems to have originated about two thousand years ago with the Greeks. Taking as a focal point for their endeavour the Museum, a magnificent center of Hellenic scholarship situated in the Brucheum quarter of Alexandria on a hill overlooking its great harbor, the Greeks attempted to gather together in one place a copy of every extant work. The resulting Alexandrian Library, founded about 300 B.C. and possibly modeled after the personal library of Aristotle, alternately enjoyed and endured a long history of splendor and near-destruction.

With a practically unlimited book budget, and licensed to employ acquisitions techniques at which contemporary librarians might well blush, the Alexandrian Library reputedly accumulated some two hundred thousand volumes in the first ten years of its existence and seven hundred thousand volumes by 47 B.C.

By forfeiting deposits on borrowed manuscripts, confiscating books found on ships making port in Alexandria, and employing its own staff of scholars and scribes to edit and translate Egyptian and other texts, the Alexandrian Library managed an average annual accession rate of some three thousand volumes. The largest single augmentation of the Library's holdings turned on a combination of personal animosity and love when, to thwart the succession of his illegitimate brother, the monarch of Pergamum bequeathed to Rome in 133 B.C. his entire kingdom, which included the only library in the world to rival in size the Alexandrian. The two hundred thousand volumes of the library of Pergamum became, in turn, a love token bestowed by Marc Antony upon Cleopatra, and a major gift made by Cleopatra to the Alexandrian Library.

Within sixty-five years of its founding, its holdings had increased to such an extent as to cause the Alexandrian Library to spawn a branch facility of significant size, the Serapeum, in the Rhakotis, or old Egyptian, quarter of the city.

Demetrios of Phaleron, founder of the Alexandrian Library.

Credit for the founding and early aggrandizement of the Library, ten halls of white marble and stone connected to the architecturally harmonious Museum, belongs to Demetrios of Phaleron, a capable scholar wooed from Athens to Alexandria by, and installed as personal advisor to, Ptolemy I Soter. The profusion of documents accumulated therein by this enterprising expatriate Athenian bore little resemblance to the volumes that inhabit the shelves of contemporary libraries. Variously inscribed on parchment and papyrus, some rolled, some bound into books, the manuscripts frequently commenced directly with a writer's text, and sometimes contained the mixed works of multiple authors; few bore names of authors or titles of works, prefaces or introductions, chapter or running heads.

By order of the succeeding monarch, Ptolemy II Philadelphus, the Alexandrian Library embarked upon the first significant excursion into library science since that undertaken by the scribes at Nineveh. Under the librarianship of one, Zenodotus, the holdings of the great library were divided among several major categories, an enterprise from which derived lengthy lists of authors and works. What is presumed to have been the first major separation, that of prose works from verse, is a division that persists even into contemporary classification systems. Upon the foundations laid by his predecessor, the librarian Callimachus undertook the compilation of a bio-bibliographical compendium of the whole corpus of Greek literature to his time as it was represented in the holdings of the Library. Extending over one hundred and twenty volumes, the resulting work identified each author by name, date of birth, father, teachers and educators, and nicknames or pseudonyms; included a short biography; listed titles of works and offered comments on authenticity; and provided notes that gave the first words of works and total numbers of manuscript lines. Called the *Pinakes*, this first great library catalog of Western civilization employed, with some exceptions, an alphabetical ordering of entries throughout.

A variety of peoples have been implicated in the demise of the Alexandrian Library; warring enterprises of the Romans, the Christians, and the Moslems, at various periods in its history, are credited with eliminating portions of its holdings. What was left of the collection by the middle of the seventh century was incinerated by the Saracens, ending the Library's life just half a century short of its millenial birthday.

In the centuries during which the Alexandrian Library experienced its uneven dissolution, book collections throughout much of the then-known world hibernated; the sixth-century Benedictine practice of storing them in chests is at once an apt metaphor and an indicator of the extent of the period during which libraries languished.

Wooden chests, of the type used to store books in monasteries.

But though they kept their books locked up, the Benedictines were responsible for infusing some order into what has come to be known as library administration. Under the rule of Saint Benedict, the order undertook the making of an annual report and the taking of an inventory of books in the Benedictine houses. Other orders that built upon this base include the Carthusians, who first lent books away from the convent; the Cistercians, who first appointed a separate library official and designated a particular room for the storage of books; and the Augustinians, who developed rules for the binding, repairing, cataloging, and arranging of books by libraries. The practice of interlibrary loan originated with the Reformed Augustinians, whose librarians were charged with, among other things, arranging for the borrowing of books from "elsewhere."

The library as we know it evolved gradually, over a span of several centuries. The simple chests used to store books in the early monasteries were succeeded by more complex forms incorporating horizontal and vertical partitions. Later, they stood erect and backed into walls to become recessed cabinets with built-in shelves and doors. By the fifteenth century, the further evolution of library furnishings had given rise to desks and lecterns on which books were laid on their sides, attached by chains, often to an overhead crossbar which permitted lateral movement of the volumes. Later generations of this type of fixture held books, still chained, in partitioned cases mounted above the desk. A shelf list, identifying its contents, was usually provided at an end of each case.

Closed wooden cabinet for the storage of books.

Harbinger of things to come was the library founded in 1575 by Spain's Philip II in the magnificent monastery and palace of Escorial in the mountains northwest of Madrid. No chains secured the volumes on the shelves of the bookcases that stood against its walls. But Escorial's bookcases were to come into general use long before its practice of freeing books, whose chaining persisted into the early eighteenth century.

Increasing occupation by recessed cabinetry in the houses of the Cistercian monks resulted in the creation of small, windowless rooms. By the fifteenth century, consignment of an entire room to library service was fairly common in monasteries, and emulated by college libraries, whose evolution was patterned closely after that of their monastic precursors. Abetted by Johann Gutenberg's invention of moveable type, the proliferation of books increased to such an extent by the end of the fifteenth century that the erection of whole buildings, specifically for their storage, was warranted.

Chains secured books to desks or lecterns or to shelves above them.

A concomitant liberalization of access privileges accompanied the construction of library buildings at Canterbury and Durham, in England, and Citeaux and Clairvaux, in France, wherein learned strangers were permitted to use the books. The Benedictines extended the privilege of using the books at Saint Germain-des-Prés, in Paris, to students. By the seventeenth and eighteenth centuries, many monastic libraries had been enlarged and made generally accessible to outsiders.

New world libraries

Destined to become one of the greatest of the educationally-affiliated libraries in the world, the library of Harvard University began with the bequest by John Harvard of two hundred and thirty-nine titles in four hundred volumes to a newly-established college in Cambridge, Massachusetts. This fledgling collection, received by the College two years after its founding in 1636, was probably stored or shelved in Peyntree House, which was occupied by Harvard until the completion of its first building in 1643. The library probably moved into this building, later called Old College, before construction was completed, and remained there until its partial collapse in 1677, whence it moved into the College's second nearly completed building, called Harvard Hall.

The library had occupied Harvard Hall for nearly a century when a fire, in 1764, consumed both the building and most of the library's collection. Begun anew in the central chamber of a reconstructed Harvard Hall with the four hundred and four books that were out at the time of the fire, the library came to occupy the entire second floor by 1841 when it was moved to Gore Hall, the first Harvard building to be constructed specifically for library purposes.

By 1900, the Harvard Library had amassed a collection that approached, in numbers, the holdings of the Alexandrian Library at its peak. Access to the then more than half-million volumes, which by that time were catalogued by both author and subject, was granted to any respectable male, though the borrowing of books was restricted, more or less, to those associated with the College.

Some part in the further liberalization of access privileges that finds contemporary library patrons, by comparison with those of ages past, veritably unfettered, was likely played by a shift in responsibility for lost and stolen books. Replacement of books strayed or misappropriated from libraries in the American colonies was typically required to be made out of pocket by the librarian. Exemplary of the degree to which things turned about in this regard is an instance alluded to by Dixon Wecter (1950, 9), who relates the finding of a label inside a book retrieved from the shelves of the Widener Library "proclaiming its onetime theft, but the culprit caught and sentenced to five years' hard labor."

At roughly the same time that monastic and college libraries were opening their proprietary collections to outsiders, the concept of the free public library, which had slumbered for nearly two thousand years, was reawakening. A variant, the pay public library, called a *corporation,* or *subscription,* library began with the Library Company of Philadelphia, founded by Benjamin Franklin in 1731. Together with the Redwood Library of Newport, Rhode Island, founded in 1747, and the Boston Athenaeum, founded in 1807, it has survived the dissolution of a broad network of such libraries that grew up around it in the wake of the American Revolution. The remainder were either abandoned or absorbed by municipalities and converted into free public libraries, the establishment of which had, by the nineteenth century, won the support of governments. Legislation encouraging the municipal creation of free public libraries was enacted by Parliament in 1850, and by the State of Massachusetts one year later (a statewide extension of an 1848 law that created a public library in the City of Boston).

Over the twenty year period from the end of the nineteenth through the beginning of the twentieth centuries, nourished by grants from Andrew Carnegie, which alone helped to establish some fourteen hundred new buildings, municipal libraries flourished. By 1910, there were in the United States more than ten thousand such libraries with holdings of one thousand volumes or more.

Also on the ascendant during the eighteenth century was the state library. The British Museum, the national library of Great Britain (and later called the British Library), was founded in 1753. In the American colonies, the existence of state libraries in Pennsylvania and New Hampshire as early as 1777 anticipated a post-Revolutionary War trend to establish official libraries in connection with the state system. The Library of Congress, following a seeming tradition of great libraries, was established in 1800 and burned by the British Army in 1814. Rebuilt around the personal library of Thomas Jefferson, its collection grew slowly, reaching twenty thousand volumes before it was again consumed by fire in 1851.

The Library subsequently grew rapidly, absorbing the library of the Smithsonian Institution in 1866. The present Library of Congress building was, at the time of its opening in 1897, considered to be the largest, the most ornate, and the most costly building created for library purposes in the world.

If we regard the structural opulence of the Alexandrian Library as a mirror of its historical significance, then the grandness of the edifices that house them are fitting looking-glasses for the two preeminent national libraries, that of Great Britain and the de facto national library of the United States, the Library of Congress.

Seventy-eight years after its founding, the elder of these two, the British Library, offered employment to a political refugee from Italy. Probably not since Demetrios of Phaleron and the Alexandrian Library has the conjunction of an institution and an individual had such a dramatic influence on library administration. Following a twenty-five year climb through its institutional hierarchy, Antonio (later Sir Anthony) Panizzi, in 1856, assumed the position of principal librarian for the British Library. Over the course of his ten-year librarianship, Panizzi's ideas predominated in scholarly and research libraries, and much of his thinking found later expression through the Library of Congress.

To its own credit, the Library of Congress has been central in cooperative and standards-setting efforts for more than century. In 1901, with an outlet in the form of a loosely-structured network formed around the then twenty-five-year-old American Library Association, the Library of Congress inaugurated a catalog card production and distribution service. Subsequently, its book catalog and *National Union Catalog* became the embodiment of all of the bibliographic prescriptions, the rules for cataloging and classification, that had been worked out, and widely adopted, during the first half of the century. Then, in the 1950s, with librarians eyeing hopefully the evolving general-purpose computer, the Library took the lead in designing a format for machine-readable bibliographic records. The Library of Congress Machine-Readable Cataloging (LC MARC) format became the basis of first a national, and then an international, standard for storing bibliographic information in a form amenable to computer processing.

Since their inception, and notwithstanding the emphasis of successive generations on different aspects of their charge, the fundamental mission of the institutions we call libraries has remained constant. For more than two thousand years, they have engaged in the business of accumulating and making accessible to their patrons the wealth of human knowledge as it is recorded in books and, more recently, on the variety of non-print media spawned by twentieth-century technologies.

Though the sizes of the collections accumulated by the Harvard and Alexandrian Libraries within three centuries of their respective origins were roughly equivalent, by the time that Harvard amassed its first half-million volumes it had become clear that, however many books one might accumulate in one place, the number would represent but a fraction of the total number in the world at that time.

But though librarians, acknowledging the futility of its Olympian aspirations, relinquished the Alexandrian Library as a model, they never completely forsook it as an ideal. For the successors of Demetrios of Phaleron, founder of that illustrious forbear, selective acquisition has been the pound of flesh exacted because the dictates of reality must, perforce, supercede idealistic yearnings. Even so, how their gardens grew; however judiciously cultivated, they inevitably spilled over their boundaries, and as often as they were re-fenced, spilled over again. The culmination, in the mid-1970s, of a decade of construction that constituted the biggest building boom in library history found libraries generally more direly in need of space than they had been when it began.

From the decline of the Alexandrian Library in the early centuries A.D. until the invention of moveable type in the mid-fifteenth century, library book collections grew slowly enough to be accommodated by incremental expansions of their quarters. When the monastic librarian could no longer close his book chest on its contents, he built another; when the wall shelves that replaced the chests became full, he erected more; and when the shelves, though they lined an entire room, were no longer capable of holding the library's books, the monks undertook the construction of whole buildings for their storage.

Precipitated by Gutenberg more than five hundred years ago, accelerated by the mechanization of typesetting in the eighteen hundreds, and finally driven by speed-of-light technologies that have redoubled their potential every few years for the past several decades, the automation of the printing and publishing industries has helped them keep pace with geometric expansions in the volume of output, not alone in the form of books and serials, but also, increasingly, in the various non-print media. Until very recently, libraries attempted to stay this information glut with a combination of human ingenuity and a continuing reliance on the construction industry.

Drawing on the legacy of their predecessors, librarians fastened on sharing as one technique for increasing access to their burgeoning collections. The associations and regional networks that came into being toward the end of the nineteenth century provided a structure around which practical interlibrary loan programs could be developed.

At about the same time, the concept of off-premise storage began to attract attention as a way of reducing somewhat the space requirements of existing collections. The expense of acquiring or erecting a regional facility could be shared among a group of libraries and the space allocated among them for deposit of the less-used books in their collections. Such a cooperative warehouse was proposed by then-president of Harvard University, Charles Eliot, at the turn of the century, although it was not to be realized until 1942, when Harvard, during the librarianship of Keyes D. Metcalf, entered into an agreement with six other Boston area libraries to create the New England Deposit Library.

Neither was the concept of the branch library, which the Greeks hit upon more than two thousand years ago when their Alexandrian Library quickly filled up, lost to later librarians. At Harvard, the trend to dis-

Peyntree House—1638

Old College—1642

Original Harvard Hall—1677

Contemporary Harvard Hall—1764

Gore Hall—1841

Randall Hall—1912

Widener Library—1915

Houghton Library—1941

Lamont Library—1947

Three hundred and fifty years of Harvard library buildings.

tribute the University collection among one central, and a host of satellite, facilities — which was well established before the turn of the century — today finds the nearly eleven million volumes that constitute its holdings scattered throughout more than one hundred separate libraries.

Containing their growing collections, however, was but one of a number of problems aggravated for libraries by the considerable lag between the automation of book production methods and library methods.

The year 1638 saw both the founding of the Harvard Library and the arrival of the first printing press in the American colonies. By 1770, at least a dozen establishments were vying for Boston's printing business. But not until 1901, when the Library of Congress inaugurated a program to mass produce catalog cards, whose distribution was by no means universal, was any serious attention paid to automating library methods.

Characteristic of what was going on in libraries during this century-plus interval was the evolution of the catalog of the Harvard College Library. At the very same time that libraries were cultivating dramatic liberalizations in their policies governing access, mushrooming collections were becoming an impediment to the act of access, a situation to which librarians, lacking machines to effect needed change, applied their individual organizational acuity.

The earliest of the Harvard College Library's catalogs reflected the organization of its collection by donor. The first catalog to be printed, in 1723, ordered the volumes by size. Because neither arrangement was satisfactory for locating individual volumes in a growing collection, subsequent catalogs ordered volumes alphabetically by author.

In 1822, librarian Joseph Green Cogswell reorganized the then-twenty thousand volumes into four subject collections: Theology, Philosophy (Science), Literature, and History. By 1830, his successor, Benjamin Peirce, had overseen the production of a combined author-subject index. A decade later, Thaddeus William Harris recommended the making of a card catalog of a type that had come into fairly wide use in Germany and Scandinavia by the end of the eighteenth century. Its application at Harvard came at roughly the same time that its collection, which had doubled in the less than two decades since Librarian Cogswell had reorganized it, moved to new quarters in Gore Hall. The first card catalog was constructed with low, wide drawers that held $9\frac{1}{2}'' \times 2\frac{1}{2}''$ handwritten cards. Superseded, in 1861, by a catalog devised by Ezra Abbott and Charles Cutter, which used cards of a $5'' \times 2''$ size, the original $9\frac{1}{2}'' \times 2\frac{1}{2}''$ cards were retained as an "official" catalog for staff use. The contemporary $5'' \times 3''$ catalog card, which was coming into general use toward the end of the nineteenth century, had begun to replace the $5'' \times 2''$ cards for the Harvard College Library's central collection by 1915, when the present Harry Elkins Widener Library was completed. At about the same time, the hand writing of catalog cards at Harvard began to give way to their typing.

A rising tide of technology

To the warehousing and retrieval problems of libraries was added, though it has only recently come to be recognized as such, the bane of modern, acid-based paper production methods. The high acid content of the paper used in many contemporary books and periodicals has rendered them susceptible to more rapid deterioration than their antecedents. Growing awareness of this problem elicited another significant contribution from the Library of Congress, which launched a major deacidification program for preserving copies of all books of importance. The arrival, in the 1960s, of microform technology, by means of which the storage on film of materials photographically reduced many times is made possible, offered another partial solution to the paper problem, and introduced into the bargain yet another approach to the perennial problem of collection containment.

Firms specializing in the filming of periodicals and rare documents for conversion to microfilm or microfiche came into existence and libraries began to buy some journals and periodicals only in microform, at once solving the problem of physical deterioration and reducing storage requirements. Microfilming of precious materials has enabled repositories to reduce wear on originals, and also to complete collections of rare document sets by acquiring from the institutions that hold them microform copies of the pieces they lack. However, even with recent advances that have enhanced readability — a long-standing patron complaint about the medium — and introduced color, microform remains a less-than-popular alternative to print publications for readers, and overall its applications remain limited.

Throughout the first half of the twentieth century, while librarians were preoccupied with improving compatibility among the various manual systems that governed the orderly augmentation, arrangement, and accessibility of their burgeoning collections, a confluence of chemical, electronic, mechanical, and optical innovations was being applied to the automation of commercial activities. Nineteen forty-nine saw the debut of the phototypesetter, 1950 the introduction of the Xerox Copier. By the early 1960s, automation of industrial machinery had progressed from punched paper tape and magnetic tape control to computer control. In 1965, both the first commercial telecommunications satellite and the first electronic telephone switching system went into operation. By the late 1960s, robots were becoming more populous on manufacturing assembly lines and the microcomputer had been born.

While this brief survey might lead one to infer that the library is a poor cousin of everything else that can be nurtured by the fruits of technology, such is not really the case. Rather, it is appropriate that libraries, being institutions steeped in tradition, have applied the various technologies to the automation of their venerable systems with such studied scrupulousness.

We noted earlier that the Library of Congress had introduced a degree of automation into the production of catalog cards as early as 1901 and that the Harvard College Library had begun to employ a typewriter in the production of its own catalog cards by 1915. 1927 found a teletypewriter in use by the Free Library of Philadelphia as part of a closed-circuit communication system between its loan desk and stacks. A similar application of teletypewriters connected two city libraries in Michigan in the 1940s. In 1951, the King County Library of Seattle, Washington, used punched card sorting devices, forerunners of later tabulating machines, as the basis for developing the first effective mechanized systems for producing book catalogs of holdings. It was a time of testing an unfamiliar element with a toe. Librarians did not rush to commit a whole foot to undulating technology.

During the late 1950s and early 1960s the computer was evolving from the computational tool of the scientist into the data processing machine whose generalized capabilities and ever-increasing processing capacity were beginning to be appropriated by business, government, industry, the health professions, and the administrations of colleges and universities for their respective information handling needs. At about the same time, perceiving a match between the computer's principal strength — the rapid and repetitive processing of enormous amounts of data — and the function and content of their own manual systems, librarians began to evaluate seriously the former's apparent potential for automating the latter.

Because the amount of data that must be processed relative to the acquisitions, cataloging, and circulation functions of a library is roughly proportional to the size of its collection, in the larger libraries, particularly, the processing capacity of manual systems was being severely taxed, a situation that weighed heavily upon operational efficiency as evidenced in growing backlogs in cataloging departments and inefficiencies in order processing and circulation control.

By the late 1960s, libraries had gotten their feet wet in technology and had begun to explore the currents and eddies that kept its surface astir. They were being offered computer-based acquisitions systems by at least two commercial vendors, and automated circulation systems by several. Access to an organizational computing facility provided libraries with the option of developing automated systems in-house, either by contracting for programming services with the local computing center, or by buying time on its computer and "doing-it-oneself."

Libraries that could afford none of these approaches found in the venerable library network a means to benefit from the development of computer-based library systems. The New England Library Information Network (NELINET) was formed to provide its members with access to computer-based cataloging services.

Created in 1967 by a National Library of Medicine Regional Medical Library Program grant awarded to Harvard University's Francis A. Countway Library of Medicine, the New England Regional Medical Library Service (NERMLS) proffered significant contributions, computer-supported and otherwise, to the New England medical community. Training programs developed by NERMLS, in cooperation with the

Harvard School of Public Health, led to marked improvements in the staffing and stocking of hospital libraries. The network also mounted an ambitious interlibrary loan program and undertook the development of regional programs for training medical database searchers.

A pioneer in library automation, the Harvard University Library had developed, by the early 1960s, a punched card-based circulation system that has continued in operation to the present time. The information that patrons of Harvard's Widener Library print on the computer cards they use to check out books is subsequently keypunched into the cards, which are then batched and processed against a database on the University's central mainframe computer to produce reports that are distributed daily to the circulation desk staff.

By the late 1960s, the Library had also put into operation, to handle the approximately 60,000 book orders it was then placing annually, a home-grown acquisitions system. The Computer Assisted Ordering System, contracted, with some reservation we suspect, to CAOS (pronounced "chaos"), was capable of automatically producing and tracking orders, maintaining data relative to funding levels and recalculating balances, and generating claims and follow-up letters. Within a decade, to handle a volume of orders that had grown to more than 100,000 per year, CAOS was replaced by another locally developed system called CAPS (for Computer Assisted Processing System). The CAPS system, in addition to supporting the ordering activities of the Widener Library, was also used by many of the departmental libraries.

In the early 1960s, the development of systems designed to automate library activities was usually undertaken by library staff who possessed some computer orientation. By the end of the decade, many libraries had established official departments to handle the automation of library systems. Such a progression was followed by the Harvard University Library to its contemporary Office for Systems Planning and Research.

The spirit of cooperation that libraries had begun to manifest in the late nineteenth century, and which continued to grow thereafter, served them well in what was probably the most leviathan of their undertakings, the automation of cataloging. The Library of Congress's MARC (Machine Readable Cataloging) format, a standard for facilitating the transmission of bibliographic data that became a near-universal standard for its internal storage, became the cornerstone of this endeavour. Once it was set, a variety of options developed for libraries.

The driving force behind standardization of cataloging was economy. A standard size and format evolved for catalog cards primarily because it was much cheaper for libraries to purchase cards that had been produced en masse than it was for each library to type them individually. This was true whether the cards were produced by traditional printing methods, as were those distributed by the Library of Congress at the turn of the century, or by computer, as were those which the Library began to produce in the 1960s from MARC format machine-readable records.

Standardization was not, however, and still is not, an all or nothing proposition. The Library of Congress classification system that suggested call numbers for the cards it distributed was but one of many, a goodly number of libraries having developed their own systems during the nineteenth century. But although libraries that bought catalog cards frequently typed in their own call numbers and often made other changes as well, they typically found doing so to be less expensive, overall, than producing and verifying entire cards themselves.

In 1969, the Library of Congress began offering for sale, in machine-readable form on computer magnetic tape, the MARC format data from which it prepared its cards. With this development, it became possible for libraries to undertake the computer production of catalog cards locally, and to automatically include on them local call numbers and other variations from Library of Congress card content.

Early experiments in manipulating MARC format data were made by a number of institutions, including the libraries of Stanford University and the University of Chicago, the Washington State Library, and a group of Ohio college libraries. The latter organized as the Ohio College Library Center (OCLC) and later, retaining its original initialism, incorporated as the On-line Computer Library Center, one of several major on-line cataloging services, or *bibliographic utilities*. These organizations maintain large bibliographic databases from which they provide both processing capabilities, such as the retrieval of existing, and creation of original, cataloging data, and products, such as computer magnetic tape files of cataloging data and traditional catalog cards.

Other institutional collaborations that emulated OCLC in becoming autonomous, or semi-autonomous, service organizations include: the Washington Library Network (WLN); the University of Toronto Library Automation Systems (UTLAS); and the Research Libraries Group's Research Libraries Information Network (RLIN).

Although all of these utilities were formed around collections of MARC format bibliographic data, the sophisticated retrieval systems that they employ to enable searchers to locate and retrieve single bibliographic records from databases containing millions, and to manipulate retrieved data as extensively as necessary to conform to local needs, exhibit marked differences.

Very early in the 1960s, Harvard's Widener Library experimented with the automation of its shelf list, which then consisted of large sheafs of papers held together in books. Putting the list onto the University's central mainframe computer, the Library produced, from the subject groupings that derived from the numerical ordering of call numbers, individualized bound shelf lists for specific disciplines, such as the humanities and the social sciences. The one and one-quarter million records that were converted into machine-readable form during the life of this project are still preserved by the Library, which expects to use them in future development projects. Subsequent to the automation of its shelf list, the Library built its own system for manipulating the MARC format data obtained from Library of Congress tapes.

Planning for the first comprehensive, or *Union*, catalog of Harvard's holdings coincided roughly with the breaking of ground for the Widener

Library in 1913. At a time when handwritten catalog cards were just beginning to be replaced by printed and typed cards, Harvard began the work of reconciling the contents of its two existing card catalogs, an "official" one and a "public" one, and adding cards for tens of thousands of books not yet cataloged in either.

The Union Catalog, which was to contain cards of location for every book in the University as well as for books in collections elsewhere, was to be one of two catalogs in the new library building, the other being a public catalog planned for the circulation area. Assembly of Harvard's Union Catalog 1, which was accomplished during the administration of Archibald Cary Coolidge, was expedited by making it a single (author) entry alphabetical catalog instead of the more usual multiple entry alphabetical catalog that provides access not only by author, but also by title, subject, series, editors, translators, etc.

One can, today, find intermixed in the drawers of Union Catalog 1 cards from the Library of Congress, cards provided by other Harvard libraries for titles entered into their own catalogs, cards typewritten by staff of the Widener Library, and handwritten carry-overs from the preceding public catalog. Although it includes few entries for works in non-Roman scripts, is restricted to author entries, has been minimally edited, and was officially closed to additions in 1982, the nearly six million cards of Union Catalog 1 remain a revered reference tool.

The closing of Union Catalog 1 heralded a new era of cataloging at Harvard. Union Catalog 2, the Distributable Union Catalog, or DUC, is very much a progeny of the Library of Congress's MARC format and the flourishing of bibliographic utilities. The Harvard University Library joined OCLC in 1977, and both the Harvard Law School Library and the Harvard College Library's Fine Arts Library subsequently became associate members of RLIN. Because of standardization around the MARC format, cataloging data from these sources and from Library of Congress tapes can be stored, together with original cataloging data input locally, in an on-line database on the University's central mainframe computer. It is from the accumulated data stored in this database that the DUC derives.

The physical DUC is an incredibly dense microfiche catalog that currently packs nearly three and one-half million entries onto eight hundred and sixty-nine pages of fiche. The addition of a single page of fiche to the catalog can accommodate approximately one thousand additional titles. A paragon of portability compared to Union Catalog 1, the DUC can be situated and used in any location that provides a surface area adequate to hold a fiche-reader and access to an electrical outlet.

The comprehensiveness and portability of the DUC have been achieved through a carefully planned integration of the services of bibliographic utilities, programming additions and modifications to the Library's own locally-developed system for manipulating MARC format data, and use of computer output microform (COM) capabilities.

Unlike Harvard's Union Catalog 1, of which there is only one copy in the Widener Library, there are approximately one hundred and forty-nine copies of the DUC distributed throughout the University. Each is divided into two main catalogs, author/title and subject, with entries arranged alphabetically. Full bibliographic information is provided under the author or other main entry, and abbreviated information under other access points.

Although it does not yet contain entries in all categories, the scope of the DUC includes musical scores, sound recordings, motion pictures, film strips, slide sets, and machine-readable data files, as well as monographs and serials. Entries for titles ordered but not yet received, and received but not yet cataloged help to reduce duplication of orders among the decentralized libraries and to expedite the cataloging of needed volumes, respectively. Thanks to work of the University's Judaica Department, romanized entries for works in Hebrew are being incorporated into the DUC, and the catalog may someday be opened to works in Middle Eastern and East Asian languages.

The DUC is a testimony to the spirit of cooperation among the decentralized Harvard libraries that made the University's first union catalog possible. Brought together by then-director of the Library, Douglas Bryant, and with the counsel and support of his successor, Oscar Handlin, catalog, collection development, reference, and system librarians, together with library administrators and a senior member of the University's Office for Information Technology, participated in a three year planning effort that culminated, in 1981, in the distribution of one hundred and thirty-two copies of the first DUC to Harvard libraries. Semiannual recumulations, updated by monthly cumulated supplements to the author/title catalog, have brought it from an initial cumulation of more than one million entries for 362,000 titles to nearly three and one-half million entries for 870,000 titles in its eighth cumulation in February of 1985.

Though it has waded out quietly, the Harvard University Library is among a growing number of large libraries that are presently up to their knees in technology. Around them is an unprecedented range of options for automating library processes.

Services can be purchased centrally, through a network or by direct subscription, or separately, as packages or in the form of one or more stand-alone systems. Many more commercial vendors have introduced automated systems that run on increasingly powerful and relatively inexpensive minicomputers. So-called *turn-key* systems package the requisite hardware and software to automate a particular function or combination of functions and are designed to be installed as easily, and made operational as quickly, as "turning a key." The major bibliographic utilities, having built complex and extensive networked computer systems for the provision of on-line cataloging services, have added such functions as serials control, interlibrary loan, and book-ordering to their repertoires. Meanwhile, the technical staffs of libraries have continued to refine their own skills in the development, adaptation, and interfacing of computer-based systems.

Toward integrated systems and distributed services

Following the fire that reduced Old Harvard Hall, and most of Harvard College's early book collection, to ashes, a successor collection seeded with the four hundred plus volumes that survived was, through the collective beneficence of Messrs. Hollis and Hancock, the Societies Xtian and Episcopalean, the colony of New Hampshire, and private sources, restored in a period of one year to the proportions it had achieved over the previous century. The gift of the first-named donor, Thomas Hollis, constituted more than one-quarter of the total contribution of four thousand, three hundred and fifty volumes. Descended from the Hollis family of London, England, this Hollis was one of a number of Hollises, and several Thomas Hollises, whose generous contributions to the library of books, money, advice, and criticism spanned a century from the late 1700s to the late 1800s. At his death in 1774, Thomas Brand Hollis, heir to the Thomas Hollis named above, bequeathed to the library £100 with which was established the Library's first permanent book fund.

Harvard's acknowledgement of the generosity of the Hollis family, which found earlier expression in the naming of Hollis Hall, the building next to Harvard Hall and fourth oldest in Harvard Yard, was renewed with the naming of its developing, computer-based, integrated library support system, the Harvard On-Line Library Information System, or HOLLIS.

Based on the NOTIS package, a third generation integrated acquisitions and cataloging system developed by Northwestern University that has provided its originator a decade of stable and reliable service, the HOLLIS system will eventually be capable of dispensing to Harvard's decentralized libraries an integrated package of acquisitions, cataloging, and circulation services and, ultimately, of making the resulting database directly accessible to library patrons.

Within the context of HOLLIS, data will be centralized but activity will remain decentralized. For example, data derived from the heavy volume of processing associated with serials control — that is, with initiating and cancelling subscriptions, checking-in received and claiming outstanding issues, paying invoices, and generating orders for the binding of volumes — is being centralized in HOLLIS. However, serials cataloging will continue to be done by individual libraries in conjunction with the Library of Congress's Conversion of Serials (CONSER) program, which is administered locally by the Harvard University Library's CONSER Office. The cataloging information that results from bringing these records together in HOLLIS will be shared nationally; the holdings information (i.e., information about the specific issues and volumes of periodicals held by Harvard libraries) will be shared locally.

In addition to the transfer of serials data, this first phase of HOLLIS also entails the transfer of data from CAPS, the Library's existing acquisitions system. When completed, the HOLLIS acquisitions and serials control module will become accessible to some twenty to thirty Harvard libraries through approximately one hundred and twenty terminals.

The subsequent phase of HOLLIS involves producing, from the Library's existing DUC data and data retrieved from bibliographic utilities such as OCLC and RLIN, a comprehensive, on-line, bibliographic database. HOLLIS's bibliographic module will be capable of interchanging data freely with its acquisitions and serials modules as well as generating the Library's Union Catalog. The capability of generating a fiche catalog will be retained, although a long-range target of HOLLIS is to open the catalog to on-line inquiry, first from interactive terminals in the various libraries and, eventually, to dial-up access from home terminals or personal computers of patrons.

The ability to assemble a complex system, like that under development at Harvard, by wedding components obtained variously from local development and commercial and institutional products, and making their marriage work with data obtained from a variety of sources, is characteristic of a trend in library software development that has found expression in the sharing of software between institutions and within networks.

High volume may well be the most characteristic aspect of the work of libraries. It is certainly characteristic of their principal commodity, printed works, and inasmuch as library administration consists in recording, processing, and updating large amounts of highly variable information associated with each of the individual items in their very large collections, it is severalfold characteristic of that activity.

When libraries first began to apply computers to these processes, in the early 1960s and 1970s, the state-of-the-art in computer technology was such that the storage and processing capacities requisite to their needs could be provided only by mainframe computers, of which International Business Machines Corporation (IBM) had already established its preeminence as a manufacturer. That the preponderance of development of library systems took place on IBM mainframes was to be propitious for several reasons: 1) mainstream IBM equipment proved to be extremely reliable over subsequent generations, 2) a consistent hardware architecture and operating system philosophy facilitated the transfer of software forward to newer machines, and 3) many competing manufacturers found it in their interest to build into their own products compatibility with IBM's computers.

Though unplanned, this circumstance yielded significant benefits for many libraries. For example, a circulation system developed by the Ohio State University Libraries was subsequently employed by the libraries of both the State University of New York at Albany and the University of Illinois at Urbana-Champaign. Similarly, library system software developed by Guelph University in Ontario was eventually adopted by other libraries in the province.

An example of two systems developed independently by separate institutions being combined into a hybrid system for a third institution is provided by the Hennepin County, Minnesota, Public Library System, which interfaced a University of California Institute for Library Research system for creating and maintaining a machine-readable, MARC format, cataloging database with a New York Public Library system for producing book catalogs.

At Harvard, systems development efforts of the Library progressed relatively uninterrupted through three generations of IBM mainframe computers operated by the Harvard University Computing Center.

While the high-capacity systems for managing library acquisitions, cataloging, and circulation have tended to grow apace with the mainframe computers they were developed on, the mid-1970s found a growing body of library systems, both commercially- and institutionally-developed, running on minicomputers.

Although the minicomputer had its debut in the late 1960s, several years of hardware evolution, followed by a few more years to bring operating system and application development software up to an adequate level of sophistication, had to pass before the minicomputer would become a viable tool for library use.

Early commercial systems developed on minicomputers tended to focus on particular subsystems, predominantly circulation control, although acquisitions and cataloging modules were later added to some. To expand the scope of such systems, minicomputers were variously employed in multiples in a network configuration or linked to mainframe computers. In the latter arrangement, the minicomputer would typically function as a *front-end,* or pre-processor, to the mainframe; that is, it would perform a particular function, for example, circulation control, possibly using an optical character recognition (OCR) scanner to retrieve the input data, and interact with the mainframe for storing accumulated transactions for subsequent report generation or integration with bibliographic data.

Most recently, libraries have recognized the utility of the increasingly capable microcomputer for managing a host of the less voluminous facets of library administration. Word processing and electronic spreadsheet software are routinely used by larger libraries for traditional administrative housekeeping chores, such as handling internal correspondence and reports, preparing brochures and pamphlets for patron familiarization and instruction, and managing local operating budgets.

Not a new phenomenon, machine-readable databases that are accessible on-line to terminals and personal computers are becoming an increasingly visible extension of the traditional research services of libraries. Microcomputers have an advantage over terminals as hooks into such search services in that they can, from those databases that permit it, download retrieved information onto their disks or diskettes for subsequent manipulation and/or printing.

By the early 1960s, the computer had been enlisted in the formidable task of indexing the burgeoning body of scientific and technical literature; printed bibliographic aids for this vast body of knowledge had begun to be recorded on computer magnetic tape to automate their compilation and phototypesetting. Rendered in machine-readable form, the data could also, with the development of appropriate retrieval software, be transferred from computer tape to high-speed disk and made accessible interactively.

Large-scale development projects aimed at making such access a reality, sponsored by the world's largest clearinghouse for scientific and technical information, the United States government, gave birth to the two largest contemporary commercial providers of on-line database access. Major contracts were awarded for the development, in 1963, of an interactive storage and retrieval system for some two hundred thousand bibliographic records maintained by the Department of Defense's Advanced Research Projects Agency (ARPA) and, in 1966, of an interactive system to handle bibliographic information for the publications of the National Aeronautics and Space Administration. The respective recipients of these contracts were the System Development Corporation of Santa Monica, California, and Lockheed Missles and Space Company of Palo Alto, California. The commercial service that grew out of Lockheed's government work is called DIALOG, that which grew out of System Development Corporation's, SDC Search Service. These were joined, in the late 1970s, by a third major provider, Bibliographic Retrieval Services (BRS) of Scotia, New York.

Save for their origins, there is little that one can say categorically about machine-readable databases. Though they had their foundation in large-scale conversions of scientific and technical bibliographic data, and though the level of financial support for publishing in these fields will foster a continuing preponderance of scientific and technical databases, many compilations of bibliographic data related to business and the professions, notably law and medicine, have been developed and made available. Some early on-line databases, having come about as a byproduct of the computerization of the photocomposition process, had printed counterparts. Some of these printed sources persisted in the face of their evolution into machine-readable form while others were rendered extinct by the process. Many of the later machine-readable databases were conceived as such, with no printed antecedents. Extensive reference databases today enable searchers to retrieve bibliographic information for a wide range of subject matter, whether published in the form of books, conference papers, dissertations, journal articles, or technical reports, and directory information on contracts, grants, organizations, people, and research projects. Complementing these is a growing number of source databases, including dictionaries, some of them adjunct to the use of complex bibliographic databases, numerical databases containing statistical or other numeric data drawn from business, government, and science, and full-text databases that contain complete texts of documents such as newspaper and magazine articles, court decisions, and municipal, state, and federal laws.

Some machine-readable databases are produced by commercial firms, some are produced by non-profit institutions and organizations. Some database producers make access available directly, others lease their product to a distributor who provides access, and still others do both.

Some distributors produce some of the databases to which they sell access and lease others, other distributors are exclusively resellers.

Libraries find themselves in this disordered realm another level of distributor, or broker, an unfamiliar role for institutions steeped in a tradition of not billing patrons directly for their services. Making on-line search capability available, however, entails a commitment of staff resources, an investment in one or more terminals or personal computers and related communications equipment, and payment of the subscription fee(s) associated with the service(s) to be used and for connect time and printing charges incurred by each use. Because their budgets often preclude absorbing the full cost of providing such services, libraries that do so are usually constrained to either charge back to their patrons some portion of the cost or to restrict the patronage or scope of the service offered, or both.

The range of strategies employed by the dozen or so Harvard libraries that offer on-line search services reflects the variegation in the panoramic view of the machine-readable database landscape. Some of the departmental libraries at Harvard provide search services for their faculty and students at no charge, others absorb the fixed costs, such as equipment, overhead, and subscription fees, and bill patrons for the recurring charges associated with connect time and printing. Some libraries, particularly the smaller departmental libraries, limit their search services to immediate faculty and students, others offer their services to the entire Harvard community, and still others will perform searches, for a nominal surcharge, for non-Harvard persons.

Collectively, Harvard libraries access more than one hundred and twenty-five databases in business, current events, education, energy and environment, the humanities, law, medicine and health, and the natural and social sciences.

With these databases, one can undertake retrospective searches by topic, author, document type or title, or can perform a comprehensive search that will cross all of these boundaries in order to gather from as many sources as possible references to a particular topic. One can order a highly selective search for the purpose of examining, for example, the financial status of a particular company, or investigate the state-of-the-art in a given area of research or product development. Interdisciplinary searches, especially, are made much easier by simultaneous access to multiple reference sources.

The ability to walk away, after a few moments at a computer terminal, with a neatly printed bibliography drawn from millions of entries derived from a multiplicity of sources compiled by divers institutions and organizations comes to us but a few decades after the first clunky, but automated, punched card circulation systems went into operation in libraries. It is as if technology, suddenly realizing after four centuries that in coming to the aid of those charged with the recording of human knowledge it had confounded the lot of those charged with its preservation and dissemination, were trying to compensate for its oversight.

Harvard's fractioned information resource is a microcosm of the great global web by which the preservation, use, and further augmentation of the body of knowledge is effected, and the most recent half-century of its three and one-half century existence is a map of the shift from informational self-sufficiency to interdependence that has been occasioned by the sudden and focused attention of technology on the library arts. The numerous independent libraries that have, since the turn of the century, served Harvard's disciplinally and geographically disparate population presaged this shift from institutional warehousing to inter-institutional distribution.

That no serious attempt was ever made to unite Harvard's many libraries was due, in part, to the recognition that no single building could contain their collective holdings, but also to an appreciation for an inherent strength in their separateness: that the staff and librarians of the individual libraries are, by virtue of their proximity to them, more sensitive to the needs of their patrons.

Harvard's venerated Union Catalog 1 was compiled with the intention of realizing the virtues of a central collection without disturbing the status quo. It was, in an era of manual library methods, a bibliographic database to the University's many scattered full-text databases.

Today, through the agency of the microfiche Union Catalog 2 whose virtues were extolled earlier, patrons of the Harvard libraries have access to bibliographic information for the bulk of the collection cataloged since 1977 and selected portions from earlier dates. In addition, some two thousand requests per year by Harvard patrons for titles not held by one of the University's libraries are filled through interlibrary loan, usually within a week of their receipt whether processed manually or through the automated interlibrary loan modules of one of the bibliographic utilities to which the Harvard libraries subscribe. In reciprocation, Harvard libraries honor approximately three thousand requests per year from other libraries for the loan of titles in their collections. The automated acquisitions and cataloging systems evolved by the Harvard University Library have contributed to overall collection enhancement by reducing the amount of duplication of titles among libraries and thereby making funds available for acquiring additional titles, and as the independent Harvard libraries press on with the transfer of their serials records into the emerging HOLLIS system, realization of an on-line, up-to-date-as-of-the-very-minute catalog that can be queried from terminals in the homes of patrons as well as in the library moves gradually closer.

Libraries are no longer the animals that they were. If they were mules, now they are horses. If they were owls, now they are eagles. Their response to the information explosion is faster and their field of vision broader. Those who haven't visited a major library recently should do so.

But though many are capable of conducting much of their business at the speed of light, though they are wont to deal with vast stores of virtual information whose very existence is as ephemeral as an electric current, and though, through the agency of international telecommunications, they have been put veritably in touch with the world, one should not take leave of this discourse with the impression that libraries have evolved from the cloistered rooms of the medieval friaries to the user rooms of the computing centers of the 1970s, all terminals and a handful of dog-eared reference manuals in disarray on a table or stuffed into wall-mounted wire racks.

Notwithstanding the growth of full-text databases, the sources cited in the neatly composed bibliographies output by on-line search services are still predominantly printed documents. Behind, or to the side of, or above or below every circulation desk, and likewise for reference desks, one will continue for some time to find books — stacks upon stacks of them. Nor is there any near-term prospect for putting on-line the wealth of materials published prior to the age of machine-readable composition. Neither should we expect libraries to rush to put a terminal on every table. Those who long for the quiet alcove, the heft of a book, and the feel of its pages will continue to be accommodated throughout their lifetimes, and it is not unlikely that their children, too, will know books. If we allow that libraries have become horses from mules or eagles from owls, we should not lose sight, in crediting their speed or loft, of the fact that they are yet animals, and warm within.

Bibliographic Database Access Through the Microcomputer

A lready opened by some distributors to the individual user at a home computer, the door to the vast stores of bibliographic information variously maintained by the major bibliographic utilities, including OCLC, RLIN, and WLN, and commercial bibliographic database vendors, such as BRS, DIALOG, and SDC, is being pushed wider by a host of recently introduced software packages. Designed to take advantage of the inherent processing and storage capabilities of microcomputers, these *personal bibliographic systems* make it possible to search multiple bibliographic databases, download and store selected bibliographic information, and operate on it in a variety of ways — without forsaking the comfort of one's home or the familiarity of one's personal computer.

Although different packages emphasize different facets of the overall activity, and some leave certain functions, like file transfer and word processing, to interfaces with existing software, the systems share similar operating characteristics and equipment requirements. With most personal bibliographic systems, a user can expect to be able to:

• organize search strategies at the microcomputer level, thereby reducing the length and associated expense of the on-line connection to the search service;
• access and search any of the databases of supported search services;
• view retrieved citations on the microcomputer's video display, save them on disk, and/or print them;
• add the retrieved citations to a locally stored database in which they can subsequently be searched, edited, and organized into formatted bibliographies;
• print raw bibliographic information, selected citations, and/or formatted bibliographies on the attached printer.

The base of operations for most personal bibliographic systems is a database stored on a microcomputer's floppy or hard disk. One can expect to manage about one thousand citations in a floppy disk resident database, and as many as thirty thousand citations in a database that resides on a hard disk.

Databases associated with personal bibliographic systems typically provide local editing, search and retrieval, and formatting capabilities, and most are designed to accept both keyboarded entries and machine-readable citations transferred from compatible microcomputers or word processors, and/or downloaded from commercial databases or institutional mainframe computers. At least one is capable of capturing data directly from optical character scanners.

Manual entries into a personal bibliographic system's database are typically typed onto a full-screen menu. Transferred or downloaded data

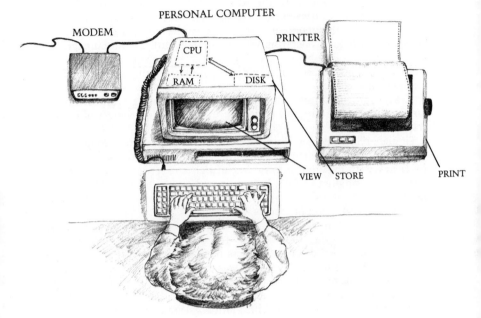

Figure 1: How personal bibliographic software systems work

(a) Personal bibliographic software is loaded into a microcomputer's random access memory (RAM) from disk. (b) This software enables a user to select a database to be searched and organize a search strategy on a microcomputer, and then dial the appropriate search service, log on to its computer, and transmit a formulated search request. By reducing the amount of time a user needs to remain connected to the search service's computer, the software reduces the charges that accumulate for the connection, as well as those assessed for use of the network while the connection is maintained. (c) The user's modem converts the digital representation of the search request produced by the microcomputer into analog signals that can be transmitted over voice-grade telephone lines into the sprawling telecommunications network. The signals might undergo several additional digital-to-analog (D-A) and analog-to-digital (A-D) conversions over the course of their trek through the network before a final A-D conversion in the search service's modem make them processable by the attached mainframe computer that holds its database. (d) Sophisticated retrieval software on the mainframe identifies appropriate citations in the database and creates images of these, which the computer transmits back to the user over the path whence the search request came. Arriving at the user's modem, the downloaded citations undergo a final A-D conversion that renders them processable by the microcomputer. (e) At this point, a user can view the citations on the microcomputer's display screen, preserve them on, or delete them from, disk, and/or print them, individually or altogether, in a variety of formats, on an attached printer. Downloaded citations can be accumulated in a personal database on the microcomputer's disk and augmented with citations keyed in manually. This database can be searched, edited, and used to generate reports independently of being connected to an on-line search service.

is usually brought into the database by a separate module and frequently requires some editing; both the structure of the data and the inherent reformatting capabilities of the database will bear on the amount.

Interaction with supported on-line search services is usually handled by another module, operating in conjunction with a communications program that is capable of recording on the microcomputer's disk the dialogue between the search service's computer and the microcomputer.

Some packages rely on, and others provide interfaces to, existing word processing programs for editing, formatting, and printing. Output formats can usually be customized by the user to conform to a variety of bibliographic styles.

Though relatively new things under the sun, personal bibliographic systems that run on personal computers are emerging from shadows that are heavy with experience in on-line search and retrieval. One of these systems is a product of BRS, one of the major resellers of bibliographic database access. Another was developed by an information brokering firm to expedite production of reports for its clients.

Increasingly sophisticated retrieval techniques being employed on the mainframe computers that contain the databases of the large bibliographic utilities and database vendors have combined with the growing capability of the microcomputer to spawn these pint-sized systems that boast a range of utility from managing a personal reprint file, through gathering references for research, to supporting the cataloging requirements of a small library or the information-gathering and reporting needs of a modest information brokering business. Personal bibliographic systems are part of a growing trend being driven by the ability of the minute central processing units of microcomputers to handle tasks of ever-greater volume and complexity.

12

Learning From the Technology or Learning With It:

Being a Brief History Of, and Inquiry Into, the Presence of Computers on Campuses

John Simon, 1985

A succession of rapid courtships finds several institutions of higher learning betrothed to one or another manufacturer of personal computers. Whether this introduction of machine genes will bring about fundamental changes in the progeny of such institutions — the clutches of learned youth they have spawned for more than eight centuries — will be determined, to some extent, by whether contemporary educators use computers or defer to them, on whether they promote "learning from the technology, or learning with it.

Take an apple to my teacher? But my teacher *is* an Apple. A cute remark, perhaps, this, but one which represents, to some ways of thinking, the worst possible case in the computers in education scenario.

Computer lineage

From antiquity (that is, approximately forty years ago), computers have served up facts and figures to those who input the requisite data. They have variously supplied solutions to complex equations; calculated means, averages, and percentiles for rows and columns of raw statistical data; printed pages upon pages of employee salary and benefit information for institutional administrations. Scientists, researchers, and administrative officials have learned from this material. The numbers they derive perhaps replace variables in yet other equations, or lend numerical support to theses presented in social science journals, or validate an institution's employee payroll. In all cases, a computer has proffered output from some set of input.

The distinction being pursued is subtle; the nature of learning *with* an instructor, *with* a fellow student, even *with* the printed works of a great thinker, is substantively different from what most often takes place with a computer. One can learn with the aid or help of a computer, but that is not the same thing as learning *with* it. The difference may not be reducible to anything more than the experience of thinking in the presence of another being, or some residue of one, that thinks, or thought, like one.

Most educational applications developed for computers to date have followed the input/output paradigm; they have been characterized by fixed and predictable exchanges between students and machines. The worry associated with the simplistic portrayal in the opening paragraph has to do with the fact that, by and large, computers are still input/output-oriented machines, machines that one can, in a way that is more than less rigid and formalized, learn *from*.

Contemporary computers, even those that incorporate elaborate configurations of parallel processors and are imbued with artificial intelligence of the highest sort, cannot create, empathize, intuit, or sense in any way related to the cognitive or emotional makeup of students. Indeed, one does learn *from* a human instructor, but one also, in ways that do not lend themselves to existing modes of quantification, learns *with* her or him.

The foregoing exercise in semantics is intended only to affirm that educational applications of computers are, as yet, bounded, not to diminish the value of what has been learned from computers. Business, government, industry, science, and society have, to varying degrees and in ways that range from subtle to revolutionary, changed as a result of knowledge gained from what has poured from the "mouths" of computers over the course of the past few decades.

To extrapolate a solution, however popular and cheap, to a problem that might be of a fundamentally different nature, entails a risk, not alone that the solution might prove ineffective, but that its attempted implementation might aggravate the problem. The computer has not slighted education; institutional research and administration were among its early benefactors. Nor was instruction slighted, although benefits thereto have been, to a great extent, discipline-specific. At risk in positing the computer — because it has proved efficacious in so many applications and is now inexpensive enough for individual ownership — as a general solution to myriad and long-standing problems associated with formalized education, is not alone the failure of the proposed solution, but the possible confounding of a process that is at best little understood.

Today's liaisons between educational institutions and computer manufacturers are brought about by the arrows of more than one Cupid; amid the flurry are shafts loosed by the Cupids of capital gain and institutional peer pressure, as well as by the Cupid of educational enhancement.

Because education at the primary and secondary levels is largely public and mandated, its purveyors are not obliged to recruit their charges. At the post-secondary level, however, the economic vitality of institutions in the business of providing education can be significantly affected by competition for students. Educational benefits need not be substantiated, but only perceived, to render the incorporation of computers into an institution's educational strategy an economically sound move.

If students, and those who their tuition, are affected as intended by the messages being promulgated by manufacturers — that computers can provide an educational advantage — colleges that, for reasons financial or otherwise, do not elect to be washed by this wave could find their admissions declining as students gravitate toward institutions whose shores it has strewn with the flotsam and jetsam of technology. That the messages are having the intended effect is evident in the increasing familiarity of elementary and high school students with computers, either purchased for them, at no trifling expense, by their parents, or made available by their schools through grants, taxes, or the fund-raising efforts of parents who do not want to place their children at risk by doubting the touted educational virtues of the machines.

Computers are not new to schools. As early as the 1950s, researchers at colleges and universities were using computers, at other institutions if their own did not possess one, to support scientific inquiries in such fields as chemistry, engineering, and mathematics. Then the computer was, like the electron microscope, an expensive and limited-application tool of research. Computing capability, because the equipment that delivered it was enormously expensive, was usually provided centrally and the expense shared among the departments and operating units that used it.

Generalization of the computer's utility beyond that of a high-speed solver of complex equations turned on its programmability; if different equations could be solved by writing different programs, then by writing yet other programs the computer could be applied to other numerically-based activities. With the birth of electronic data processing, the computer became a tool not only of accounting departments of businesses and corporations, but also of college and university administrations. Without forsaking its utility as a computational device, the computer entered the 1960s as a general-purpose "information processor."

The principal academic users of computers at this time were students in college engineering courses, who would keypunch computer programs into cards, drop them off at the campus computing center to be processed, along with dozens of other programs, on the institutional computer, and later pick them up together with pages of fan-folded, continuous-forms paper on which were printed the results of their programming efforts. This mode of interaction with a computer is termed *batch processing*.

Occurring during a period of heightened anxiety about the potential automation of much human endeavour and the reduction of human beings to numbers for purposes of storing and processing information about them, the nominal penetration of the campus by the computer in the early 1960s was protested by students at a number of universities, even to the point of bombing a number of computer rooms. Philosophical objections to the new technology, however, were gradually eroded by the computer's incredible efficiency coupled with an increased accessibility that served to diminish its apparent threat.

The earliest manifestation of decentralization, that is, putting the computer resource in the hands of its users, took the form of remote, self-service card readers. It was of the nature of a baby step compared to the reorientation, in the mid-1960s, around timeshared computing, by which many individuals are afforded simultaneous use of a centrally-located *mainframe*, or high-capacity computer, sans punched cards, by communicating with it interactively via remote, typewriter-like computer terminals.

These developments were enabled and supported by the increasing sophistication of computer *operating systems*, complex sets of programs that enable a computer to handle much of the low-level detail of its operation. An operating system, one or more *compilers* (e.g., FORTRAN, COBOL, etc.), and a number of *utilities* (i.e., programs for automating general tasks, such as sorting and copying of files) were usually bundled with computers sold during this time. Additional *applications* software (programs for automating specific tasks, such as solving scientific equations or processing accounting or payroll data) was available separately, either from computer manufacturers or from one of a growing number of

Figure 1: The evolution of computing on campuses

(I) In the beginning, computing was done behind closed doors. Those who wanted information from a computer or had problems for it to solve generally got no closer than a person at a counter who carried their problems or requests, as they had keypunched them into cards, into the computer room. (II) Remote computing established access points to a central computer outside of the room that contained it. Common by the late 1960s were remote card readers that enabled users to read their own cards into computers that were located elsewhere, cabled to the readers from other rooms or even other buildings. (III) Card decks are queued, or batched, by a computer and processed sequentially as a series of jobs. By contrast, time-sharing, which began to appear in the late 1960s and early 1970s, allowed multiple users operating typewriter-like terminals to interact seemingly simultaneously

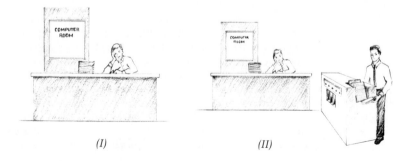

(I)   *(II)*

"software houses" (firms that specialize in writing and marketing applications software for a variety of common applications). Fed by the latter, the base of applications software expanded rapidly leading, by the late 1960s, to litigation against computer manufacturers that resulted in the unbundling of computers and software.

Successive generations of computers, each with capabilities manyfold greater than their immediate predecessors, held promise for automating more and more scientific and administrative activities, and programming blossomed as the profession through which the creation of the requisite applications programs was realized.

From a time in the very early evolutionary stirrings of computers, when some among those associated with their development were led to speculate that a dozen or so machines would saturate the world market, it had become exceedingly apparent that computers were destined to proliferate far beyond such expectations. Fields of study associated with the further understanding and application of computers melded into a new discipline — computer science. Its subject matter consisted of such elements as: computer architecture (the study of the application and performance of computer systems from the perspective of their underlying structure); numerical methods, (the mathematical substantiation of the computational approaches used in computing); and artificial intelligence, (the realization of characteristics usually associated with human intelligence — such as language comprehension, problem-solving, learning, and reasoning — in machines).

with a central computer. At first, terminals were cabled directly to computers and batch and timesharing processing was usually done alternately. Later computers handled both kinds of processing simultaneously, and the development of modems and other telecommunications devices enabled terminals to be located anywhere they could access telephone lines. (IV) With the proliferation of micro, or personal, computers, in the 1980s, computing retreated back into the computer room, but the computer room can now be a dormitory room, a bedroom, even an ample closet. Miniaturization of the computer and its quarters notwithstanding, much of what has gone before remains. At many institutions, strategies for taking central computing facilities into the personal computing era are being formulated within earshot of the hum and drone of traditional computer room sounds, occasionally punctuated, even yet, by the primal chatter of a card reader.

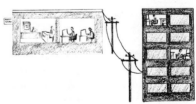

(III)   *(IV)*

By the end of the 1970s, library ordering systems, statistical packages, and collections of routines for solving sets of complex equations in chemistry, engineering, and other sciences had joined the manifold applications that programmers were employed in the creation, maintenance, and refinement of. Text processing, a mainframe-based version and antecedent of word processing, had begun to elicit interest in the capabilities of central computers in non-traditional quarters. During the 1970s, the numbers of adventuresome faculty in college and university liberal arts departments petitioning their computing centers for computer terminals and timesharing accounts increased significantly.

For fully two decades, provision of computing was marked by an ebb and flow of such issues as centralization versus decentralization, and consolidation versus separation, of academic and administrative computing facilities, and by debates over whether computing should be provided in the library tradition, as a "free" service, or charged back as in the bookstore model, either directly to students in the manner of lab fees, or to the academic departments offering courses that make use of the computer.

In general, computing centers encouraged diversified use of their equipment. As the further sophistication of operating systems, applications programs, and computer terminals combined to make connected mainframe computers more tractable, the number of users multiplied.

Although their designation as "mainframes" gave central computers an aura of unlimited capacity, in fact, there were limits, reached with increasing frequency over time, to how much processing such computers could handle. Considerations relative to making significant upgrades to equipment in-place and/or seeking replacement machines of still more behemoth proportions, became standard fare for computing center administrators. It was at this juncture that academic and administrative computing, at those institutions where they had grown up together, often parted company, with a new machine being acquired for one or the other, thereby reducing the load on the extant computer. Meanwhile, decentralization had rounded another corner with the advent of minicomputers, relatively modestly-priced systems of modest capacity that enabled some departments to satisfy their computing requirements independently of the institutional computing center.

Yet, for all their increasing presence, and increasing drain on institutional budgets, computers contributed little to the mainstream academic mission of colleges and universities. Not that the idea that computers could be used to teach had not occurred to anyone. Plato, a computer-based teaching system developed at the University of Illinois and marketed by Control Data Corporation, was in use in the very early 1960s but, in part because it relied on expensive, special-purpose equipment and employed a complex authoring language for development of programmed instruction, it never became the widespread teaching phenomenon that some had forecast.

With computerized instruction more or less a laboratory activity, the computer of the 1960s and early 1970s, despite its increasing costs and use, and though indispensable for what it did, was to the administration little more than an automated set of books and files; to the scientific and research communities, an impressive calculator; to the computer science curriculum, the object of a course of study; and to the rest of the academic community that availed itself of it, a replacement for the venerable typewriter.

Those who argued for free, or "open," access to the computer chose a good analogy in the library. As traditionally employed by academics at colleges and universities, the computer, like the library, has been an important and useful adjunct to the educational mission. Like the library, it has been "over there," a place one goes on occasion when an assignment warrants. Also like the library, it has been both more intimidating to some students than to others, and more useful to some than to others. As some students have successfully completed college without ever visiting the library, so, today, students graduate without ever tapping on the keyboard of a terminal or a personal computer.

There is another aspect of the library analogy that is germane. In an era in which an "information explosion" is said to be taking place, libraries are hard-pressed to keep pace because of physical and logistical constraints. So, too, as latent demand for each new application of the computer surfaced, capacity was quickly exhausted. Getting time on timeshared computers became a major frustration for all concerned. Faculty who could do without the computer often did; those who wanted or needed access to it for their students either limited the amount of work that required such access or pressed for priority use for their students, and computing center administrators became computing center arbitrators, whose time not spent mediating among committees variously representing the interests of the academic, administrative, and research communities (for which, it was becoming apparent, there could never be enough computer resources) was devoted to plying their systems programmers for creative new ways to divide and prioritize available resources and to negotiating with their institutional administrations for funds for more of the same.

That some small part of the overburden bringing timesharing computers to their collective knees around the late 1970s and early 1980s was relief for libraries is another story (told, in part, in "The late, great handshake of libraries and technology"). Relief for the timesharing computer operated by the campus computing facility came from within its own cadre — the microcomputer that had been a project of electrical engineering students and a toy of home electronics enthusiasts during the early 1970s came of age just in time to allay the woes of its precursor.

A computer in every dormitory room?

Although year by year, micro, or personal, computers have grown increasingly powerful (that is, have become capable of processing more information faster, and storing it in ever greater quantities), their principal application in the educational environment has been, and continues to be, in writing, or, as reduced to its computational equivalent by the computer community, "word processing." It is a matter of curiosity that this application, one of but a few whose educational value shows some promise of being demonstrable, fell into disfavor when things got tight on central timesharing computers; some computing centers considered word processing non-essential work and severely restricted, or even totally banned, it during periods of peak use.

Personal computers have put this application, along with a number of others, including instructional computer programming, into the hands of individual students. To the extent that a school's students have, or have access to, personal computers, the pressure on computing centers to make value judgements regarding the legitimacy or relative worth of applications on their timesharing computers is reduced. Instead, such centers can get on with the business of their own further evolution, for the personal computer, despite its amazingly rapid proliferation, is not the be-all and end-all of computing. There are still many tasks that require machines of the proportions of contemporary mainframes; indeed, there are computationally complex research tasks for which even mainframes must defer to a class of machine that is larger still, the scarce — but equally essential for what it does — supercomputer.

Even as personal computers relieve their larger siblings of some of the routine tasks for which users have traditionally been required to contend, they make other, and often novel, demands not only on central computers but on the support staffs of the computing centers that operate them. Both centralized storage for purposes of backing up microcomputer-resident data and file service for distributing and collecting assignment-related data for academic courses require networking capability significantly more sophisticated and reliable than was called for to support hosts of timesharing computer terminals. Many users of personal computers, being former, and perhaps still occasional, timesharing users turn quite naturally to computing center staff for help with, and advice on, personal computer-related matters. Their abetting influence notwithstanding, personal computers are engendering service and support needs that many computing centers are finding they cannot meet with existing resources and within existing budgets.

The potential pervasiveness of the personal computer derives directly from its self sufficiency. Computer terminals could not have effected so wholesale an occupation of student dormitories as personal computers have on some campuses because of limitations in the number of *ports*, or points of entry, on central timesharing computers; the number of simultaneous users that even the largest such systems can support is in the low hundreds. Although most personal computers can be used as terminals into timesharing computers, such use is ancillary to their ability to function as stand-alone computers.

While personal computers haven't the full power of contemporary timesharing computers, because most students can do on them most everything they would have occasion to do on an institutional machine, the personal computer creates a potential for doing what was just a few years ago unimagineable — providing each student with not only access to a computer, but the computer itself.

Personal computers have become as affordable as good second-hand cars or first-rate stereo systems. But just as cars and stereo systems are not in every college student's budget, so neither might a several thousand dollar personal computer be. Schools are helping; in addition to procuring discounted computers for students, some are taking computer purchases into consideration when assembling financial aid packages. Others are helping students to arrange for low-interest loans from outside lending institutions. It is fitting that they do so; a computer purchase is overburden for a student, not fill for an expense that has been eliminated. Students are still required to buy books, to pay laboratory fees, etc. Now, additionally, they are being asked to subsidize the cost of providing computing from which, admittedly, they are expected to derive some educational benefit.

Notwithstanding that a machine equivalent in capability to what an institution might have struggled to pay for a decade ago is now affordable by an individual, the total cost of providing institutional computing has gone up. The plummeting cost of hardware has been offset by the rising cost of software development and a vastly increased use computers, and sellers, as well as buyers, of the machines are being driven to some creative reassessments.

Having successfully put its computer on a sliver of silicon and packaged it in a box that can sell for several thousand, instead of several hundred thousand, dollars, a manufacturer finds that time becomes an expensive commodity; unlike mainframes, which can warrant weeks, or even months, of sales effort, personal computers can be afforded only minutes if their sale is to yield a profit. If a high volume of sales can be generated by conceding substantial discounts in that few minutes, because the resulting penetration might help a vendor to establish itself in the educational marketplace and breed loyalty for its products in the students who use them, the vendor might exchange a short term loss for longerterm profitability. The institution that negotiates such a discount is coping with the rising cost of providing computing by reducing the cost of doing so if it makes the machines available directly, and by redeploying some of the expense if it resells them to students.

The ultimate cost of promoting the proliferation of personal computers, and of providing the centralized services, underlying network facility, and logistical and human support necessitated by their proliferation, will not be known for some time. For now, it is generally considered that personal computers are affordable by students, and that students should be encouraged to acquire them. Indeed, many who arrive at college today bring with them personal computers acquired while they were in high school.

But though it be capable of putting into the hands of each student all of the capability that most ever demand from a timesharing computer, in a package that is much easier to use and far more available, will the personal computer revolutionize education? We noted earlier that the most frequently used application of personal computers is word processing. Have we simply altered our earlier analogy, substituted for the lofty library the utilitarian typewriter and correspondingly denigrated the value of the proliferating personal computer?

As a writing "medium" — and that, to date, has been its most widespread academic application — the personal computer has many advantages over traditional implements of the craft. Software has been developed that can analyze grammar and sentence structure and advise writers of potentially awkward or inappropriate constructions, that can perform word counts that might alert writers to overused words, and that can proffer substitutes for multi-syllabic and compound words. Such software lends a faint lumination to the horizon. It is not, however, the software being used by the great multitudes of personal computer users; theirs is a conventional, and far more rudimentary, kind of word processing software that is as darkness to it. A glorious dawn is portended but, withal, the use of the computer to *teach* writing must, like every other application of the computer to the teaching of complex subject matter, await significant further developments in the field of artificial intelligence.

For the present, as applied to writing, the personal computer is at best a great facilitator. By eliminating the need to retype the bulk of altered text, it reduces resistance to revision. Resistance overcome, the writer finds in personal computer word processing software the greatest boon to revision since scissors and tape. Without affecting the original manuscript, an author can effect everything from a subtle refinement of a single sentence to a wholesale reorganization of a lengthy text by rearranging the transitory images — of words, sentences, paragraphs — on a video display screen. The author can then read the reordered material through, alter it further if desired, and repeat the process ad infinitum, all the while preserving the original intact.

Although one can make a xerographic copy of a typed or handwritten manuscript handily enough, in the cutting apart and rearranging of it, scissors work one's hand much harder at the word and sentence levels, and tape becomes increasingly intractable with each iteration. Further, with a typewriter one must sit down at the machine, set margins, tabs, etc., and then commence hammering away at the keys to effect the transformation from draft to finished manuscript (or pay someone to do it for one). A word processor, given access to a compact, electronic version of a draft manuscript, needs only to be instructed as to the parameters of the final format — margins, lines per page, etc. — into which it will flow the copy like so much gelatin into a mold. This, too, it will do over and over again, to varying specifications and the ultimate satisfaction of the writer. In addition, most contemporary word processing packages are provided with a *dictionary* (computer vendor vernacular for "word list") against which it can compare the words in a manuscript for the purpose of checking spelling.

Does such utility make students better writers? Certainly, there is no inspirational component to word processing software. It cannot comment upon the meaning that derives from the arrangement and rearrangement of words that it so ably facilitates, nor can it discourse on the nature of the art of writing. The making of a writer is still a thing that is achieved by an individual, perhaps with the guidance and encouragement of another individual. For the present, the virtue of word processing has to do with the mechanical aspects of writing, with the physical acts of writing or typing, revising and reorganizing, formatting and reformatting. A blank video display screen is no more inspiring, and every bit as intimidating, as a blank piece of paper in a typewriter or under a pencil or a pen. Word processing cannot make a student a better writer but it can make it easier for a student to become a better writer.

Such utility might be worthy, but it is not the stuff of which marriages between institutions of higher learning and major corporations, some attended by multi-million dollar dowries, are made. There must be, and, in fact, are, greater expectations for the role of the computer in higher education.

Such expectations are held by colleges and universities that have established institution-wide computer literacy requirements, as fifteen thousand student Southwestern Michigan University and thirteen hundred student Alverno College in Wisconsin have, by schools that have instituted curricular changes that have led them to require, or strongly encourage, every incoming student to purchase a recommended personal computer as the Stevens Institute of Technology in New Jersey, and the Harvard Graduate School of Business Administration have, and by institutions that have allied themselves with one or more of the major manufacturers of personal computers in cooperative ventures involving very large sums of money and significant commitments of corporate and institutional staff and resources, as Brown University in Rhode Island, Carnegie-Mellon University in Pennsylvania, and the Massachusetts Institute of Technology have.

These schools are merely representative of a widespread perception among institutions of higher learning that the role of computer-related technology in education is going to become increasingly important and fundamental. When college administrators talk about computer technology and tomorrow's students they are referring, quite literally, to the students who will be enrolling tomorrow; the students who enrolled yesterday are the guinea pigs of today's technology. The situation reflects, quite simply, the fast pace of development in the computer industry.

Taking advantage of the baby computer boom

The investments that educational institutions are today making in computing are, to a large extent, proportional to their historical investments in computing. Those institutions that strove to provide the greatest base of computer hardware and to encourage the broadest possible access to it were the ones most often beleaguered by demand; major upgrades and banks of additional disk drives and terminals spelled mainframe time-sharing computers for as much as a year or two at first, then for but a few months.

Institutions coped with saturation of computing facilities, which was a way of life at many of them before the microcomputer was even a gleam in an engineer's eye, by periodically infusing large sums of money into equipment upgrades, by scheduling or restricting access, by charging back rigorously for use, or by some combination of these approaches. That these same institutions, when it came of age, should have sought succor from the personal computer is not surprising.

Dartmouth College in Hanover, New Hampshire, is one institution that did so. Dartmouth's tack through the choppy seas of personal computing is altered little from that which bore it across the undulating swells of timesharing. Albeit slight, the alteration — which has to do primarily with cables and the nature of the traffic through, and physical connections to, them — is significant.

A pioneer in providing timeshared computing, and of the library parallel of free or open access, Dartmouth began to feel the hard pinches of space and dollars in the late 1970s. The problems have been alluded to earlier: demand was exceeding capacity; space in which to locate additional terminals, which would increase the load upon, and necessitate upgrades to, the College's mainframe, was wanting; the costs of the upgrades, terminals, and space were becoming prohibitive. With a long

Figure 2: Timesharing versus . . . a distributed network

(I) Once upon a timesharing paradigm, computers were sliced up like great pies and those who wanted a piece of one queued up for it. Networks, like kitchen tables, were utilitarian things intended to accommodate only as many people as there were pieces of computer pie. (II) The coming of the personal computer afforded individuals an opportunity to have their own individual pies. This reduced demand on, but not the need for, great pies, leading many institutions to tack on extensions to their kitchen table networks, and others to build, or buy, banquet table networks that can seat entire institutional hosts, enabling those sharing great pies to sit down with those eating their own individual ones.

tradition of timesharing, and with attendant miles of wire and cable that had snaked through the campus, Dartmouth was already a largely "wired" college.

Recognizing that the evolving personal computer would soon overtake timesharing as the unquestionably most effective means for providing academic computing, Dartmouth decided, in the early 1980s, to make intentional the inevitable crossover.

Among the centrally-supported services available to users of Dartmouth's timesharing system were an on-line catalog of the holdings of the College library and an electronic mail system. Access to these resources would have to be preserved in any extensive shift from timesharing to personal computing. This could be accomplished by ensuring that students' personal computers possessed the ability to function as terminals into the timesharing system and by providing the necessary network connection to enable them to do so.

Dartmouth considered its institutional role in precipitating the shift from timesharing to personal computing to be to identify considerations such as distinctions between centrally- and locally-supportable services; to retain responsibility for maintaining, enhancing, and increasing access to, the former; and to make recommendations regarding appropriate complements of equipment for the latter. The College's first conclusion was that a student-owned computer should possess: 1) sufficient capability to do locally much of what can be done on its timeshared computers, and 2) the ability to communicate as a terminal to do the rest. Expectations for a machine's local capabilities included word processing, graphics, and BASIC-language programming, and its remote capabilities, personal computer-to-personal computer and personal computer-to-timesharing computer communications.

Precursor to the widespread introduction of personal computers at Dartmouth was a small-scale introduction of International Business Machines Corporation (IBM) PC personal computers to the Amos Tuck School of Business Administration, which already had a bank of teaching materials on the Dartmouth timesharing system used by all first year, and some second year, students. Although no purchase requirement was established when the PCs were introduced, approximately forty percent of incoming Business School students acquired one. Subsequently, on the College's recommendation, approximately eighty percent of Dartmouth's incoming freshmen acquired an Apple Macintosh personal computer.

For its part, the College commissioned the writing of software that would enable the Macintosh to be operated as a terminal into the timesharing system and undertook to extend the wiring of the campus, which already ran to almost every academic and administrative office, into the dormitory buildings with a network tap per desk or bed, as the case might be. To achieve the wide range of personal computer-to-personal computer and personal computer-to-timesharing computer communications it considered necessary, Dartmouth implemented a variety of networking protocols, including asynchronous, Appletalk, X.25, and Ethernet.

The College's long experience with computing is perhaps responsible for the exceedingly practical, albeit informal, projection of the completion of the network by the turn of the century. The flexibility being built into it is a conscious hedge against the inevitable shifts and developments that can occur over so protracted a period.

By its dictionary definition, technology was spawned with the first application of science to the furtherance of some human endeavour. Its root system is extensive, and even if we look only at what is above ground — what the scientific leaps and bounds of recent history have thrust up and spread over us — our gaze cannot be contained in the twentieth century. Institutionalized study of technology, for example, harkens back to the previous century, the year 1870 marking the founding of the Stevens Institute of Technology, one of the original private institutions devoted to the study of technology in the United States.

The Stevens curriculum having broadened, over its history, from mechanical engineering to include other engineering disciplines, science, management, and computer science, its early appropriation of, and growing reliance upon, computers is consonant with its institutional raison d'etre. That Stevens faculty had concluded that use of computers in engineering was altering in a fundamental way engineering practice was reflected in the adoption of a revised core curriculum in the late 1970s. Convinced that a new cognitive style for problem solving, analysis, and design in engineering was being engendered by increasing utilization of computers, but convinced as well that the curriculum could not accommodate additional courses to provide students with the requisite grounding in computers, Stevens engineering faculty moved to make computing an integral part of the engineering student's undergraduate experience.

The approach was intended to make computing pervasive and to beget in students a level of understanding and appreciation that Stevens termed computer "fluency." As distinguished from computer literacy, computer fluency has as its objective to impart to students the following attributes:

- a natural inclination to turn to the computer when appropriate and to interact comfortably with it;
- the ability to identify capabilities and limitations of computer systems and software;
- the ability to develop higher-level language programs for significant engineering problems;
- competence in implementing professional techniques, including numerical methods, modeling, simulation, computer graphics, data acquisition, and process control.

Because timesharing was still the predominant mechanism for delivering computing services when Stevens embarked on this course, its campaign to foster widespread computer fluency was promptly run aground by saturation of resources. At Stevens, as at so many other institutions that promoted academic computing, the all-too-consistent theme of utilization outstripping hardware expansion was played out. The Stevens response was a counterpoint that is increasingly being picked up by other institutions.

In making ownership of an Atari 800 personal computer with tape drive and television monitor requisite for the eighty students entering its Science, Management, and Computer Science programs in the fall of 1982, Stevens became the first college in the country to establish a personal computer requirement. The following year, extension of the requirement to the engineering program, with its need for a professional engineering workstation-equivalent, led to the Digital Equipment Corporation (DEC) Professional 325 being designated as the required machine.

In addition to negotiating special pricing for required computers, Stevens further sought to keep student costs down by establishing a computer peripheral center that provides access to a handful of DEC Professional and Atari computers with attached printers and serves as a point of transfer for data, programs, and assignments from faculty to student floppy disks.

In ways both similar and different, the Milwaukee Area Technical College is providing another genre of education in technology (Tucker 1983-84, 34-36). Engaged in the training of technicians rather than professionals, the College recruits its student body from the ranks of those laid off by old-line industries and those who must adapt to retain their jobs in growing, and changing, companies, as well as from the graduating classes of high schools.

Like the Stevens Institute of Technology, the Milwaukee Area Technical College expects its students to derive substantive benefits from their interaction with the devices of technology. According to the latter, in contemporary industry,

> the greatest need is for the "super tech," who can install, operate, maintain, and repair systems that may incorporate combinations of electrical motors, digital circuits, mechanisms, hydraulic actuators, lenses, light sources, and transducers. Many of these systems are controlled by microcomputers and are part of huge computerized databases requiring persons skilled in information management, including documentation development, storage, retrieval, and decision making.

The College regards its mission to be to insure that persons with the requisite interdisciplinary skills and knowledge to serve this need emerge.

Unlike Stevens, the Milwaukee Area Technical College relies heavily on institutionally-owned equipment acquired largely through aggressive pursuit of partnerships with area industries. Individual pieces of equipment supplied to the College by various of its industrial partners have ranged in value from one hundred thousand to more than one million dollars. In return for their beneficence, representative technical employers from the industries are invited to participate in a steering committee charged with reviewing, and making recommendations on, the relevance of the College's curriculum and the effectiveness of the training it is delivering.

Industry observations constitute only a part of the College's broad evaluation scheme, which also includes specific measurements, as of the efficiency of student workstation scheduling, common assessments, as those made by faculty regarding improvements in the teaching of scientific and engineering principles, and reviews of bodies of data, ranging from annual enrollment statistics, through student achievement and course completion surveys, to follow-up surveys conducted post-employment.

Whether on a professional or a technical track, students of technology, in the course of their continuing relationship with it, can expect to have to use the devices of technology as well as understand them. The places that school such students most effectively will provide them with both theoretical comprehension and practical operational skills, weighted according to the perceptions of their institutional missions. Thus, at the Stevens Institutes of Technology and Milwaukee Area Technical Colleges of this country, computers and other devices of our so-called hi-tech society are, to varying degrees, both a means and an end.

At other institutions, in other disciplines, we can find computers employed in another way, as means to ends that are only tangentially, or not at all, related to the technology that occasioned them. An example, selected from many possible others, follows.

In 1980, Dr. Donald Thursh, at the University of Illinois College of Medicine, initiated a project aimed at breathing life into a textbook of pathology (ibid., 32-33). Dr. Thursh's earliest work on The Living Textbook of Pathology was carried out on a mainframe computer using the PLATO system. The object of the work was to produce a knowledge-base that could be used widely by medical schools whose particular faculties could regulate student access to it and modify or replace with locally-authored versions such parts of it as they wished.

The original implementation, which accumulated several thousands of hours of student use over a five-year period, provided for all of the following:

- Constructing author-specified outlines of information;
- Displaying this information in discrete units called frames;
- Accepting and displaying student comments and questions in context;
- Marking places in the text for future study;
- Linking learning objectives and references to specific text;
- A source of preparation of hard copies of standard linear text;
- Segregating information (knowledge-base) from system (managing programs);
- Using a simple command language by knowledge-base authors;
- Flexibly accepting new programs to support authoring functions.

Experience with the original implementation, coupled with such new developments as powerful personal computers and enhanced videodisc interfaces, led Dr. Thursh to undertake a reimplementation aimed at making the user interface "friendlier" to first-time users and making the overall structure of the system more apparent to users (Thursh 1985, 402-406). Called KAMES (for Knowledge Access Management and Extension System), the newer implementation of the on-line pathology textbook, begun on a DEC VAX 11/780 minicomputer and later adapted to run on a Cadmus 9000 series microcomputer, is intended to generalize its applicability from undergraduate studies to postgraduate and continuing professional education. To date, the redesign effort has yielded a system that is: 1) capable of supporting both systematic study of a large body of subject matter by beginning students and directed inquiries by more sophisticated learners, and 2) capable of running on increasingly smaller computers. A version that will run on an IBM PC-AT has performed student-oriented system operations in a manner comparable to that in which they are performed by versions that run on VAX and Cadmus computers, and a version that runs on the less-powerful PC-XT has successfully performed all tested operations, albeit with some degradation as compared with larger machines. A version that will run on an upgraded Apple Macintosh personal computer is eventually expected.

Among the 1.8 Megabytes of machine-interpretable information that comprised the KAMES system in February of 1985 are some twenty thousand lines of text suitable for viewing by other academic pathologists. A related demonstration videodisc contains about twenty-five hundred color illustrations from the teaching collection of the Illinois College of Medicine at Urbana-Champaign and from the personal collection of Dr. Thursh.

Future development will be directed at imbuing the system with sophisticated capabilities — derived from applications of artificial intelligence — for automatically propagating changes throughout the knowledge-base, for controlling inadvertent redundancy within it, for automatically cross-referencing frames that are logical parts of more than one hierarchy, and for making English language access easier and more flexible. Ultimately, the system is expected to be able to take on the role of a collaborator in research by postulating relationships unnoticed by the content expert, and to evaluate the completeness of knowledge bases and ask content experts for missing information. Underway is an effort the put the system in touch with established bibliographic databases, such as MEDLINE, in order to facilitate literature searches. This work is consistent with the overall direction of the system; according to Dr. Thursh:

> Our long-range vision for KAMES is a mini-library of biomedical science, "staffed" by a small but efficient expert system in lieu of a human librarian. It will include textbooks of anatomic and clinical pathology, basic biomedical science, and the major clinical specialties, and a user-directed abstracts service plus whatever available on-line journals are desired — all of which will be "aware" of each other's contents and able to access each other as readily as they access themselves. The library will also have an extensive audio-visual section that will be fully and automatically indexed through its textbooks and journals.

Besides students and teachers, interns, physicians, and medical researchers might be expected to use and augment the text of KAMES. Growing and changing thus, it will truly be a "body" of knowledge.

Choosing partners

The "marriages" alluded to earlier occur when an institution undertakes to make the personal computer ubiquitous and to wire the campus so that each can, if it wants to, communicate with any other as well as with any of the institution's shared computing facilities. For so leviathan an undertaking an institution needs not just a mate, but a very particular mate.

Like Dartmouth College, Carnegie-Mellon University evolved an extensive network of timeshared computing (Tucker 1983-84, 3-10). Third-ranked among private universities in total dollar volume of industrial research, Carnegie-Mellon — with a tradition of emphasizing maximum access to computing resources for students, researchers, and computer scientists — held a leadership position in computing as it entered the 1980s. But resources and leadership notwithstanding, Carnegie-Mellon faced the same stark reality that confronted so many other institutions — that to provide sufficient computing capability to every member of the University community under the timesharing model was becoming prohibitively expensive. Although Carnegie-Mellon, too, would embrace networked personal computers as the solution to its computing dilemma, it began by seeking what its President, Richard Cyert, described as "a broadly based view and a sense of perspective about where we want to go."

Before focusing on hardware, Carnegie-Mellon assessed its existing and desired states. Working from the assumption that computing is fundamentally good for it, the University discovered that major attributes of an optimally operating timesharing system continue to have relevance, for example, enough terminals (workstations), generally adequate response times, sufficient storage, and quick and convenient printing.

Inasmuch as growth would inevitably have to accommodate a mix of large and medium-size computers required to support services with high-volume storage requirements, as well as terminals and stand-alone workstations for the bulk of local uses, extension and refinement of, and simplification of access to, an underlying communication network were deemed essential.

An information system of sufficient scope to index the profusion of computing resources available to the university community was also deemed necessary, as was access to appropriate databases and to relevant and well-conceived documentation and human consultation.

Carnegie-Mellon suspects the computer of having a potential for educational usefulness that approximates, and might someday rival, that of the book, but it also suspects that it has a greater potential than the book to get in the way of education if used inappropriately or if access is difficult or use is perceived to be tedious or time-consuming. The University regards many existing educational uses of the computer as demonstrated, including, among others: management of education, as in scheduling and grading; display of information in classrooms; application to writing, in general, and composition, in particular; numerical analysis in data-rich disciplines such as social science and computation-rich fields such as engineering; tutorial delivery in drill-and-practice domains, such as music and language training; simulation of all manner of complex systems.

Carnegie-Mellon's interpretation of "computer literacy," like that of the Stevens Institute of Technology, stresses fluency. Anticipating that the overwhelming majority of users of computing will be consumers, not writers, of programs, it focuses on promoting competence with available tools, such as electronic mail, word processing, simulation, and statistical packages, and computer-aided-design and database systems. Underlying these skills should be an appreciation for what constitutes the appropriate application of them, and underlying that, an elementary understanding of what a computer can and cannot do. The University regards student competence with institutional computing facilities, of which network access is a fundamental component, to be a matter of practical exigence.

Although it anticipates that the computer will have an increasingly profound effect on the nature of education, Carnegie-Mellon expects use to be diverse and extremely uneven and supports the primacy of the role of the teacher in determining how best to educate.

As the computer becomes more integral to the delivery of education, reliability of the institutional framework of computing resources becomes more crucial. Carnegie-Mellon contrasts the replaceability and interchangeability of conventional educational facilities — such as classrooms, books, pens, and paper — with the computer.

Although acknowledging that the personal computer's infiltration of academic life must be attended by questions of a social nature, Carnegie-Mellon suspects that the most significant and profound of these might not be anticipated. While it waits for them to emerge, the University will ponder questions whose broad apprehension renders them seemingly intuitive. Answers posited to many of these questions, like the Roman god Janus, face in two directions at once. Overreliance or overindulgence might be limiting; a readiness to adapt everything to the problem-solving methodologies of the computer could lead a student to allow personal skills and abilities to atrophy. Yet, as it becomes, like the telephone and television before it, an accoutrement of daily life, the computer, even when used obsessively, might pose no more threat to an individual than those other household contrivances.

Among other questions are those that are seemingly antithetical one to another. Some fear that computers might violate students' desirable or rightful privacy, intruding on already crowded living space and/or opening students, through their machines and the data thereby contributed to and withdrawn from "the network," to unrestrained scrutiny by faculty and university officials. Others worry that pervasiveness of the personal computer will lead to student isolation by reducing the need for, and denigrating the role of, direct interpersonal contact.

Figure 3: A personal computer . . .

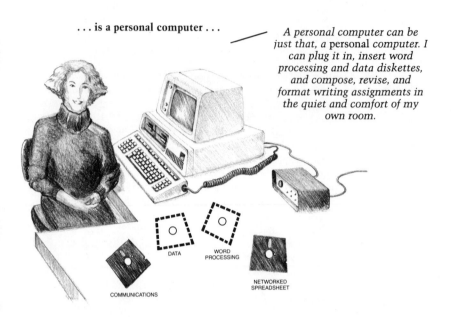

. . . is a personal computer . . .

A personal computer can be just that, a personal computer. I can plug it in, insert word processing and data diskettes, and compose, revise, and format writing assignments in the quiet and comfort of my own room.

DATA

WORD PROCESSING

NETWORKED SPREADSHEET

COMMUNICATIONS

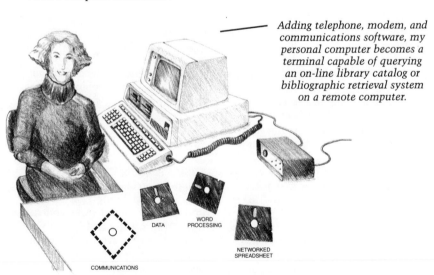

. . . is a computer terminal . . .

Adding telephone, modem, and communications software, my personal computer becomes a terminal capable of querying an on-line library catalog or bibliographic retrieval system on a remote computer.

DATA

WORD PROCESSING

NETWORKED SPREADSHEET

COMMUNICATIONS

. . . is a distributed processor . . .

Unlike a terminal, my personal computer can send information to, and retrieve it from, other computers; it can, for example, send text files to a typesetting computer or process stored information after disconnecting from the source computer.

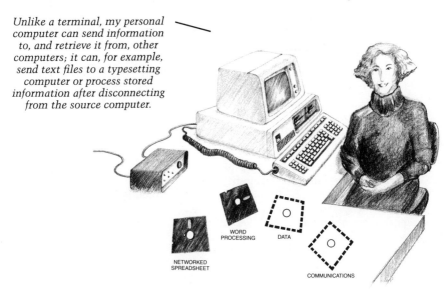

. . . is a networked workstation . . .

Networked software allows my computer to dynamically access information stored in another computer; a networked spreadsheet program, for example, can manipulate data in a remote computer and display the results on my personal computer screen.

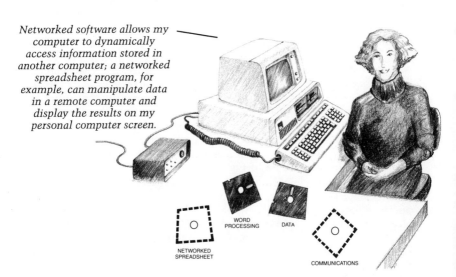

Having taken stock of itself and its mission, and taken under advisement such issues of implementation as could be identified, Carnegie-Mellon purposed to reshape its computing resource around a sophisticated telecommunications network capable of supporting easily initiated interconnections among and between the primary computing resource, distributed among the entire University community in the form of powerful workstations, and larger, centrally- or departmentally-administered computers. A comprehensive formal proposal sent to several major corporations in 1980 asked for:

> (a) funding for a software development center, (b) equipment and/or financial support to implement an advanced prototype environment at Carnegie-Mellon University, and (c) a commitment for a complementary development effort within the company.

Its interest piqued, IBM announced, in 1981, a six-month engagement during which it undertook a joint feasibility study with, and quartered a small staff at, Carnegie-Mellon. The two subsequently consummated the relationship and work toward the realization of the University's computing environment of the 1980s is proceeding apace. In addition, Carnegie-Mellon has allied itself with some fifteen other universities in a consortium whose intended purpose is to promote the development of useful educational software and the sharing of networked personal computer applications.

Brown University, a liberal arts college in Rhode Island, also established a compact with IBM (ibid., 11-17).

Brown's computing background is comparable to those of other institutions that have sought liaisons with major corporations. It shares the dual tradition that has proved to be self-defeating at so many; providing as much computing resource as possible, and promoting the institution-wide access to, and use of, the resource that inevitably consume it. Like others that have attempted to make computing pervasive, Brown has faced the declining prospects for timesharing to meet, in an affordable way, the exploding demand that its computing policies has engendered.

Like Carnegie-Mellon, Brown University was possessed of an extensive telecommunications network when it began deliberating the future of computing on its campus. Dubbed BRUNET, Brown's broadband network, in 1982, consisted of some fourteen hundred ports in one hundred and thirty-five buildings, which originated traffic variously related to energy management, security, television, and high-speed, terminal-to-mainframe timeshared computing.

But unlike Carnegie-Mellon's efforts, which reflect that school's technical orientation, activity at Brown has achieved a utilization of computers across a broader range of academic disciplines. The School had already, for example, employed an innovative technique, based on a concept evolved by Theodor Nelson, in both poetry and energy management courses. Called "hypertext," the technique consists of related bodies of text joined by predefined links. As used in the poetry course, hypertext enabled students to call up simultaneously on a screen, with a couple of keystrokes, a stanza of poetry and attendant professorial critique. The work of another critic, cited in the latter, could additionally be called up, and personal comments of the student entered in and appropriately linked, with equal facility.

Like Carnegie-Mellon and Dartmouth, Brown saw in the networked workstation model a way to preserve the positive aspects of timesharing (primarily inter-user communication and access to centrally-supported services) while eliminating its negative characteristics (periodic exhaustion of the computer's capacity by increased demand). In addition, workstations can afford students capabilities, such as real-time graphics and animations, that are impractical to implement on timesharing computers. As early as 1982, Brown's Department of Computer Science had initiated an experiment in which students in introductory computer science courses were afforded access to a laboratory of sophisticated Apollo workstations on which to run locally-developed, graphics-based instructional software capable of animating the concepts it described.

Brown looked to IBM's substantial corporate resources for a large part of the funding and support that would be required to transform the workstation model into an institutional schema for providing educational computing. Among the attributes that Brown would bring to the partnership were: a liberal arts environment in which to explore the potential of networks of powerful workstations to further educational objectives; a demonstrated interest in making computing an intrinsic part of the educational experience of its students; and a pervasive communications network that attested to that interest.

Relationships between colleges and corporations are seldom monogamous. IBM is involved in at least three major partnerships and eighteen additional alliances through its Advanced Education Projects, while Brown University has acquired equipment with an aggregate value in excess of one million dollars from relationships with Apollo Computer and Apple Computer, and has secured a three-year, million and one-half dollar Annenberg/Corporation for Public Broadcasting grant to support educational software development.

Corporations and universities have evolved variant patterns in their search for relationships. Corporation-initiated liaisons tend to be by invitation and hence somewhat exclusive, whereas universities are disposed to make overtures to several partners at once, but with the object of securing non-exclusive unions that will not preclude their search for other companions.

A considerable amount of the effort being expended at Brown is related to the development of a family of "scholars' workstations" and educational software to run on them. This activity has been centralized at Brown in the Institute for Research in Information and Scholarship (IRIS). IRIS is being fertilized by basic research carried on in the Department of Computer Science and its seeds carried throughout the University by the agent that heretofore distributed timesharing computing to the Brown community, its Computing and Information Services organization.

IRIS has already propagated. A development effort carried out during the summer of 1984, in which faculty from several academic departments at Brown cooperated with IRIS staff, yielded a "sampler" of subject-specific applications programs with consistent interactive characteristics.

A common development vehicle is essential if educational programs are to be consistent and generalizable. Just as library patrons are not required to learn a new way of interacting with a book each time the library acquires a new one, so users of educational software should not be expected to learn a whole new way of interacting with each new piece of educational software. Brown has achieved the first part of its two-part goal for educational software — consistency. Students taught to use one of the programs from the IRIS "sampler" have been able to use all of the others without additional instruction. This has been achieved, in part, by creating all of the subject programs in the same software environment.

Future educational program development at Brown will emphasize its other targeted goal — generalizability. The consistent software development environment is planned as a total environment, which instructors will be able to use in their daily work as well as in the building of educational software that can be easily adapted from one course, or even discipline, to another by simply adding, changing, modifying, or eliminating text, graphic displays, animations, and/or associated references.

With a goal of one workstation for every student, faculty, and staff member by the end of the decade, an estimated ten thousand machines, work toward the identification of a family of affordable workstations continues within IRIS. "Identifiable" is a key word, since it is not the goal of IRIS to create new hardware.

For the present, IRIS has settled on surrogate machines that either fall short of its workstation criteria or are too expensive to ultimately satisfy its volume requirements. Brown's requirements are for a machine that can provide:

- power equivalent to that which a user can obtain via a terminal into a mainframe;
- sufficient memory to support the graphics environment;
- a large bitmapped display capable of supporting full-page textual displays;
- a mouse-type user interface;
- sufficient local hard-disk capacity to store book-length works;
- and hardware to interface it to the campus computing network.

A need is perceived for three levels of machine that take these requirements as a starting point:

- a low-end machine affordable by individual students and faculty members;
- a mid-range machine capable of supporting general teaching and research activities;
- and a high-end machine with an advanced and extended set of capabilities that will support endeavours of greater complexity.

An hour north of Brown, but on the same tack, the Massachusetts Institute of Technology (M.I.T.) is paired with IBM and DEC in a five-year effort to create a cohesive computational environment incorporating some two thousand high-performance workstations (equivalent to what Brown views as medium- to high-end machines) and a pervasive communications network (Tucker 1983-84, 17-22).

Because, like Carnegie-Mellon University, it expects that it will have to continue to accommodate computer equipment from a variety of manufacturers, M.I.T. has adopted a two-tiered networking scheme. To be promulgated through a network, data must conform to a specified format, or *protocol*. A number of manufacturers offer local area networks as products; clusters of a particular manufacturer's equipment are often most expeditiously interconnected using these products. A proliferation of such networks, which it considers inevitable, constitutes the lower tier of M.I.T.'s networking scheme.

But because they frequently employ different protocols, local area networks from different manufacturers can seldom communicate with one another directly. In order to realize a network that is truly pervasive, M.I.T. must provide a means for interconnecting dissimilar local area networks. This it will achieve through the upper tier of its scheme, a common spine, or backbone, network provided with a single established protocol and a varied and changeable set of *gateways* (programs that enable communications traffic to "change clothes," exchanging one network's protocol for that of another).

Notwithstanding the considerable financial commitment associated with implementation of the technical elements of its project, the Massachusetts Institute of Technology, like other institutions similarly engaged, reserves its greatest concern for the educational ramifications of the project. Central to that concern is the development of software to be used in the educational process.

An internal grant program, together with a substantial Annenberg/Corporation for Public Broadcasting grant, is providing the principal source of funding for educational software development. More than fifty individual development projects, as varied as the schools and departments that have proposed them, are currently underway throughout the M.I.T. One of these is an "electronic journal."

The conceptual basis for M.I.T.'s electronic journal, the software for which is being developed by the School of Architecture and Planning, is the artist/engineer's journal as used by Leonardo da Vinci. The electronic journal is intended to serve students in much the same way that personal journals have served them — as a place to collect and manipulate clipped, and perhaps annotated, passages and pictures, class and personal notes, and sketches that can variously provide inspiration and spur creativity. In electronic form, a journal's content can be shared, in toto or selectively, as immediately as it is compiled. It can be extended beyond what one can write or paste into a notebook to include, for example, photographic prints and slides and videotape frames; and it is much more amenable to editing, and to interleaving with materials drawn from the journals of others, than an equivalent paper journal. There is hardly an academic discipline in which such a journal would not have utility.

At least two of M.I.T.'s other projects involve videodisc technology: in mechanical engineering, to enable entering students with varied backgrounds to fill in, outside of class time, gaps in their experience; and in biology, to enhance the presentation of vast amounts of pictorial material and data that is only amenable to presentation in time-lapse microphotography.

And out of these unions...?

Though representative, activities and concerns related in this article are, of necessity, selective. The handful of large-scale, multi-million dollar projects being fostered by college-corporation-foundation partnerships have much in common, but they constitute only a brief, if bold, stroke in a pattern with many variations.

For instance, all of the major efforts described above are being built on the model of distributed networks of intelligent workstations, or personal computers. Far from being dead, or even obsolete, timesharing remains an acknowledged component of this model, and even, for some institutions, a viable alternative to it. Union College in Lincoln, Nebraska, for example, has wired, and installed timesharing terminals in, all four hundred and ten of its dormitory rooms with the intention of providing timeshared computing to the school's liberal arts students from a Hewlett-Packard mainframe computer. Union President, Dean Hubbard, opines that his school is "probably at the top edge of a size of institution that could do this"(Fiske 1984).

As the rush to offer the "computer advantage" proceeds apace, colleges and universities, large and small, are casting about for ways to fund hardware and foster development of useful software. Even those institutions that have garnered substantial infusions of capital from major computer manufacturers, recognizing that that reservoir will not long persist, and concerned about being perceived to be diverting monies raised to meet other institutional obligations, such as faculty salaries, building construction and maintenance, and library needs, have concomitantly launched fund-raising drives the proceeds of which are targeted for continued support of their respective projects. For the rest, fund-raising can be supplemented with grant proposals, compromises in the operating budget, increases in already high tuitions, and such less grand deals as can be struck with equipment manufacturers.

In what is increasingly becoming a two-tiered arrangement, institutions are assuming responsibility for providing the network component and some set of central support services and are encouraging, or insisting, that students supply the complementary computing component. Some worry that a stratification of computer "haves" and "have-nots" among educational institutions might be reflected in a corresponding stratification among college graduates.

One might conclude, from the paucity of really good educational software presently available, that for all the fanfare associated with it the "computer advantage" could come to naught. Classical "computer-aided instruction," or CAI, after all, has over its twenty-year history had little effect upon education. Of the innovative software described earlier, some is in use, but much more of it is "under development." Some of the latter will never be completed or, being completed, will prove ineffectual. Yet, some might prove so successful as to effect radical changes in the mode of presentation, and even the content, of a given subject area.

Reviewing the ambitious computing strategies of a number of institutions of higher learning and the stakes, as well as the expectations, that accrue to them, education editor for *The New York Times*, Edward Fiske, observed that "it may be significant that Harvard University has done little more than appoint some task forces to study the issue" (ibid.). That Harvard has since, though its footfalls have hardly been heard, taken steps toward the integration of personal computers into its academic curricula was reflected in the observation of its President, Derek Bok, in a talk delivered prior to publication of the 1984-85 *Annual Report of the President to the Board of Overseers of Harvard Collge*, that "even at stodgy old Harvard things are beginning to happen" (Bok 1985). In this talk, one of several on the subject of education and technology invited by the Harvard Graduate School of Education during the second semester, 1985, Mr. Bok enumerated uses of personal computers in several of Harvard's professional schools, including the Harvard Medical School, the Harvard Law School, and the Harvard Graduate School of Business Administration.

Bok's further remarks, together with the observations of subsequent speakers, which included Elliot Soloway, a computer scientist at Yale University, Lauren Resnick, a member of the faculty of psychology at the University of Pittsburgh and past director of Harvard's Learning and Development Center, and Paul Evans, of IBM's Educational Systems Planning Group in Boca Raton, Florida, contributed greatly to a sense of perspective on the level of attainment thus far achieved in advanced instructional computing.

Dr. Soloway explained that his inquiry into the nature of computer programming has led him to conclude that it consists primarily in learning to construct explanations and invent mechanisms, activities that correspond roughly to the setting of goals, and implementing of plans to achieve them, that people engage in continually. If, like the latter, the fundamental skills taught in computer programming are generic in nature, then perhaps, he posits, they are transferable.

In fact, the focus of much of Dr. Soloway's research has been to determine whether cognitive skills learned in programming courses will transfer to other problem-solving disciplines, whether programming might be, as some suggest, the "new Latin," which, "to be able to learn is to be able to learn anything."

Having found that even among engineering students, presentations of simple algebraic expressions, whether in words or pictures, elicit a surprisingly high percentage of incorrect solutions, Dr. Soloway endeavoured to determine whether inculcating in a group of such students the semantics of programming, which tend to be highly descriptive and procedural, might reduce the degree of ambiguity that seemed to account for their errors. In theory, the students would treat the expressions as equations to be solved in a program, regard their solutions as commandments to act, apply the appropriate functions, and derive correct solutions, much as if they were writing code in a programming language to act upon an instruction, call an appropriate subroutine, and print out an answer. Though rigorously organized, and incorporating pre- and post-testing of participants, this attempt to find transfer from the learning of computer programming to the learning of algebra was inconclusive in all respects but one; it hinted at gender differences. Undaunted, Dr. Soloway purposed to repeat the experiment, with a different sample, in a different school.

Dr. Resnick, observing that there is empirical evidence that weaker readers will be slower to recognize individual words, described an experiment in which computer software was used to drill students on word recognition with the object of improving overall reading abilities. Although the experiment failed to demonstrate improvements beyond speed of word recognition, later experiments with game-style programs that keyed on spaces between words showed some evidence of transfer and hinted at the potential efficacy of computer software in remedial reading applications. Later laboratory experiments achieved transfer up to the sentence, but not the paragraph, level posing questions as to what is special about this juncture.

Researchers inquiring into how children invent rules are tapping into work in artificial intelligence that attempts to understand why particular courses of action are followed. Like computer programs, the rules children invent frequently have bugs; there is a great deal of interest in why this is so, and in how buggy rules are debugged. Although conceptual (theory-forming) and procedural (rule-making) processes are suggested, where one begins and the other ends, and how the two interact, is not at all clear.

Dr. Resnick described an experiment that attempted to gain insight into these phenomena by yoking two representations of a borrowing problem such that a solution carried out in one resulted in presentation of the corresponding solution in the other. Children who solved the problem as represented with blocks saw a corresponding change in a numeric representation.

Only one-half to one-third of the children who used the sophisticated combination of hardware and software that delivered this instruction showed evidence of acquiring the subject principles, and of these, only half were able to make the transfer of the acquired principles to correction of previously-held buggy rules.

The idea that providing children with graphic tools that enable them to perceive analogies between multiple representations of a single quantity will lead to development of higher level concepts seems plausible enough, but results of experiments conducted to date do not seem to support the hypothesis.

Much of the research described by Dr. Resnick shows a dichotomy between rule-development and theory-formation. Well-designed computer software has demonstrated some utility for fostering the former, but little potential, so far, for effecting the latter.

Parent-child reading activities, Dr. Resnick explained, exemplify a scaffolding type of learning experience in which a child takes command, a little at a time, of an object of learning that is present in its entirety from the outset. At first, the parent does most of the reading, the child little, but over time the roles reverse. Because it requires one-on-one or one-on-a small group contact, this paradigm is usually not feasible in school settings. A computer, Dr. Resnick observed, could deliver individualized reading instruction by allowing a child to read from a textual display those parts with which he or she is familiar, and reading for the child, in a sufficiently sophisticated, synthesized voice, unfamiliar parts identified by the child with a light pen or some such device.

Most of the software referenced by Dr. Resnick was a long time in development and much of it runs on what are currently fifty-thousand dollar machines. Machines of equivalent capability that are affordable enough for classroom use, she suggested, will probably be available in five years.

Mr. Evans has suggested that educational software is still in an early stage of evolution, that it is just making the transition from the teaching-machine stage that has predominated since the 1960s, in which the machine is in control, to a learning machine stage in which control is shifting gradually to the learner. Mutations begun in the mid-1970s that could lead to a still higher evolutionary stage, in which the machine might function as concept builder, continue. Products of artificial intelligence — expert analysis systems that can seek out information and explain their reasoning — are a key component in the development of machines that can serve as true partners in learning.

According to Mr. Evans, the market for educational software has, to date, proved less lucrative than anticipated. A leading purveyor of educational software products, he noted, went from a nine million dollar business one year to near-bankruptcy the next. That most contemporary educational software is based on the old CAI paradigm he attributed to the failure of research to provide technical assessment models. Presumably, some, at least, of the network, workstation, and software development projects in which colleges and universities, both individually and in partnership with major corporations, are engaged will yield models for appropriate uses of technology in education.

Derek Bok, in the conclusion of his *Annual Report* for 1984-85, stressed the importance for university administrations to persuade their best teachers, with funds and technical assistance as well as with equipment, to devote their energies to the design and development of imaginative educational software. The best teachers, he observed, will "have thought most about how students learn and will attract the widest interest and command the greatest respect for the work they do in using technology in their courses." Nor does he neglect the complementary component of software development — evaluation — observing that, "with ingenuity . . . and a modest use of funds, a determined administration may be able to evaluate the new technology and thus learn to use it with discrimination."

Identification of appropriate models for academia, and a burgeoning market for training in industry and the military, will probably spur development of educational software, but a thorn under the saddle that could make the ride bumpy is the issue of ownership.

Commercial software is protected by copyright law; hence, copying it without permission is illegal. That illicit copying is rampant, nonetheless, deprives vendors of their due and lowers the ethical standards of those who indulge in the illegal giving and taking.

Software distribution is much simpler under the timesharing model; though it might be expensive, one (or perhaps two, if a university operates a second processor) package(s) can serve an entire user population. Use of the software is usually provided "free," the computing service organization billing, instead, for such things as connect time, processing cycles, and consumables (magnetic tapes, paper, etc.). Bills are typically paid by a department or an office. Students are seldom required to do more than qualify, usually by virtue of being enrolled in an appropriate course, for a computer account.

When the processor is no longer a large, shared, centrally-owned machine, but myriad smaller, individually-owned ones, the number of individual copies of each piece of software required for a given population to share a particular computing experience. is greatly increased. In an instructional environment, in which students might have occasion to use a number of different software packages, some of them for only a short time and then never again, the cost of obtaining or providing enough copies for an entire class can be prohibitive if prices are high. Often they are.

The principal sources of commercial software products are so-called "software houses," whose prices, and protection schemes for preventing illicit reproduction and distribution, reflect high overhead and promotional expenses and a need to realize rapid profit growth; and computer manufacturers, which might price software somewhat more reasonably if only because their primary product is computer systems. Traditional book publishers, which see software publishing as an important part of their long-term strategies, are just beginning to exert an influence on the market.

Free of copyright restrictions is a wealth of software, much of it developed by universities or under government contract, which is in the public domain. Such software, besides being often difficult to identify and locate, is seldom of the quality of good commercial software, usually proliferates in a multiplicity of versions, and is often documented, if at all, only perfunctorily. Nevertheless, some universities have expended considerable effort to develop software internally, or to adapt public domain software, for applications that already exist as commercial products because the latter are deemed prohibitively expensive in the quantities required and the institution wishes to skirt the issue of illegal copying.

The interests of all concerned would be better served if such perceived needs for redundant development were eliminated allowing universities to apply their efforts to the creation of innovative and novel applications, some of which might later serve as prototypes or models for new commercial products.

William Arms, while Vice Provost for Computing and Planning at Dartmouth College, summarized in a report prepared for the Interuniversity Communications Council, Incorporated (EDUCOM) of Princeton, New Jersey, issues related to software licensing for personal computers and types of agreements by means of which commercial software can be made affordable to educational users. Included in his report were:

• agreements for bulk purchase with discounts, whereby a university might buy in quantity from a manufacturer standard copies of software at list price per copy less some (usually significant) discount;

• agreements to buy copies for all computers, by which a university might agree, in exchange for a low price, to buy a copy of a manufacturer's software product for every computer that it distributes (a useful arrangement for such utilitarian software as word processing packages);

• campus licenses, a type of agreement preferred by many universities, in which individual copies of a product can be purchased at a low, marginal cost following an up-front payment (usually of several thousand dollars) to the supplier by the institution;

• agreements whereby an institution, in exchange for a low price, assumes responsibility for duplicating and distributing software and manuals, (sometimes employed in the case of preliminary versions of packages accompanied only by manuscripts of manuals);

• student packages, which exchange a lower price for lower product functionality, different packaging, a partial set of manuals, of some combination of these elements.

Dr. Arms' report suggests that major software packages and large textbooks are comparable in the amount of effort required to produce, and the cost of distributing, them and that the pricing of software will follow the pattern of textbooks, with prices kept relatively low by competition among several good products for every important market niche. He notes the availability of good compilers and word processing packages for about fifty dollars and predicts similar pricing for spreadsheet, database, and statistical packages in the near term. Some products, he allows, will remain expensive because of inherent complexity or application specificity, or simply because the market for them is not price sensitive.

Overall, the effect of competition and widespread adoption of creative licensing agreements should be to reduce the incentive for making unlicensed copies of commercial software products. Dr. Arms suggests in his report that, just as few people will take the trouble to photocopy a two hundred-page book, even though to do so would be much cheaper than to buy it, when software packages consisting of a disk, a back-up disk, and a couple of manuals can be purchased for less than fifty dollars, a similar disinclination will obtain.

Paul Evans, of IBM, expects that the evolution of easy-to-use, state and national telecommunications networks will foster a return to the time-sharing model of distribution for much of educational software. State departments of education, he posited, might purchase packages that would, in effect, become state property, like state vehicles, with equivalent penalties for unauthorized use. Network access to such packages might be metered, like a utility, and the various users billed, according to their respective amounts of use, by the departments of education.

When the criteria for selecting equipment becomes network compatibility, and the network is the principal provider of software, the tendency for hodge-podges of limited-application machines to accumulate and rapidly become obsolete might be reduced, and some balance and consistency introduced to the use of computers in the educational mission statewide.

What the pedagogical value of commercial educational software will be, however affordable or available it might be made, remains to be seen. Certainly, there is, amongst the panoply of software currently available to students, much that can reduce what has been called the "drudge work" of the educational process. Word processing packages, on-line library catalogs, and bibliographic search services can save students, faculty, and researchers a great deal of time and effort that they can presumably redirect to being more creative and prolific.

With our ability to make rote much of what we do in order to concentrate on other things even as we do it, we might ponder, as we compose our litany to the computer (preserver from mental drudgery, boon intellectual companion, etc.), what the elimination of earlier forms of drudgery has yielded.

The scribe's pen freed philosophers and poets from the need to exercise their vocal chords in the delivery of long orations and the recantation of lengthy epics. The printing press eliminated the need for scribes to copy, in a flowing hand, and with successive adornments and embellishments of both copy and content, the written works that earlier eliminated the need for philosophers and poets to exercise their vocal chords in the delivery of long orations and recantation of lengthy epics. Might not there be some loss in our concomitant freedom from truly great orators and beautifully inscribed documents?

A recurring tendency to posit lofty intellectual ends from the elimination of tedious labor by mechanized means was expressed in an extreme form by Oscar Wilde in *The Soul of Man Under Socialism:*

> There is no doubt at all that this is the future of machinery: and just as trees grow while the country gentleman is asleep, so while humanity will be amusing itself or enjoying cultivated leisure — which, and not labor, is the aim of man — or making beautiful things or reading beautiful things or simply contemplating the world with admiration and delight, machinery will be doing all the necessary and unpleasant work.

Education is, at best, a hopeful process. It attempts to inculcate in many and diverse individuals, through somewhat fewer diverse individuals, some heightened sense of the world they must inhabit and some basic set of tools by which they might further their comprehension of that world in order that their occupancy of it might be relatively comfortable and productive. One need not look widely to see how far short it falls of achieving its ends. Whatever help it can get should be welcomed.

The potential of the computer for education may be greater outside of the classroom than in it. The overwhelming use of contemporary computers on college and university campuses takes place in dormitory rooms and in "common areas" in which shareable equipment is provided. Some correspondence schools are beginning to distribute courseware via computer and novel, profit-making enterprises are relying on computers to deliver teaching services through "one-room electronic schoolhouses" already established in a handful of retail malls and office buildings. Computers have been appropriated, too, by a growing number of parents who are choosing the alternative of educating their children at home.

Notwithstanding its promise, the computer should not be embraced as *the* enhancer of education to the exclusion of other, traditional and demonstrated, abettors of the process. Field-study, work-study, and foreign-exchange programs can provide invaluable experiences that can be realized in no other way. Academic competitions — "mental decathlons" comprising written tests, interviews, speeches, and aural quizzes — are gaining in popularity, generating enthusiasm among parents as well as students, and garnering publicity for participating schools. Several such competitions have become national in recent years.

As for the computer, how it can serve education is a question that can have many, and varied, answers. Some have already been supplied by students, some by institutions of higher learning. Many more are being posited by researchers.

Israel Scheffler, Professor of Education and Philosophy at Harvard, has spoken of, among other things, computers and hammers (R). Of the latter, he said that the uses that can be made of them are not limited by the implements' stereotypic application to the driving of nails. Of a certainty, there are things that a hammer cannot do, he conceded, such as serving as a soup ladle, but there are other things, such as serving as a doorstop, a bookend, or a paperweight for which it is suited, albeit not by design. "Its suitability," he explains, "for such non-conventional uses is neither guaranteed nor precluded by its stereotype but must be independently established for each case." So, too, for the computer.

SELECTED BIBLIOGRAPHY

Cited works

American Telephone and Telegraph Company. *Principles of Electricity applied to Telephone and Telegraph Work.* American Telephone and Telegraph Company, 1939.

Bernold, T., and G. Albers, eds. *Artificial Intelligence: Towards Practical Application.* New York: Elsevier Science Publishing Company, Inc., 1985.

Bok, D. *The President's Report to the Board of Overseers of Harvard College.* Cambridge, Massachusetts: Harvard University, 1985.

Clark, A. *Wireless World 51.* 10, October, 1945.

Conigliaro, L. *13th International Symposium on Industrial Robots and Robots 7.* Dearborn, Michigan: Society of Manufacturing Engineers, 1983.

Dessauer, J., and H. Clark, eds. *Xerography and Related Processes.* London: Focal Press Ltd., 1965.

Dreyfus, H. *What Computers Can't Do.* New York: Harper and Row, 1979.

Fiske, E. "Computers in the Groves of Academe." *The New York Times.* 13 May 1984.

Harvard University. *The Annals of the Computation Laboratory of Harvard University,* vol. 1. Cambridge: Harvard University Press, 1946.

Hofstadter, D. *Gödel, Escher, Bach: An Eternal Golden Braid.* New York: Basic Books, Inc., 1979. Reprint. New York: Vintage Books, 1980.

Jaki, S. *Brain, Mind and Computers.* New York: Herder and Herder, 1969.

Kidder, T. "Less (and More) Than Meets the Eye." *The New York Times Book Review.* 29 December 1985.

Lattimore, R. *Homer's Iliad.* Chicago: University of Chicago Press, 1951.

McCorduck, P. *Machines Who Think.* San Francisco: W. H. Freeman and Company, 1979.

McCulloch, W. and W. Pitts. "A Logical Calculus of the Ideas Immanent in Nervous Activity." *Bulletin of Mathematical Biophysics 5.* 1943.

Michie, D. *On Machine Intelligence.* New York: John Wiley & Sons, 1974.

Michie, D., and R. Johnston. *The Knowldege Machine.* First published in a slightly different form as *The Creative Computer.* Harmondsworth, Middlesex, England: Penguin Books, Ltd., 1984. New York: William Morrow and Company, Inc., 1985.

Mishkoff, H. *Understanding Artificial Intelligence.* Dallas: Texas Instruments Information Publishing Center, 1985.

Morison, S. *Harvard in the Seventeenth Century.* Cambridge, Massachusetts: Harvard University Press, 1936.

Oettinger, A. "Programming a Digital Computer to Learn." *Philosophical 7.* 43, 1952.

Rose, Frank. *Into the Heart of the Mind.* New York: Harper and Row, 1984.

Schaffert, R. *Electrophotography.* London: Focal Press Ltd., 1965.

Shockley, W. *Electrons and Holes in Semiconductors.* New Jersey: D. Van Nostrand Company, Inc., 1950.

Thursh, D., F. Mabry, and A. Levy. "The Knowledge Access, Management, and Extension System in Pathology." *Proceedings of the AAMSI Congress, 1985.* American Association of Medical Systems and Informatics, 1985.

Tucker, S. "Computer on Campus: Working Papers." *Current Issues in Higher Education.* 2, American Association of Higher Education, 1983-84.

Wecter, D. "General Reading in a University Library." *The Place of the Library in a University.* Cambridge, Massachusetts: The Harvard University Library, 1950.

Weiner, P. *Leibnitz Selections.* New York: Charles Scribner's Sons, 1951.

Winston, P. *Artificial Intelligence*. Reading, Massachusetts: Addison-Wesley, [1981] 1985.
Winston, P. and K. Prendergast. *The AI Business*. Cambridge, Massachusetts: The M.I.T. Press, 1984.

Other references

Chapters 1 and 2

Blakeslee, T. *Digital Design with Standard MSI and LSI*. New York: John Wiley and Sons, 1975.
Healey, M. *Minicomputers and Microprocessors*. New York: Crane, Russak and Company, Inc., 1976.

Chapter 3

Bell Telephone Laboratories. *Transmission Systems for Communications*. Winston-Salem, North Carolina: Western Electric Laboratories, Inc., 1971.
Bennet, W. *Introduction to Signal Transmission*. New York: McGraw-Hill Book Company, 1970.
Black, H. *Modulation Theory*. Princeton, New Jersey: D. Van Nostrand Company, Inc., 1962.
Crowley, T., G. Harris, S. Miller, J. Pierce, and J. Runyon. *Modern Communications*. New York: Columbia University Press, 1967.
Hartley, G., P. Mornet, F. Ralph, and D. Tarran. *Techniques of Pulse-Code Modulation in Communication Networks*. Great Britain: Cambridge at the University Press, 1967.
Pierce, J. *Signals The Telephone and Beyond*. San Francisco: W. H. Freeman and Company, 1981.
———. *Waves and Messages*. Garden City, New York: Anchor Books, Doubleday and Company, Inc., 1967.
The Royal Society. *Telecommunications in the 1980s and After*. London: The Royal Society, 1978.
Schwartz, M. *Information Transmission, Modulation, and Noise*. New York: McGraw-Hill Book Company, Inc., 1959.
Smith, A. *Automatic Telephony*. New York: McGraw-Hill Book Company, Inc., 1921.
Talley, D. *Basic Telephone Switching Systems*. Rochelle Park, New Jersey: Hayden Book Company, 1979.

Chapter 4

Jaffe, L. ed. *Satellite Communication in the Next Decade: 14th Goddard Memorial Symposium*. San Diego, California: Univelt, Inc., 1977.
Martin, J. *Communications Satellite Systems*. Englewood Cliffs, New Jersey: Prentice-Hall, Inc., 1978.

Chapter 5

McLean, T. and P. Schagen. *Electronic Imaging*. New York: Academic Press, 1979.

Chapter 7

Rice, P., and R. Dubbe. "Development of the First Optical Videodisc." *SMPTE Journal*. March 1982.
3M Optical Recording Project. *Premastering/Post Production for Scotch Videodiscs*. Minnesota, Missouri: Minnesota Mining and Manufacturing Company, 1981.

266

Chapter 8

Barsky, B. "A Description and Evaluation of Various 3-D Models." *IEEE Computer Graphics and Applications.* January, 1984.

Berg, C. "Computer Graphics Displays: Windows for Process Control." *IEEE Computer Graphics and Applications.* May/June, 1983.

Foley, J., and A. Van Dam. *Fundamentals of Interactive Computer Graphics.* New York: Addison-Wesley Publishing Company, 1982.

Fugimoto, A., and K. Iwata. "Jag-free Images on Raster Displays." *IEEE Computer Graphics and Applications.* December, 1983.

Grotch, S. "Three-dimensional and Stereoscopic Graphics for Scientific Data Display and Analysis." *IEEE Computer Graphics and Applications.* November, 1983.

Hahn, G., and C. Morgan. "Color Face Plots for Displaying Product Performance." *IEEE Computer Graphics and Applications.* May/June, 1983.

Hall, R., and D. Greenberg. "A Testbed for Realistic Image Synthesis." *IEEE Computer Graphics and Applications.* November, 1983.

Hubschmann, H., and S. Zucker. "Frame-to-frame Coherence and the Hidden Surface Computation." *ACM Transactions on Graphics 1:2.* April, 1982.

Kajiya, J. "New Techniques for Ray Tracing Procedurally-Defined Objects." *ACM Transactions on Graphics 2:3.* July, 1983.

Knuth, D. *TEX and METAFONT.* Digital Press, 1979.

Lores, M. "Evaluation of 3-D Graphics Software, A Case Study." *IEEE Computer Graphics and Applications.* November, 1983.

Max, N. "Computer Representation of Molecular Surfaces." *IEEE Computer Graphics and Applications.* August, 1983.

McLaughlin, H. "Shape-preserving Planar Interpolation: An algorithm." *IEEE Computer Graphics and Applications.* May/June, 1983.

Newman, W., and R. Sproull. *Principles of Interactive Computer Graphics.* New York: McGraw-Hill Book Company, Inc., 1979.

Pavlidis, T. "Curve Fitting with Conic Splines." *ACM Transactions on Graphics 2:1.* January, 1983.

Potmesil, M., and I. Chakravarty. "Synthetic Image Generation with a Lens and Aperture Camera Model." *ACM Transactions on Graphics 1:2.* April, 1982.

Sabella, P., and M. Wozny. "Toward Fast Color-Shaded Images of CAD/CAM Geometry." *IEEE Computer Graphics and Applications.* November, 1983.

Shimomura, T. "A Method for Automatically Generating Business Graphs." *IEEE Computer Graphics and Applications.* September, 1983.

Turkowski, K. "Anti-aliasing through the Use of Coordinate Transformation." *ACM Transactions on Graphics 1:3.* July, 1982.

Van Wyck, C. "A High-level Language for Specifying Pictures." *ACM Transactions on Graphics 1:2.* April, 1982.

Wixson, S. "Four-dimensional Processing Tools for Cardiovascular Data." *IEEE Computer Graphics and Applications.* August, 1983.

Chapter 9

Albus, J. *Brains, Behavior, and Robotics.* Peterborough, New Hampshire: McGraw-Hill, BYTE Books, 1981.

Hayes, J., and D. Michie. *Intelligent Systems.* Chichester, England: Ellis Horwood Ltd., 1984.

McCorduck, P., and E. Feigenbaum. *The Fifth Generation: Artifical Intelligence and Japan's Computer Challenge to the World.* Reading, Massachusetts: Addison-Wesley Publishing Company, 1983.

Gardner, *The Mind's New Science: A History of the Cognitive Revolution.* New York: Basic Books, 1985.

Chapter 10

Dorf, R. *Robotics and Automated Manufacturing.* Reston, Virginia: Reston Publishing Company, Inc., 1983.

Hartley, J. *Robots at Work: A practical guide for engineers and managers.* United Kingdom: IFS Publications Ltd., North Holland Publishing Company, 1983.

Hunt, V. *Industrial Robotics Handbook.* New York: Industrial Press Inc., 1983.

Osborne, D. *Robots: An Introduction to Basic Concepts and Applications.* Midwest Sci = Tech Publishers, Inc., 1983.

Tanner, W. ed. *Industrial Robots: Volume 1/Fundamentals.* Dearborn, Michigan: Robotics International of SME, 1981.

Tanner, W. ed. *Industrial Robots: Volume 2/Applications.* Dearborn, Michigan: Robotics Inernational of SME, 1981.

Chapter 11

American Council of Learned Societies. *On Research Libraries.* Cambridge Massachusetts: The M.I.T. Press, 1969.

Bentinck-Smith, W. *Building a Great Library.* Cambridge, Massachusetts: Harvard University Library, 1976.

Boss, R. *The Library Manager's Guide to Automation.* White Plains, New York: Knowledge Industries Publications, Inc., 1979.

Gore, D. *Farewell to Alexandria.* Westport, Connecticut: Greenwood Press, 1976.

Knowledge Industry Publications. *Books, Libraries and Electronics.* White Plains, New York: Knowledge Industry Publications. 1982.

Knowledge Industry Publications. *Changing Information Concepts and Technologies.* White Plains, New York: Knowledge Industry Publications. 1982.

Knowledge Industry Publications. *The Professional Librarian's Reader in Library Automation and Technology.* White Plains, New York: Knowledge Industry Publications. 1980.

Knowledge Industry Publications. *Telecommunications and Libraries: A Primer for Librarians and Information Managers.* White Plains, New York: Knowledge Industry Publications. 1981.

Morison, S. *The Development of Harvard University.* Cambridge, Massachusetts: Harvard University Press, 1930.

———. *The Founding of Harvard College.* Cambridge, Massachusetts: Harvard University Press, 1935.

Chapter 12

Education Section. *The New York Times.* 14 April 1985.

Meyrowitz, N. *Networks of Scholar's Workstations: End-User Computing in University Community, Preliminary Report.* Brown University, Institute for Research in Information and Scholarship, 1985.

Project Athena. *Project Athena: Faculty/Student Projects.* Massachusetts Institute of Technology, 1985.

Yankelovich, N. *The Sampler Companion.* Brown University, Institute for Research in Information and Scholarship, 1985.

ILLUSTRATIONS AND PHOTOGRAPHS

By permission of the Association for Computing Machinery (© ACM):
134 (Whitted, T., Bell Labs, ACM SIGGRAPH Slides, 1982), 135 (top, Fuchs, H., G. D. Abram, and E. D. Grant, *Computer Graphics*, July 1983; bottom, Whitted, T., *ACM Transactions on Graphics*, January 1982)

Courtesy Automatix, Incorporated:
192 (inset photo)

The Book of Knowledge, The Grolier Society, New York, 1912:
42

Eleanor Bradshaw, Harvard University Office of the University Publisher:
37, 43, 44, 46, 47, 48, 52, 62, 118, 120, 125, 127 (after Newman, W. M., and R. F. Sproull), 128 (after Knuth, D. E.), 129 (after Barsky, B.), 130-131 (after Foley, J.D., and A. Van Dam), 138, 143, 148, 155, 161, 171, 175, 186, 190, 192, 196, 197, 198, 200, 207, 208, 209, 213, 229, 234, 235, 242, 250-251

Greg Byrne:
82

Courtesy Cincinnati-Milacron:
188, 192 (photo)

Armand Dionne, Cruft Photo Lab, Harvard University:
72

Institute of Electrical and Electronic Engineers (© 1983 IEEE):
123 (Hahn, G. J., C. B. Morgan, and W. E. Lorensen), 124 (Grotch, S.)

Pioneer Video:
101

Diane Shar:
105

Nathan Simon:
115

Texas Instruments, Incorporated:
12

Unimation, Incorporated:
183

Henry Valentinas, Media Graphics, Newton Highlands, Massachusetts:
4, 16, 22, 26, 31, 66, 69, 70, 74, 87, 88 (after Schaffert, R.M., and M.J. Langdon), 94

ABOUT THE AUTHORS AND EDITOR

John Simon, a Portsmouth, New Hampshire-based writer, editor, and publications consultant, developed technology-oriented publications for a number of institutions and organizations prior to founding the Harvard University *Information Technology Newsletter* in 1982. Mr. Simon served as editor and chief writer for the *Newsletter* for four years, through its transformation into the *Information Technology Quarterly.*

Madeleine L. Butler is a principal partner in Butler, Raila & Company, a firm specializing in the design and development of interactive media, including interactive videodisc. Ms. Butler managed the Harvard Television Production Center at Harvard University for five years, prior to which she produced and directed broadcast television programming for WYES-TV, a Public Broadcasting Service station in New Orleans, Louisiana.

George H. Stalker (A.B. Harvard, 1967) is a private consultant. Upon completing his Ph.D. at the University of Michigan in 1975, Mr. Stalker joined the Education Development Center in Newton, Massachusetts. He subsequently became manager of academic computing at Tufts University and, in 1981, was appointed University Consultant for Research and Instructional Computing.

Donald S. Bradshaw (A.B. Harvard, 1944) is a retired business executive living in Weston, Vermont. During his business career, Mr. Bradshaw became interested in questions regarding human behaviour and is currently developing some ideas on the nature of perception and its role as a function of the mind.